SOCIAL SECURITY LEGIS
SUPPLEMENT 2006/2

General Editor
David Bonner, LL.B., LL.M.

Commentary by
David Bonner, LL.B., LL.M.
Professor of Law, University of Leicester
Formerly Member, Social Security Appeal Tribunals

Ian Hooker, LL.B.
Lecturer in Law, University of Nottingham
Formerly Member, Social Security Appeal Tribunals

Richard Poynter B.C.L., M.A. (Oxon)
Solicitor, District Chairman,
Appeals Service, Deputy Social Security Commissioner

Mark Rowland, LL.B.
Social Security Commissioner

Robin White, M.A., LL.M.
Professor of Law, University of Leicester,
Deputy Social Security Commissioner

Nick Wikeley, M.A.
Barrister, Professor of Law, University of Southampton,
Deputy Social Security Commissioner, Deputy District Chairman, Appeals Service

David Williams, LL.M., Ph.D., C.T.A.
Solicitor, Social Security and Child Support Commissioner, Deputy Special Commissioner of Income Tax and part-time Chairman of VAT and Duties Tribunal

Penny Wood, LL.B., M.Sc.
Solicitor, District Chairman
Appeals Service

Consultant to Vol. II
John Mesher, B.A., B.C.L., LL.M.
Barrister, Professor Associate of Law,
University of Sheffield,
Social Security and Child Support Commissioner

Consultant Editor
Child Poverty Action Group

LONDON
THOMSON
————✱————™
SWEET & MAXWELL
2007

Published in 2007 by
Sweet & Maxwell Limited of
100 Avenue Road, Swiss Cottage,
London NW3 3PF
(http://www.sweetandmaxwell.co.uk)
Typeset by Interactive Sciences Ltd, Gloucester
Printed in England by
MPG Books Ltd, Bodmin, Cornwall

No natural forests were destroyed to make this product.
Only farmed timber was used and re-planted.

A catalogue record for this book is
available from the British Library

ISBN-10 0-421-96320-4
ISBN-13 978-0-421-96320-7

All rights reserved. Crown Copyright Legislation is reproduced under
the terms of Crown Copyright Policy Guidance issued by HMSO.

No part of this publication may be reproduced or transmitted,
in any form or by any means, or stored in any retrieval system
of any nature without prior written permission, except for
permitted fair dealing under the Copyright, Designs and
Patents Act 1988, or in accordance with the terms of a licence
issued by the Copyright Licensing Agency in respect of
photocopying and/or reprographic reproduction.
Application for permission for other use of copyright material
including permission to reproduce extracts in other published
works shall be made to the publishers. Full acknowledgement
of author, publisher and source must be given.
Application for permission for other use of copyright material
controlled by the publisher shall be made to the publishers.
Material is contained in this publication for which publishing
permission has been sought, and for which copyright is
acknowledged. Permission to reproduce such material
cannot be granted by the publishers and application
must be made to the copyright holder.

Commentators have asserted their moral rights under
the Copyright, Designs and Patents Act 1988 to be identified
as the authors of the commentary in this Volume.

©
THOMSON

SWEET & MAXWELL

2007

CHILD POVERTY ACTION GROUP

The Child Poverty Action Group (CPAG) is a charity, founded in 1965, which campaigns for the relief of poverty in the UK. It has a particular reputation in the field of welfare benefits law derived from its legal work, publications, training and parliamentary and policy work, and is widely recognised as the leading organisation for taking test cases on social security law.

CPAG is therefore ideally placed to act as Consultant Editor to this 4-volume work—**Social Security Legislation 2006 and Supplement 2006/2007**. CPAG is not responsible for the detail of what is contained in each volume, and the authors' views are not necessarily those of the CPAG. The Consultant Editor's role is to act in an advisory capacity on the overall structure, focus and direction of the work.

For more information about CPAG, its rights and policy publications or training courses, its address is 94 White Lion Street, London N1 9PF (telephone: 020 7837 7979—website: *www.cpag.org.uk*).

PREFACE

This is the combined Supplement to the 2006 edition of the four-volume work, *Social Security Legislation*, which was published in September 2006.

Part I of the Supplement contains new legislation (Acts and Regulations), presented in the same format as the main volumes. This will enable readers to note very quickly new sets of legislation.

Parts II, III, IV and V contain the updating material—a separate Part for each volume of the main work—which amends the legislative text and key aspects of the commentary so as to be up to date as at December 6, 2006. Part VI, the final section of the Supplement, gives some notice of changes forthcoming between that date and the date to which the main work (2007 edition) will be up to date (mid-April) and some indication of the April 2007 benefit rates, and takes account of changes known to us as at December 6, 2006.

As always we welcome comments from those who use this Supplement. Please address these to the General Editor, David Bonner, at the Faculty of Law, The University, Leicester LE1 7RH.

David Bonner
Ian Hooker
John Mesher
Richard Poynter
Mark Rowland
Robin White
Nick Wikeley
David Williams
Penny Wood
December 12, 2006

CONTENTS

	Page
Preface	*iv*
Using the Updating Material in this Supplement	*vi*
Pages of Main Volumes Affected by Material in this Supplement	*vii*
Table of Abbreviations used in this Series	*xiv*
Table of Cases	*xvii*
Table of Social Security Commissioner's Decisions	*xxi*
Table of European Materials	*xxiii*
Table of Statutes	*xxv*
Table of Statutory Instruments	*xxix*
Part I: New Legislation	1
Part II: Updating Material Volume I: Non Means Tested Benefits	9
Part III: Updating Material Volume II: Income Support, Jobseeker's Allowance, State Pension Credit and the Social Fund	41
Part IV: Updating Material Volume III: Administration, Adjudication and the European Dimension	93
Part V: Updating Material Volume IV: Tax Credits, Child Trust Funds and Employer-Paid Social Security Benefits	123
Part VI: Forthcoming Changes and Up-rating of Benefits	147

USING THE UPDATING MATERIAL IN THIS SUPPLEMENT

The amendments and updating contained in Parts II–V of this Supplement are keyed in to the page numbers of the relevant main volume of Social Security Legislation 2006. Where there have been a significant number of changes to a provision, the whole section, subsection, paragraph or regulation, as amended, will tend to be reproduced. Other changes may be noted by an instruction to insert or substitute new material or to delete part of the existing text. The date the change takes effect is also noted. Where explanation is needed of the change, or there is updating to do to existing annotations but no change to the legislation, you will also find commentary in this Supplement. The updating material explains new statutory material, takes on board Commissioners' or court decisions, or gives prominence to points which now seem to warrant more detailed attention.

This Supplement amends the text of the main volumes of Social Security Legislation 2006 to be up to date as at December 6, 2006.

David Bonner, General Editor

Index to the Social Security Legislation 2006 Volumes

This year the Index has been removed from all four volumes of Social Security Legislation in order to provide the space necessary for the legislation and commentary. The alternative, given the continued growth in case law and legislation, would have been the more expensive option of adding another volume to the series.

The index is now online and the file can be accessed from the following location on the internet: *http://www.sweetandmaxwell.co.uk/books/ss/*. The index can be printed off for use, accessed directly from the above location or downloaded onto the desktop.

For the first time the separate indexes have been amalgamated into a single main index covering all four volumes. This will enhance searching, making it faster, since paragraph locations across all four volumes are given beside each reference. The index is now much easier to search as the "find" functionality in Adobe Acrobat can be used to locate a specific term. This tool highlights all instances of the term making it quicker to find the correct reference and location.

Information can be easily located in the volumes using methods other than the index. These are:

- The combination of the "How to Use This Book" section and the running heads text at the top of each page enable lawyers, and non-lawyers alike, to navigate the material effectively.
- The Arrangement of Sections at the beginning of each statute can offer further aid. Similarly, the mass of Regulations have been grouped according to type of benefit and each set has its own "Arrangement of Regulations", enabling readers to locate the relevant material.

If you would like to give feedback on the index or any other matter relating to the volumes, I would be very interested to hear from you.

Fiona Keyte
Publishing Editor
Sweet & Maxwell
100 Avenue Road
London, NW3 3PF

Fiona.Keyte@thomson.com

PAGES OF MAIN VOLUMES AFFECTED BY MATERIAL IN THIS SUPPLEMENT

Main volume page affected	Relevant paragraph in supplement

VOLUME 1

Main volume page affected	Relevant paragraph in supplement
4	2.001
44–46	2.002
56	2.003
60	2.004
87	2.005
89	2.006
131	2.007
159	2.008
160	2.009
190–192	2.010
216–219	2.011–2.012
404	2.013
419	2.014
440	2.015
447	2.016
465	2.017
504	2.018
508	2.019
516	2.020
533	2.021
535	2.022
542	2.023
569	2.024
570	2.025
609	2.026–2.027
634	2.028
635–636	2.029
639	2.030
644–645	2.031
660	2.032
662	2.033
679–680	2.034
681–683	2.035
688	2.036
690–691	2.037
694	2.038
705–708	2.039
712	2.040
718–720	2.041
731–735	2.042
757–758	2.043

Pages of Main Volumes Affected by Material in this Supplement

Main volume page affected	Relevant paragraph in supplement
768–772	2.044–2.045
775	2.046
777	2.047
778	2.048
788	2.049
794	2.050
796	2.051
802	2.052
857–862	2.053
923–925	2.054
928	2.055
937–938	2.056

VOLUME II

Main volume page affected	Relevant paragraph in supplement
91–94	3.001
113	3.002
154	3.003
156	3.004
225	3.005
235	3.006
237	3.007
264	3.008
266	3.009
274	3.010
279–280	3.011
282	3.012
300	3.013
301	3.014
302	3.015
305	3.016
308	3.017–3.018
334	3.019
375	3.020
387	3.021
388	3.022
398	3.023
449	3.024
452	3.025
455	3.026
458	3.027
462	3.028–3.029
470	3.030
485	3.031–3.032

Pages of Main Volumes Affected by Material in this Supplement

Main volume page affected	Relevant paragraph in supplement
494	3.033–3.034
501	3.035
502	3.036
519	3.037
521	3.038
526	3.039
531–532	3.040
533	3.041
539–540	3.042
544	3.043
547	3.044
554	3.045
561	3.046
564–568	3.047
577	3.048
588	3.049
589	3.050
595	3.051–3.052
598	3.053
599	3.054–3.055
611–614	3.056–3.057
626	3.058
626	3.059
628	3.060
642	3.061–3.062
648	3.063
656	3.064
662	3.065
683	3.066
768	3.067
792	3.068
794	3.069
810–813	3.070
814	3.071
825	3.072
830–832	3.073
845	3.074
868	3.075
913	3.076
919	3.077
930	3.078
935	3.079
951	3.080
973	3.081
974	3.082
996	3.083
997	3.084

Pages of Main Volumes Affected by Material in this Supplement

Main volume page affected	Relevant paragraph in supplement
999	3.085
1002	3.086
1003	3.087–3.088
1038	3.089
1043	3.090
1048	3.091
1049	3.092
1055	3.093
1057	3.094
1066	3.095
1068	3.096
1073	3.097–3.100
1084	3.101
1085	3.102
1090	3.103
1092	3.104–3.105
1095	3.106
1096	3.107–3.108
1103	3.109–3.110
1105	3.111–3.112
1108	3.113
1112–1113	3.114–3.116
1123	3.117
1124	3.118
1127	3.119
1133	3.120
1149	3.121
1171	3.122
1172	3.123
1174	3.124
1183	3.125
1204	3.126
1207	3.127
1231–1232	3.128–3.129
1235	3.130
1238	3.131
1243	3.132

VOLUME III

Main volume page affected	Relevant paragraph in supplement
50	4.001
52	4.002

Pages of Main Volumes Affected by Material in this Supplement

Main volume page affected	Relevant paragraph in supplement
201	4.003
206	4.004–4.005
211–213	4.005a
213–220	4.006
233–239	4.007
240–241	4.008
241–242	4.009
247	4.010
248–249	4.011
253	4.012
326	4.013
378	4.014
380	4.015
381	4.016
382	4.017–4.018
398	4.019
405	4.020
407	4.021
417	4.022
452	4.023
472	4.024
484	4.025–4.026
536	4.027
538	4.028
556–562	4.029
563	4.030
576–577	4.031
595	4.032
599	4.032a
601	4.033
603	4.034
614–615	4.035
621	4.036
624	4.037
628–631	4.038
632	4.038a
636	4.039
642	4.039a
645–647	4.040
660	4.041
676	4.041a
704	4.042
715	4.043
716	4.044
812	4.045
816	4.046
912	4.047

Pages of Main Volumes Affected by Material in this Supplement

Main volume page affected	Relevant paragraph in supplement
924	4.048
927	4.049
942	4.050
950	4.051
953	4.052
982	4.053
991	4.054
1192	4.055
1200	4.056
1211	4.057
1220	4.058
1239	4.059
1258	4.060
1263	4.061
1275	4.062

VOLUME IV

Main volume page affected	Relevant paragraph in supplement
8	5.001
28	5.002
50	5.003
51	5.004
56	5.005
62	5.006
66	5.007
69	5.008
71	5.009
74	5.010
77	5.011
80	5.012
134	5.013
164	5.014
174	5.014a
214	5.015
215	5.016
238	5.017
248	5.018
260	5.019
323	5.020
324	5.021
331	5.022
380	5.023
401	5.024
403	5.025

Pages of Main Volumes Affected by Material in this Supplement

Main volume page affected	Relevant paragraph in supplement
413	5.026
414	5.027
440	5.028
450	5.029
452	5.030
478	5.030a
479	5.031
488	5.032–5.033
489	5.034
494	5.035
575	5.036
638	5.037
639	5.038
670	5.039
674	5.040
679	5.041
680	5.042
687	5.043
712	5.044
741	5.045
743	5.046
744	5.047
748	5.048
817	5.049
819	5.050
826	5.051
877	5.052

TABLE OF ABBREVIATIONS USED IN THIS SERIES

1982 Regulations	Social Security (General Benefit) Regulations 1982
1992 Act	Social Security Contributions and Benefits Act 1992
A.C.	Appeal Cases
A.C.D.	Administrative Court Digest
All E.R.	All England Reports
Attendance Allowance Regulations 1991	Social Security (Attendance Allowance) Regulations 1991
B.H.R.C.	Butterworths Human Rights Cases
B.L.G.R.	Butterworths Local Government Reports
Benefits Act	Social Security Contributions and Benefits Act 1992
C.E.C.	European Community Cases
C.M.L.R.	Common Market Law Reports
CPAG	Child Poverty Action Group
Claims and Payments Regulations 1987	Social Security (Claims and Payments) Regulations 1987
Computation of Earnings Regulations	Social Security Benefit (Computation of Earnings) Regulations 1996
Contributions and Benefits Act	Social Security Contributions and Benefits Act 1992
Decisions and Appeals Regulations	Social Security and Child Support (Decisions and Appeals) Regulations 1999
Dependency Regulations	Social Security Benefit (Dependency) Regulations 1977
Diseases Regulations 1985	Social Security (Industrial Injuries) (Prescribed Diseases) Regulations 1985
Disability Living Allowance Regulations 1991	Social Security (Disability Living Allowance) Regulations 1991
E.C.R.	European Court Reports
E.G.C.S.	Estates Gazette Case Summaries
E.H.R.R.	European Human Rights Reports
Eur.L.R.	European Law Reports
F.C.R.	Family Court Reporter
F.L.R.	Family Law Reports
Fam.Law	Family Law
General Benefit Regulations 1982	Social Security (General Benefit) Regulations 1982

Table of Abbreviations used in this Series

Graduated Retirement Benefit Regulations	Social Security (Graduated Retirement Benefit) Regulations 2005
H.L.R.	Housing Law Reports
HMRC	Her Majesty's Revenue and Customs
H.R.L.R.	Human Rights Law Reports
I.C.R.	Industrial Cases Reports
I.N.L.R.	Immigration and Nationality Law Reports
IS	Income Support
I(EEA) Regulations	Immigration (European Economic Area) Regulations 2006
Imm.A.R.	Immigration Appeals Reports
Incapacity Benefit—Increases for Dependants Regulations 1994	Social Security (Incapacity Benefit—Increases for Dependants) Regulations 1994
Incapacity Benefit Regulations 1994	Social Security (Incapacity Benefit) Regulations 1994
Incapacity Benefit (Transitional) Regulations 1995	Social Security (Incapacity Benefit) (Consequential and Transitional Amendments and Savings) Regulations 1995
Incapacity for Work (General) Regulations 1995	Social Security (Incapacity for Work) (General) Regulations 1995
JSA	Job Seekers Allowance
Jobcentre Plus Interviews Regulations	Social Security (Jobcentre Plus Interviews) Regulations 2001
L.S.G.	Law Society Gazette
Maternity Allowance Regulations 1987	Social Security (Maternity Allowance) Regulations 1987
NACODS	National Association of Colliery Overmen Deputies and Shotfirers
N.L.J.	New Law Journal
N.P.C.	New Property Cases
NVQ	National Vocational Qualification
Overlapping Benefits Regulations 1979	Social Security (Overlapping Benefits) Regulations 1979
P. & C.R.	Property, Planning & Compensation Reports
Pens.L.R.	IDS Pensions Law Reports
Prescribed Diseases Regulations 1985	Social Security (Industrial Injuries) (Prescribed Diseases) Regulations 1985
S.C.	Session Cases
S.C.L.R.	Scottish Civil Law Reports
S.J.	Solicitors Journal
S.J.L.B.	Solicitors Journal LawBrief
S.L.T.	Scots Law Times

Table of Abbreviations used in this Series

SPC	State Pension Credit
SSA 1998	Social Security Act 1998
SSAC	Social Security Advisory Committee
SSCBA 1992	Social Security Contributions and Benefits Act 1992
U.K.H.R.R.	United Kingdom Human Rights Reports
USI Regs	Social Security (Unemployment, Sickness and Invalidity Benefit) Regulations 1983
W.L.R.	Weekly Law Reports
Widow's Benefit and Retirement Pensions Regulations 1979	Social Security (Widow's Benefit and Retirement Pensions) Regulations 1979
Working Neighbourhoods Regulations	Social Security (Working Neighbourhoods) Regulations 2004

TABLE OF CASES

Abdirahman, Abdirahman and Uluslow v Secretary of State for Work and Pensions, unreported, CA 4.048
Arathoon v Secretary of State for Work and Pensions [2005] EWCA Civ 942, CA (Civ Div) 3.045
B v Secretary of State for Work and Pensions [2005] EWCA Civ 929; [2005] 1 W.L.R. 3796; *The Times*, September 16, 2005, CA (Civ Div) 4.001, 4.002
Barrow v United Kingdom (42735/02); *The Times*, September 11, 2006, ECHR 4.061
Belgium v Humbel (263/86) [1988] E.C.R. 5365; [1989] 1 C.M.L.R. 393; *The Times*, October 25, 1988, ECJ 4.048
Calvin v Carr [1980] A.C. 574; [1979] 2 W.L.R. 755; [1979] 2 All E.R. 440; 123 S.J. 112, PC (Aus) 4.001
Carpenter v Secretary of State for the Home Department (C60/00) [2003] Q.B. 416; [2003] 2 W.L.R. 267; [2003] All E.R. (EC) 577; [2002] E.C.R. I–6279; [2002] 2 C.M.L.R. 64; [2003] 2 F.C.R. 711; [2002] I.N.L.R. 439; *The Times*, July 20, 2002, ECJ 4.048
Chief Adjudication Officer v Astle, unreported, CA (Civ Div) 2.002
Chief Adjudication Officer v Sherriff (1995) 92(22) L.S.G. 41; (1995) 139 S.J.L.B. 131; *The Times*, May 10, 1995, CA (Civ Div) 4.001
Chief Supplementary Benefit Officer v Leary [1985] 1 W.L.R. 84; [1985] 1 All E.R. 1061; (1984) 81 L.S.G. 3596; (1984) 128 S.J. 852, CA (Civ Div) 4.007
Cockburn v Chief Adjudication Officer; Joined Cases Secretary of State for Social Security v Halliday; Secretary of State for Social Security v Fairey [1997] 1 W.L.R. 799; [1997] 3 All E.R. 844; (1997) 94(24) L.S.G. 32; (1997) 147 N.L.J. 794; (1997) 141 S.J.L.B. 122; *The Times*, May 26, 1997, HL 2.007
Collins v Secretary of State for Work and Pensions (C138/02) [2005] Q.B. 145; [2004] 3 W.L.R. 1236; [2004] All E.R. (EC) 1005; [2004] E.C.R. I–2703; [2004] 2 C.M.L.R. 8; [2004] C.E.C. 436; [2005] I.C.R. 37; *The Times*, March 30, 2004, ECJ 4.048, 4.050
Collins v Secretary of State for Work and Pensions [2006] EWCA Civ 376; [2006] 1 W.L.R. 2391; [2006] Eu. L.R. 981; [2006] I.C.R. 1033; *The Times*, May 2, 2006, CA (Civ Div) 4.048, 4.050
Couronne v Crawley BC [2006] EWHC 1514, QBD (Admin) 4.061, 4.057
De Cuyper v Office National de l'Emploi (ONEM) (C406/04) [2006] All E.R. (EC) 947; [2006] 3 C.M.L.R. 44, ECJ 4.048
Duggan v Chief Adjudication Officer; *The Times*, December 19, 1988, CA (Civ Div) 4.001
Elo v Finland (App.30742/02), unreported, ECHR 4.059
Esfandiari v Secretary of State for Work and Pensions; Joined Cases Latif v Secretary of State for Work and Pensions; Nessa (Hawarun) v Secretary of State for Work and Pensions; Nessa (Momirun) v Secretary of State for Work and Pensions [2006] EWCA Civ 282; [2006] H.R.L.R. 26; *The Times*, May 29, 2006; *Independent*, March 29, 2006, CA (Civ Div) 4.058, 4.061
Fenton v J Thorley & Co Ltd [1903] A.C. 443, HL 2.010
Francis v Secretary of State for Work and Pensions [2005] EWCA Civ 1303; [2006] 1 All E.R. 748; [2005] 3 F.C.R. 526; [2006] H.R.L.R. 9; *The Times*, November 17, 2005; *Independent*, November 17, 2005, CA (Civ Div) 4.061
Gillies v Secretary of State for Work and Pensions; sub nom. Secretary of State for Work and Pensions v Gillies [2006] UKHL 2; [2006] 1 W.L.R. 781; [2006] 1 All E.R. 731; 2006 S.C. (H.L.) 71; 2006 S.L.T. 77; 2006 S.C.L.R. 276; [2006] I.C.R. 267; (2006) 9 C.C.L. Rep. 404; (2006) 103(9) L.S.G. 33; (2006) 150 S.J.L.B. 127; 2006 G.W.D. 3–66; *The Times*, January 30, 2006, HL 4.059

xvii

Table of Cases

Grant v United Kingdom (App.32570/03), unreported, ECHR 4.060
Grzelczyk v Centre Public d'Aide Sociale d'Ottignies Louvain la Neuve (C184/99) [2003] All E.R. (EC) 385; [2001] E.C.R. I–6193; [2002] 1 C.M.L.R. 19; [2002] I.C.R. 566; *The Times*, November 16, 2001, ECJ 4.048
Howker v Secretary of State for Work and Pensions [2002] EWCA Civ 1623; [2003] I.C.R. 405; (2003) 100(2) L.S.G. 32; *The Times*, November 19, 2002; *Independent*, November 12, 2002, CA (Civ Div) 2.042, 2.044
Jones v Secretary of State for Social Services; sub nom. R. v National Insurance Commissioner Ex p. Hudson; R. v National Insurance Commissioner Ex p. Jones; R. v National Insurance Commissioner Ex p. Lloyd-Jones; Joined Cases Hudson v Secretary of State for Social Services [1972] A.C. 944; [1972] 2 W.L.R. 210; [1972] 1 All E.R. 145; (1971) 116 S.J. 57, HL 2.011
Kay v Lambeth LBC; sub nom. Lambeth LBC v Kay; Leeds City Council v Price; Joined Cases Gorman v Lambeth LBC; Constantine v Lambeth LBC; Barnett v Lambeth LBC; Cole v Lambeth LBC; Price v Leeds City Council; Dymny v Lambeth LBC [2006] UKHL 10; [2006] 2 W.L.R. 570; [2006] 4 All E.R. 128; [2006] 2 F.C.R. 20; [2006] H.R.L.R. 17; [2006] U.K.H.R.R. 640; 20 B.H.R.C. 33; [2006] H.L.R. 22; [2006] B.L.G.R. 323; [2006] 2 P. & C.R. 25; [2006] L. & T.R. 8; [2006] 11 E.G.C.S. 194; (2006) 150 S.J.L.B. 365; [2006] N.P.C. 29; *The Times*, March 10, 2006; *Independent*, March 14, 2006, HL 4.067
Levy v Secretary of State for Work and Pensions [2006] EWCA Civ 890, CA (Civ Div) 4.018, 4.028, 4.040
Lloyds Bank Plc v Waterhouse [1993] 2 F.L.R. 97; (1991) 10 Tr. L.R. 161; [1991] Fam. Law 23; *Independent*, February 27, 1990, CA (Civ Div) 4.001
Mallinson v Secretary of State for Social Security [1994] 1 W.L.R. 630; [1994] 2 All E.R. 295; (1994) 144 N.L.J. 604; (1994) 138 S.J.L.B. 112; *The Times*, April 28, 1994; *Independent*, April 26, 1994; *Guardian*, April 25, 1994, HL 2.007
Manning v Revenue and Customs Commissioners [2006] S.T.C. (S.C.D.) 588; [2006] S.T.I. 1920, Sp Comm 4.061
Packer's Case, unreported 2.007
Pearson v United Kingdom (App No. 8374/03) unreported, April 27, 2004 .... 4.061
R. v Wicks (Peter Edward) [1998] A.C. 92; [1997] 2 W.L.R. 876; [1997] 2 All E.R. 801; (1997) 161 J.P. 433; (1997) 9 Admin. L.R. 349; [1997] 2 P.L.R. 97; [1997] J.P.L. 1049; (1997) 161 J.P.N. 628; (1997) 94(35) L.S.G. 34; (1997) 147 N.L.J. 883; (1997) 141 S.J.L.B. 127; [1997] N.P.C. 85; *The Times*, May 26, 1997; *Independent*, June 4, 1997, HL 4.001
R (Iran) v Secretary of State for the Home Department; sub nom. R. (on the application of R) v Secretary of State for the Home Department; Joined Cases A (Afghanistan) v Secretary of State for the Home Department; M (Afghanistan) v Secretary of State for the Home Department; T (Afghanistan) v Secretary of State for the Home Department; T (Eritrea) v Secretary of State for the Home Department [2005] EWCA Civ 982; [2005] Imm. A.R. 535; [2005] I.N.L.R. 633; *The Times*, August 19, 2005, CA (Civ Div) 2.043
R. (on the application of Anufrijeva) v Secretary of State for the Home Department [2003] UKHL 36; [2004] 1 A.C. 604; [2003] 3 W.L.R. 252; [2003] 3 All E.R. 827; [2003] H.R.L.R. 31; [2003] Imm. A.R. 570; [2003] I.N.L.R. 521; (2003) 100(33) L.S.G. 29; *The Times*, June 27, 2003; *Independent*, July 1, 2003, HL 3.030
R. (on the application of Carson) v Secretary of State for Work and Pensions; sub nom. Carson v Secretary of State for Work and Pensions; Joined Cases R. (on the application of Reynolds) v Secretary of State for Work and Pensions [2005] UKHL 37; [2006] 1 A.C. 173; [2005] 2 W.L.R. 1369; [2005] 4 All E.R. 545; [2005] H.R.L.R. 23; [2005] U.K.H.R.R. 1185; 18 B.H.R.C. 677; *The Times*, May 27, 2005, HL 4.061
R. (on the application of M) v Secretary of State for Work and Pensions [2006] EWHC 1761, QBD (Admin) 4.061
R. (on the application of National Association of Colliery Overmen Deputies and Shotfirers) v Secretary of State for Work and Pensions [2003] EWHC 607; [2004] A.C.D. 14, QBD (Admin) 2.054
Racal Communications Ltd, Re; sub nom. Company (No.00996 of 1979), Re [1981] A.C. 374; [1980] 3 W.L.R. 181; [1980] 2 All E.R. 634, HL 4.001

Table of Cases

Richards v Secretary of State for Work and Pensions (C423/04) [2006] All E.R. (EC) 895; [2006] 2 C.M.L.R. 49; [2006] C.E.C. 637; [2006] I.C.R. 1181; [2006] 2 F.L.R. 487; [2006] 3 F.C.R. 229; [2006] Pens. L.R. 123; [2006] Fam. Law 639; *The Times*, May 5, 2006, ECJ (1st Chamber) 4.056
Secretary of State for Work and Pensions v Bhakta [2006] EWCA Civ 65; (2006) 103(10) L.S.G. 26; *The Times*, March 20, 2006, CA (Civ Div) 4.020
Secretary of State for Work and Pensions v Doyle; sub nom. Doyle v Secretary of State for Work and Pensions [2006] EWCA Civ 466; (2006) 103(19) L.S.G. 27; (2006) 156 N.L.J. 761; *Independent*, May 2, 2006, CA (Civ Div) 2.013, 2.038
Secretary of State for Work and Pensions v Menary-Smith [2006] EWCA Civ 175 .... 4.008
Secretary of State for Work and Pensions v Walker-Fox; sub nom. Walker-Fox v Secretary of State for Work and Pensions [2005] EWCA Civ 1441; [2006] Eu. L.R. 601; *The Times*, December 8, 2005, CA (Civ Div) 4.047, 4.053
Sodemare SA v Lombardia (C70/95) [1997] E.C.R. I–3395; [1998] 4 C.M.L.R. 667; [1997] 3 C.M.L.R. 591; [1997] C.E.C. 1128, ECJ (1st Chamber) 3.014
Stec v United Kingdom (65731/01) 20 B.H.R.C. 348; *The Times*, May 26, 2006, ECHR (Grand Chamber) 4.061, 4.057
Steymann v Staatssecretaris van Justitie (C196/87) [1988] E.C.R. 6159; [1989] 1 C.M.L.R. 449; *The Times*, November 26, 1988, ECJ (6th Chamber) 3.014
Szoma v Secretary of State for Work and Pensions [2005] UKHL 64; [2006] 1 A.C. 564; [2005] 3 W.L.R. 955; [2006] 1 All E.R. 1; [2006] Imm. A.R. 48; [2006] I.N.L.R. 88; (2005) 102(43) L.S.G. 31; *The Times*, November 1, 2005, HL; reversing [2003] EWCA Civ 1131; *The Times*, August 22, 2003, CA (Civ Div) 4.055
Tehrani v Secretary of State for the Home Department; sub nom. Tehrani, Petitioner [2006] UKHL 47; [2006] 3 W.L.R. 699; *The Times*, October 24, 2006, HL 4.009
Trojani v Centre Public d'Aide Sociale de Bruxelles (CPAS) (C456/02) [2004] All E.R. (EC) 1065; [2004] E.C.R. I–7573; [2004] 3 C.M.L.R. 38; [2005] C.E.C. 139, ECJ 4.048
W (China) and X (China) v Secretary of State for the Home Department [2006] EWCA Civ 1494 .... 4.048
Walker v United Kingdom (Admissibility) (37212/02) (2004) 39 E.H.R.R. SE4, ECHR 4.061
Walker-Fox v Secretary of State for Work and Pensions. *See* Secretary of State for Work and Pensions v Walker-Fox.
Westgate v Secretary of State for Work and Pensions [2006] EWCA Civ 725, CA (Civ Div) 2.055
Wirth v Landeshauptstadt Hannover (C109/93) [1993] E.C.R. I–6447, ECJ (5th Chamber) 3.014, 4.048
Yunying Jia v Migrationsverket (C–1/05), unreported, January 9, 2007, ECJ 4.048
Zalewska v Department for Social Development, unreported, CA (NI) 4.048
Zhu and Chen (C–200/02)[2004] E.C.R. 1–9925 .... 4.048

TABLE OF SOCIAL SECURITY COMMISSIONERS DECISIONS

C1/05–06(TC)(T)	5.023	CIB/3108/2005	2.039, 4.012
C1/05–06(WB)	4.060	CIB/0960/2006	2.043
C1/06–07(IS)	4.001	CIB/1064/2006	2.041
C2/05/06(WB)	4.060	CIB/1374/2006	2.046, 2.047, 2.048
C3/05/06(WB)	4.060	CIB/1635/2006	2.002, 2.036
C5/05–06(IB)	4.059	CIB/2357/2006	2.040
C6/05–06(IS)	4.048	CIS/222/1991	4.001
C8/06–07(IB)	4.062	CIS/759/1992	4.018
CA/2298/2005	4.002	CIS/17020/1996	2.014
CA/2650/2006	4.011, 4.031	CIS/5327/1998	3.044
CAF/3326/2005	4.007	CIS/3846/2001	4.001
CCS/1876/2006	4.007, 4.038	CIS/4498/2001	3.131
CDLA/156/1994	2.022	CIS/203/2002	4.001
CDLA/1804/1999	2.009	CIS/764/2002	4.001
CDLA/2680/2001	2.007	CIS/4422/2002	4.001
CDLA/5413/1999	4.059	CIS/306/2003	4.018
CDLA/2807/2003	4.023	CIS/3228/2003	4.001
CDLA/1420/2004	2.007	CIS/488/2004	4.053
CDLA/2974/2004	2.007	CIS/1335/2004	3.130, 3.132
CDLA/2999/2004	1.011, 4.003, 4.004	CIS/1491/2004	4.053
CDLA/395/2005	2.007	CIS/1814/2004	4.039
CDLA/845/2005	2.009	CIS/2901/2004	3.048, 3.124
CDLA/1707/2005	4.027	CIB/3327/2004	4.011
CDLA/2142/2005	2.008	CIS/1363/2005	4.007, 4.010, 4.033, 4.034, 4.036
CDLA/3941/2005	2.023		
CDLA/145/2006	4.037	CIS/1916/2005	4.061
CDLA/393/2006	4.027	CIS/2559/2005	4.048
CDLA/1480/2006	4.006, 4.035	CIS/2574/2005	3.124
CDLA/1639/2006	2.008, 2.021	CIS/2680/2005	4.048
CF/1727/2006	4.054	CIS/2726/2005	4–017, 4–018
CG/2054/2004	4.061	CIS/3182/2005	3.013, 3.016, 4.048
CG/2973/2004	4–018, 4.040	CIS/3315/2005	3.013, 4.048
CG/20454/2004	2/004	CIS/3573/2005	3.016, 4.048
CG/1752/2006	2.014	CIS/3605/2005	4.001, 4.011
CH/2484/2005	4.048	CIS/3875/2005	3.014, 4.048
CH/3314/2005	4.048	CIS/3890/2005	4.049
CH/687/2006	4.027	CIS/4096/2005	3.131
CH/1400/2006	3.014, 3.015, 4.048	CIS/176/2006	3.030
CH/1822/2006	3.023	CIS/624/2006	4.005a, 4.006, 4.029, 4.032a, 4.038a
CH/2484/2006	4.006, 4.039a		
CI/34/1993	2.011	CIS/933/2006	3.044
CI/3511/2002	2.009	CIS/1757/2006	3.023, 4.057
CI/3565/2004	2.056	CIS/1807/2006	3.023
CI/1804/2005	4.007, 4.008	CIS/1867/2006	4.001
CI/2930/2005	2.011, 2.053	CIS/2317/2006	3.008
CI/142/2006	2.010	CJSA/3304/1999	3.001
CI/421/2006	2.054	CJSA/1703/2006	3.001, 4.006
CI/954/2006	2.012, 4.005, 4.029, 4.032	CPC/0206/2005	3.003, 3.004, 3.120, 4.027
CIB/6244/1997	2.040	CPC/968/2005	3.124

xxi

Table of Social Security Commissioners Decisions

CPC/1820/2005	3.048, 3.124	R(G)1/06	2.004, 4.061
CPC/1928/2005	3.003, 3.004, 3.120	R(G)2/06	4.018, 4.028, 4.040
CPC/2574/2005	3.048	R(H)1/05	4.057
CPC/2920/2005	3.018, 3.118, 3.130, 4.048	R(H)6/06	4.006
		R(H)1/07	4.006
CSA/164/2004	2.019	R(I)12/75	4.007
CSA/469/2005	2/019	R(I)7/94	4.006
CSDLA/867/1997	2.007	R(I)4/03	2.012, 4.005
CSDLA/832/1999	2.007	R(I)1/06	2.055
CSDLA/860/2000	2.007	R(I)2/06	4.007, 4.008, 4.039
CSDLA/12/2003	2.008	R(IB)2/04	4.005a
CSDLA/133/2005	2.007	R(IB)3/04	2.042
CSDLA/399/2005	2.022	R(IB)1/06	2.013, 2.038
CSDLA/242/2006	4.021	R(IB)2/06	2.039, 4.012
CSDLA/427/2006	2.007	R(IS)13/89	4.001
CSIB/1521/2001	2.048	R(IS)14/96	4.001
CSIB/0148/2005	2.042	R(IS)12/98	3.013
CSIB/196/2005	2.042	R(IS)6/04	5.030a
CSIB/803/2005	2.042, 2.044, 2.045	R(IS)2/06	4.055
CSIB/808/2005	4.008	R(IS)3/06	4.047, 4.053
CSIB/818/2005	4.008	R(IS)4/06	4.001
CSIS/48/1992	4.018	R(IS)6/06	4.061
CSJSA/23/2006	3.020	R(IS)7/06	4.020
CTC/2065/2004	5.030	R(IS)8/06	4.053
CTC/4390/2004	5.030	R(IS)9/06	4.002
CTC/31/2006	5.014, 5.030a	R(IS)10/06	4–017, 4–018
CTC/869/2006	5.031	R(IS)11/06	4.058, 4.061
R4/01(IS)	4.006	R(IS)12/06	4.061
R(A)2/06	4.002	R(IS)1/07	4.038
R(DLA)3/03	2.007	R(IS)2/07	3.044
R(DLA)1/04	2.007	R(IS)3/07	3.048
R(DLA)2/06	4.037	R(JSA)3/06	4.048, 4.050
R(DLA)3/06	2.007	R(P)1/06	4.062
R(DLA)5/06	4.059	R(P)1/07	4.056
R(DLA)7/06	2.009	R(PC)1/07	3.048, 3.124
R(DLA)1/07	2.007	R(SB(6/85)	4.007

TABLE OF EUROPEAN MATERIALS

Treaties and Conventions
1950 Human Rights Convention 4.001, 5.031
    Art.6 .... 4.059, 5.030a
    Art.6(1) 4.059
    Art.8 .... 4.060, 4.061
    Art.14 .... 3.012, 3.130, 4.060, 4.061, 4.062, 5.030
    First Protocol
    Art.1 .... 3.012, 3.130, 4.061, 4.062, 4.057
1951 Convention relating to the Status of Refugees
    Art.1 .... 3.017, 3.079, 3.117
    1967 Protocol
    Art.1(2) 3.017, 3.079, 3.117
1957 EC Treaty
    Art.18 .... 4.048
    Art.39 .... 3.017, 3.018, 3.117, 4.049
    Art.43 .... 4.048
    Art.50 .... 3.014

Regulations
1968 Reg.1612/68 [1968] O.J. L257/2 .... 4.050
1971 Reg.1408/71 [1971] O.J. L149/2 .... 4.048, 4.054
    Art.4 .... 4.053
    Art.13 .... 4.054
2003 Reg.859/2003 [2003] O.J. L124/1
    Art.1 .... 4.055

Directives
1964 Dir.64/221 [1964] O.J. L56/850 .... 3.018
1968 Dir.68/360 [1968] O.J. L257/13 .... 3.018
1972 Dir.72/194 [1972] O.J. L121/32 .... 3.018
1973 Dir.73/148 [1973] O.J. L172/14 .... 3.014
    Art.1(1)(d) 4.048
    Art.6(b) 4.048
1975 Dir.75/34 [1975] O.J. L14/10 .... 3.018
1975 Dir.75/35 [1975] O.J. L14/14 .... 3.018
1979 Dir.79/7 [1979] O.J. L6/24 .... 4.056
1990 Dir.90/364 [1990] O.J. L180/26 .... 3.018, 3.118. 4.048
    Art.2 .... 3.018, 3.130
    Art.32 .... 3.118
    Annex VIII 3.118
1990 Dir.90/365 [1990] O.J. L180/28 .... 3.018
1993 Dir.93/96 [1993] O.J. L317 .... 3.018, 4.048
2004 Dir.2004/38 [2004] OJ L158/77 .... 3.017, 3.018, 3.117, 3.129, 4.048, 4.051
    Art.1 .... 4.052
    Art.2 .... 1.003, 3.079, 3.117
    Art.2(a)–(c) 3.017, 3.129
    Art.6 .... 3.017, 3.018, 3.079, 3.117
    Art.7(3) 3.017, 3.079, 3.117, 3.129
    Art.7(3)(a) 4.049
    Art.17 .... 3.017, 3.079, 3.117, 3.129
    Art.17(1)(b) 4.049

TABLE OF STATUTES

1952	Prison Act (15 & 16 Geo.6 & 1 Eliz.2 c.52) 3.011, 3.078	1988	Income and Corporation Taxes Act (c.1)	
1968	Health Services and Public Health Act (c.46)		ss.1–1B	5.021
			s.336	5.002
	s.71(1)	2.034	s.336(1A)(b)	**5.002**
1970	Taxes Management Act (c.9)		s.573	5.002
			s.609	5.002
	s.8(1A)	5.001	s.610	5.002
	s.8A(1A)	5.001	s.611	5.002
	s.9ZA	5.001	s.629	5.002
	s.9A	5.001	s.633	5.002
	s.9A(4)–6	**5.001**	1989	Prisons (Scotland) Act
	s.17	5.022		(c.45) 3.011, 3.078
	s.18	5.022	1990	Finance Act (c.29)
1971	Immigration Act (c.77)		s.25	5.025
	s.3(2) 3.017, 3.079, 3.117	1990	Enterprise and New Towns (Scotland) Act (c.35)	
1972	European Communities Act (c.68)		s.2(3)	2.028
	s.2	4.047	1992	Social Security Contributions and Benefits Act (c.4)	2.017
1973	Employment and Training Act (c.50)			
	s.2 .... 2.028, 3.006, 3.007		Pt 8 .... 3.038, 3.094	
	s.2(1)	2.028	s.6 .... 5.007, 5.010	
1975	Social Security Act (c.14) 1.010, 4.003		s.6(1)(b) 5.007, 5.010	
			s.30C 2.001, 2.036	
	s.14	1.010	s.30C(1)	2.035
	s.15	1.010	s.35	2.003
	s.16	1.010	s.35(5)	2.003
	s.35	1.010	s.36	2.004
	s.37A	1.010	s.36(1)	2.004
1976	Supplementary Benefits Act (c.71) 1.010, 1.011, 4.003		s.36(1)(a)	4.061
			s.43	4.061
1978	Interpretation Act (c.30)		s.44 .... 2.005, 2.006	
	s.7	4.018	s.44(5A)(a)	2.005
1979	Vaccine Damage Payments Act (c.17) 1.005, 1.007		s.44(6)	2.005
			s.44(7A)	2.005
	s.1(2)	2.001	s.64	4.031
	s.1(2)(i)	1.005	s.64(2),(3)	4.031
1980	Education (Scotland) Act (c.44)		s.68	3.121
			s.70	3.121
	s.73(f) 3.028, 3.087		s.72 .... 2.007, 4.031	
1983	Mental Health Act (c.20) 3.011, 3.078		s.73 .... 2.008, 4.031	
			s.73(8)	2.008
1984	Public Health (Control of Disease) Act (c.22)		s.73(12)	2.009
			s.89(1)	2.015
	s.20(1)	2.034	s.89(1A)	2.015
1984	Police and Criminal Evidence Act (c.60)		s.94	2.010
			s.94(1)	2.011
	s.118(2) 3.070, 3.073		s.103 .... 2.011, 2.012	
			s.103(1)	2.011
			s.103(2)	2.011

xxv

Table of Statutes

1992 Social Security Contributions and Benefits Act —*cont.*
- s.123(1)(a) 1.001
- s.123(1)(d) 1.001
- s.123(1)(e) 1.001
- s.131(3)(b) 1.001
- s.135(1) 1.001
- s.135(2) 1.001
- s.137(1) 1.001
- s.137(2) 1.001
- s.138(1)(a) 1.001
- s.138(4) 1.001
- s.152 .... 2.035
- s.165 .... 5.003, 5.039
- s.165(1) 5.005
- s.165(2),(3) **5.003**
- s.165(4) 5.005
- s.165(6) 5.005
- s.165(8) **5.003**
- s.166 .... 5.004
- s.166(1) 5.005
- s.166(1A) **5.004**
- s.166(4) **5.004**
- s.171 .... 5.005
- s.171(1A) **5.005**
- ss.171ZEA–171ZEE 6.002
- s.171ZE 5.006
- s.171ZE(10A) **5.006**
- s.171ZJ 5.007
- s.171ZJ(1) **5.007**
- s.171ZL 5.008
- s.171ZL(4)(b) **5.008**
- s.171ZL(4A) **5.008**
- s.171ZL(4B) **5.008**
- s.171ZN 5.009
- s.171ZN(6A) **5.009**
- s.171ZS 5.010
- s.171ZS(1) **5.010**
- s.175(1) 1.001
- s.175(3) 1.001
- s.175(4) 1.001
- Sch.5 .... 3.121
- Sch.5A 3.121
- Sch.6 para.1 .... 2.011
- Sch.6 para.1(a) 2.011
- Sch.6 para.1(b) 2.011
- Sch.6 para.1(c) 2.011
- Sch.7 para.7(1) 2.015
- Sch.11 .... 5.011
- Sch.11 para.1 .... 5.011
- Sch.11 para.2(a) 5.011
- Sch.13 .... 5.012
- Sch.13 para.3 .... 5.012
- Sch.13 para.3(2) 5.005
- Sch.13 para.3(2A) 5.012

1992 Social Security Administration Act (c.5)
- s.71 .... 1.011, 4.001, 4.002
- s.71(5A) 4.001, 4.011
- s.170(4) 2.042

1992 Social Security Administration Act—*cont.*
- s.173(1)(b) 1.008
- Sch.10 para.4(1) 1.011

1992 Tribunals and Inquiries Act (c.53)
- Sch.1 .... 3.032, 3.070, 3.073, 3.089

1994 Statutory Sick Pay Act (c.2)
- s.1(2) 5.011

1995 Jobseekers Act (c.18)
- s.4(5) 1.001
- s.4(12) 1.001
- s.6(1) 3.071
- s.19(3) 3.001
- s.19(4) 3.001
- s.19(9) 3.002
- s.20(3) 3.001
- s.35(1) 1.001
- s.36(2) 1.001
- s.36(4) 1.001
- Sch.1 para.11 .... 1.001

1995 Pensions Act (c.26)
- s.128(4)–(6) 2.006
- s.295 .... 3.070

1995 Criminal Procedure (Scotland) Act (c.46) 3.011, 3.078
- s.295 .... 3.070, 3.073

1998 Social Security Act (c.14) 1.011
- s.8(1) 2.049, 2.050
- s.8(3) 1.011, 4.003
- s.8(3)(a)–(g) 1.011
- s.8(3)(h) 1.008, 1.010, 4.004
- s.10 .... 1.011, 4.004
- s.10(1) 4.005
- s.12 .... 4.006
- s.12(1) 4.005a
- s.12(2) 4.006
- s.12(8)(b) 4.029
- s.14(1) 4.007, 4.010
- s.14(8) 4.008
- s.14(10) 4.009
- s.15(4) 4.009
- s.16(1)(3) 4.010
- s.17(1) 4.011
- s.17(2) 4.011
- s.20(3) 4.012
- s.20(3)(a) 2.039
- s.67 .... 2.003
- s.71(5A) 4.011
- s.79(1) 1.008
- s.84 .... 1.008

1998 Teaching and Higher Education Act (c.30)
- s.22 .... 3.028, 3.087

1998 Human Rights Act (c.42) 2.004, 5.014, 5.031
- s.2 .... 4.057
- s.3 .... 4.058

Table of Statutes

1999	Immigration and Asylum Act (c.33)	
	s.115(9)	3.117
2000	Finance Act (c.17)	
	s.84	5.018
	s.85	5.018
2001	Capital Allowances Act (c.2)	
	s.262	5.017
2001	Health and Social Care Act (c.15)	
	s.57	5.028
2002	State Pension Credit Act (c.16)	
	Pt 2	4.024
	s.1(5)(a)	1.001
	s.7	3.003
	s.8	4.024
	s.9	3.004
	s.17(1)	1.001
2002	Tax Credits Act (c.21)	
	s.1(3)(d)	3.010
	s.3	5.013
	s.6	5.013, 5.033
	s.9(6)	3.037, 3.038, 3.093, 3.094
	s.29	5.014
	s.38	5.014, 5.030a
2002	Adoption and Children Act (c.38)	
	s.19	5.050
	s.21	5.050
	s.144(4)	5.008
2002	Community Care and Health (Scotland) Act (asp 5.)	2.019
2003	Income Tax (Earnings and Pensions) Act (c.1)	
	Pt 7	5.015
	Pt 9	5.002
	Pt 9, Chap.9	5.026
	Pt 12	5.017
	s.3	5.015
	s.3(1)	5.015
	s.6	5.016
	s.232	5.017
	s.327	5.017
	s.327(4),(5)	**5.017**
	s.579A	5.026
	s.636A	5.027
	s.637	5.027
	s.655	5.018
	s.678	5.019
	s.679	**5.019**
2003	Finance Act (c.14)	
	s.140	5.015
	Sch.22 para.16(1)	5.015
2003	Mental Health (Care and Treatment) (Scotland) Act (asp 13.)	3.011, 3.078
2004	Finance Act (c.12)	
	s.30(9)	5.001
	s.150(2)	3.121, 5.024
	ss.188–194	5.017
	s.208(2)(a),(b)	5.026
	s.281	5.002
	s.281(1)	5.017
	s.326	5.017
	Sch.5 para.1	5.001
	Sch.29 para.7	3.121
	Sch.35 para.13	5.002
	Sch.35 para.60	5.017
	Sch.36 para.1(1)(f)	5.002
	Sch.42 Part 3	5.017
2004	Civil Partnership Act (c.33)	
	s.246	4.013
2005	Income Tax (Trading and Other Income) Act (c.5)	
	Pt 8, Chap.2	5.019
	Pt 8, Chap.3	5.019
	Pt 8, Chap.4	5.019
	s.619	5.020, 5.021
	s.619(2)	5.021
	s.781	5.018
	s.782	5.018
	s.783	5.022
	s.783(2)–(3)	**5.022**
	s.882(1)	5.016, 5.018, 5.019
	Sch.1 para.584	5.018, 5.019
	Sch.1 para.585	5.016
	Sch.1 para.612	5.018
	Sch.1 para.613	5.019
2006	Work and Families Act (c.18)	6.002
	s.1	5.003
	s.2	5.009
	ss.6–10	6.002
	s.11	5.003, 5.004, 5.005, 5.006, 5.012
	Sch.1 para.7(2)	5.003
	Sch.1 para.7(4)	5.003
	Sch.1 para.8(2)	5.004
	Sch.1 para.8(3)	5.004
	Sch.1 para.9	5.005
	Sch.1 para.16(1)	5.006
	Sch.1 para.16(3)	5.006
	Sch.1 para.21	5.009
	Sch.1 para.23	5.012
2006	Finance Act (c.25)	
	s.64(3)	5.022
	s.89	5.021
	Sch.13 para.5	5.021

TABLE OF STATUTORY INSTRUMENTS

1965 Act of Sederunt (Rules of the Court, Consolidation and Amendment) (SI 1965/321) 3.125
1971 Public Health (Aircraft) (Scotland) Regulations (SI 1971/131)
    reg.8 .... 2.034
    reg.9 .... 2.034
1971 Public Health (Ships)(Scotland) Regulations (SI 1971/132)
    reg.9 .... 2.034
    reg.10 .... 2.034
1975 Social Security Benefit (Persons Abroad) Regulations (SI 1975/563) 2.028
1977 Social Security Benefit (Dependency) Regulations (SI 1977/343)
    reg.9A 2.015
    Sch.2 para.9(1) 2.016
1978 Social Security (Categorisation of Earners) Regulations (SI 1978/1689) 5.037, 5.041, 5.047
    Sch.1 Part 3 para.7 .... 4.013
1979 Social Security (Contributions) Regulations (SI 1979/591)
    reg.18(22)–(25) 3.019, 3.080
    Sch.3 .... 3.049, 3.050, 3.075, 3.101, 3.102, 3.103
1979 Social Security (Overlapping Benefits) Regulations (SI 1979/597)
    reg.14 .... 2.017
    reg.14(1) **2.017**
1979 Social Security (Widow's Benefit and Retirement Pensions) Regulations (SI 1979/642)
    reg.3A 2.026
1979 Public Health (Aircraft) Regulations (SI 1979/1434)
    reg.8 .... 2.034
    reg.9 .... 2.034
1979 Public Health (Ships) Regulations (SI 1979/1435)
    reg.9 .... 2.034
    reg.10 .... 2.034
1982 Statutory Sick Pay (General) Regulations (SI 1982/894)
    reg.16 .... 5.037
    reg.16(1ZA) **5.037**
    reg.17 .... 5.038
1982 Social Security (General Benefit) Regulations (SI 1982/1408)
    reg.11 .... 2.011, 2.053
    reg.11(3) 2.011
    reg.11(4) 2.011
    reg.11(5) 2.011
    reg.16 ....4.041a
1983 Social Security (Unemployment, Sickness and Invalidity Benefit) Regulations (SI 1983/1598)
    regs 9–12A 3.071
1985 Social Security (Industrial Injuries) (Prescribed Diseases) Regulations (SI 1985/967)
    Sch.1 PD A11 ...... 2.054, 2,055
    Sch.1 PD D7 .... 2.056
1986 Statutory Maternity Pay (General) Regulations (SI 1986/1960)
    reg.2 .... **5.039**
    reg.9A **5.040**
    reg.17 .... 5.041
    reg.17(1A) **5.041**
    reg.20 .... **5.043**
    reg.20(2) **5.042**
    reg.28 .... 5.043
1987 Social Security (Maternity Allowance) Regulations (SI 1987/416)
    reg.2 .... 2.024
    reg.2(1)(a) **2.024**
    reg.3(2A) 2.025
1987 Social Fund Maternity and Funeral Expenses (General) Regulations (SI 1987/481)
    reg.7(9) **3.128**

Table of Statutory Instruments

1987 Social Fund Maternity and Funeral Expenses (General) Regulations—*cont.*	1987 Income Support (General) Regulations—*cont.*
reg.7(10) **3.129**, 3.130, 3.132	reg.70 .... 3.030
reg.9 .... 3.132	reg.85A(3) 3.079
reg.9(3)(a) 3.130	Sch.1B para.16 ..... 3.031, 3.033
reg.9(3)(g) 3.130	Sch.1B para.19 ..... **3.032**, 3.034
1987 Income Support (General) Regulations (SI 1987/1967) 2.014, 6.006, 6.007	Sch.2 para.9 .... 3.038
	Sch.2 para.9A 3.038
	Sch.2 para.10 ...... 3.035, 3.038
	Sch.2 para.11 .... 3.038
reg.2 .... 3.005	Sch.2 para,12 .... 3.036
reg.4ZA 3.006, 3.007	Sch.2 para.13 .... 3.038
reg.4ZA(2) 3.007	Sch.2 para.14 .... 3.038
reg.4ZA(3)(d) **3.006**, 3.007	Sch.3 para.1 .... 3.037, 3.042, 3.043, 3.097
reg.13(1)(d) 3.131	Sch.3 para.1(3)(b) **3.037**
reg.15(1) 3.008	Sch.3 para.3 .... 3.038, 3.043, 3.098
reg.16 .... 3.009	
reg.16(c)(a) 3.009	Sch.3 para.3(7)(c)(ii) 3.043
reg.17 .... 2.010, 3.025, 3.084	Sch.3 para.3(7)(c)(ii) **3.038**
reg.17(1)(a)–(d) 4.024	Sch.3 para.4 .... 3.044
reg.17(1)(e) 2.028	Sch.3 para.4(2) 3.044
reg.18(1)(a)–(e) 4.024	Sch.3 para.4(7) 3.044
reg.21 .... 3.018	Sch.3 para.4(8)–(11) 3.044
reg.21(1) 3.012, 3.013, 3.014, 3.015, 3.016	Sch.3 para.4(12) 3.044
	Sch.3 para.7 .... 3.039, 3.045
reg.21(3) **3.011**, 3.118	Sch.3 para.7(4A) **3.039**, 3.045
reg.21(3)–(3G) 3.011	Sch.3 para.7(10) 3.039, 3.045, 3.047
reg.21(3F), (3G) 3.011	
reg.21(3G) 3.118	Sch.3 para.11(5) 3.044
reg.21AA 3.011, 3.013, **3.017**, 3.018, 3.079	Sch.3 para.12 .... 3.046
	Sch.3 para.14 ...... 3.030, 3.047, 3.099
reg.21AA(3) 3.079	Sch.3 para.14(3AA)(b) 3.040
reg.21AA(3)(a) 3.018	Sch.3 para.14(10) 3.040
reg.21AA(3)(b) 3.018	Sch.3 para.17 ...... 3.041, 3.048, 3.100
reg.21AA(3)(c) 3.018	
reg.21AA(3)(d) 3.018	Sch.7 .... 3.011
reg.21AA(4)(a)–(e) 1.003, 3.018	Sch.8 para.7 .... 3.049
	Sch.8 para.15A 3.050
reg.21AA(4)(h) 3.017	Sch.9 para.13 .... 3.007
reg.21AA(4)(hh) 3.017	Sch.9 para.15 ...... 3.022, 3.051, 3.056, 3.057, 3.109
reg.21AA(4)(k) 3.017	
reg.35 .... 3.019	Sch.9 para.15(1) **3.051**, 3.055
reg.35(1)(j) 3.019	Sch.9 para.15(2) 3.051
reg.42 .... 3.020	Sch.9 para.15(4) 3.051
reg.42(6) 3.020	Sch.9 para.15(6) 3.051
reg.42(6A) 3.020	Sch.9 para.15A 3.057, 3.054, 3.057, 3.110
reg.48 .... 3.021, 3.022, 3.082	
reg.48(4) 3.021, 3.022, 3.056	Sch.9 para.16 .... 3.055
reg.51 .... 3.023	Sch.9 para.26 .... 3.053
reg.51(1) 3.023	Sch.9 para.30A 3.054
reg.62 ....3.024. 3.025	Sch.9 para.36 .... 3.055
reg.62(2)(i) 3.025	Sch.9 para.39 .... 3.051
reg.62(2A)(a) 3.024	Sch.10 para.12 .... 3.056, 3.058, 3.114
reg.62(2A)(b) 3.024	
reg.62(2B) 3.024, 3.025	Sch.10 para.12A 3.056, **3.059**
reg.65 .... 3.026	
reg.66A 3.027	
reg.66A(5)(a) 3.027	
reg.66A(5)(b) 3.027	
reg.66C **3.028**, 3.029	

xxx

Table of Statutory Instruments

1987 Income Support (General) Regulations—*cont.*
Sch.10 para.12 ..... 3.061, 3.062
Sch.10 para.12A 3.062, 3.115
Sch.10 para.44 .... **3.060**, 3.062, 3.063, 3.116
Sch.10 para.45 .... 3.062

1987 Social Security (Claims and Payments) Regulations (SI 1987/1968) 4.020
reg.4D 4–014
reg.4D(6A)–(6E) **4–014**
reg.4F(2) 4–015
reg.5 4–016
reg.6 .... 4–017, 4–018
reg.6(1) 4.018
reg.6(20) **4–017**
reg.6(21)(b) **4–017**
reg.7(3) **4.019**
reg.13A 4.021
reg.19 .... 4.022
reg.19(j) **4.022**
reg.30 .... 4.023
reg.38 .... 4.023
Sch.9 .... 4.024, 6.005
Sch.9 para.5(5) 4.024
Sch.9 para.5(5A) 4.024
Sch.9 para.6(6) 4.024
Sch.9 para.6(6A) 4.024
Sch.9 para.7(8) 4.024
Sch.9 para.7(9) 4.024
Sch.9 para.8(2) 4.024
Sch.9 para.8(2A) 4.024
Sch.9 para.8(3) 4.024
Sch.9 para.8(4) **4.024**
Sch.9A 4.025

1987 Adoption (Northern Ireland) Order (SI 1987/2203)
art.17 .... 5.050
art.18 .... 5.050

1988 Public Health (Infectious Diseases) Regulations (SI 1988/1546)
reg.3 .... 2.034
reg.9(1) 2.034
reg.9(2) 2.034
Sch.1 .... 2.034
Sch.3 .... 2.034
Sch.4 .... 2.034

1988 Social Fund Cold Weather Payments (General) Regulations (SI 1988/1724)
Sch.1 .... **3.126**
Sch.2 .... **3.127**

1989 Social Security Benefit (Dependency) Amendment Regulations (SI 1989/523)
reg.5 .... 2.015

1991 Social Security (Attendance Allowance) Regulations (SI 1991/2740)
reg.2 .... 2.018
reg.2(1)(b) 2.018
reg.2(4) 2.018
reg.7 .... 2.019

1991 Social Security (Disability Living Allowance) Regulations (SI 1991/2890)
reg.2 .... 2.020
reg.2(1)(b) 2.020
reg.2(3) 2.020
reg.9 .... 4.041
reg.12 .... 2.022, 2.023
reg.12(1) 2.021
reg.12(1)(a)(ii) 2.022
reg.12(1)(a)(iii) 2.023

1992 Social Security (Miscellaneous Provisions) Amendment Regulations (SI 1992/247)
reg.4(2) 2.015

1994 Income-related Benefits Schemes (Miscellaneous Amendments) (No.3) Regulations (SI 1994/1807) 3.064

1994 Social Security (Incapacity Benefit-Increases for Dependants) Regulations (SI 1994/2945)
reg.9 .... 2.032
reg.9(2B) **2.032**
reg.9(2C) **2.032**
reg.9(2D) **2.032**
reg.11 .... **2.033**

1994 Social Security (Incapacity Benefit) Regulations (SI 1994/2946)
reg.4 .... 2.028
reg.4(2) **2.028**
reg.4(2)(d) 2.028
reg.4(3) **2.028**
reg.5A 2.029
reg.8 .... 2.030, 2.031

1995 Social Security (Incapacity for Work) (General) Regulations (SI 1995/311)
reg.3 .... 2.034
reg.11 .... **2.034**
reg.13A 2.035, 3.005
reg.13A(1) 2.035
reg.13A(3) **2.035**
reg.13A(3A) **2.035**

xxxi

Table of Statutory Instruments

1995 Social Security (Incapacity for Work) (General) Regulations—*cont.*
reg.16 .... 2.002
reg.16(1) 2.036
reg.16(3) 2.036
reg.16(3)(a) 2.036
reg.16(3)(b) 2.036
reg.16(5) 2.036
reg.17 .... 2.037, 2.038
reg.24 .... 2.039
reg.25(3) 2.040
reg.27 .... 2.041
Sch.1 .... 2.042
Sch.1 Part I 2.043, 2.044, 2.045
Sch.1 Part II 2.046, 2.047, 2.048

1995 Children (Northern Ireland) Order (SI 1995/755)
art.119(4) 5.023
art.119(6) 5.023

1995 Social Security (Incapacity Benefit) (Consequential and Transitional Amendments and Savings) Regulations (SI 1995/829)
reg.11 .... 2.049
reg.11(6) **2.049**
reg.17 .... 2.050
reg.17(5) **2.050**
reg.17B 2.051
reg.23(2) 2.052

1996 Social Security (Persons from Abroad) Miscellaneous Amendments Regulations (SI 1996/30)
reg.12 .... 1.004, 3.065

1996 Jobseeker's Allowance Regulations (SI 1996/207) 6.006, 6.007
reg.1(3) 3.067, 3.071
reg.4 .... 3.071
reg.5 .... 3.069
reg.5(1) **3.068**
regs 5–17 .... 3.071
reg.14 .... 3.070, 3.071
reg.14(1)(r),(s) **3.070**
reg.14(2B) **3.070**
reg.14(7) **3.070**
reg.15(a) 3.071
reg.15(b) 3.071
reg.15(bc) 3.071
reg.15(c) 3.071
reg.18 .... 3.072
reg.18(34)(f)(v) **3.072**
reg.19 .... 3.071
reg.19(1)(v), (w) **3.073**
reg.19(2A) **3.073**

1996 Jobseeker's Allowance Regulations—*cont.*
reg.30 .... 3.074
reg.53 .... 3.075
reg.70 .... 3.001
reg.74 .... 3.001
reg.75(1)(a)(iii) 3.076
reg.78 .... 3.077
reg.83 .... 3.084
reg.83(a)–(e) 4.024
reg.83(f) 2.028
reg.84(1)(a)–(f) 4.024
reg.84(1)(g) 2.028
reg.85(4) 3.070, 3.073, **3.078**
reg.85(4)–(4B) 3.078
reg.85A 3.078, **3.079**
reg.85A(3) 3.018
reg.85A(4)(a)–(e) 1.003
reg.85A(4)(k) 3.079
reg.85A(4)(h) 3.079
reg.85A(4)(hh) 3.079
reg.98 .... 3.080
reg.105(13) 3.020
reg.105(13A) 3.020
reg.110 .... 3.081, 3.082
reg.131 .... 3.083, 3.084
reg.131(2)(h) 3.084
reg.131(3)(a) 3.083
reg.131(3)(b) 3.083
reg.131(3A) 3.083, 3.084
reg.134 .... 3.085
reg.136 .... 3.086
reg.136(5)(a) 3.086
reg.136(5)(b) 3.086
reg.136B **3.087**, 3.088
Sch.A1 para.15 .... **3.089**
Sch.1 para.10 .... 3.094
Sch.1 para.11 .... 3.094
Sch.1 para.12 .... 3.090, 3.094
Sch.1 para.13 .... 3.094
Sch.1 para.15 .... 3.094
Sch.1 para.16 .... 3.094
Sch.1 para.20F 3.091
Sch.1 para.20H 3.092
Sch.2 para.1 .... 3.093, 3.097
Sch.2 para.1(3)(d) **3.093**
Sch.2 para.3 .... 3.094, 3.098
Sch.2 para.3(7)(c)(ii) **3.094**
Sch.2 para.13 .... 3.095, 3.099
Sch.2 para.13(4A)(b) 3.095
Sch.2 para.13(12) 3.095
Sch.2 para.16 .... 3.096, 3.100
Sch.6 para.9 .... 3.101
Sch.6 para.19 .... 3.102
Sch.6A para.5 .... 3.103
Sch.7 .... 3.085
Sch.7 para.15 .... 3.104, 3.109
Sch.7 para.15(1) **3.104**

Table of Statutory Instruments

1996	Jobseeker's Allowance Regulations—*cont.*		1999	Social Security Act 1998 (Commencement No.9, and Savings and Consequential and Transitional Provisions) Order 1999 (SI 1999/2422)
	Sch.7 para.16 ...... 3.105, 3.107, 3.110			
	Sch.7 para.27 .... 3.106			
	Sch.7 para.32 .... 3.107			art.2(3)(b) 2.049, 2.050
	Sch.7 para.38 .... 3.108			art.3 .... 2.049, 2.050
	Sch.7 para.41 .... 3.104		2000	Social Security (Immigration and Asylum) Consequential Amendments Regulations (SI 2000/636)
	Sch.8 para.17 .... **3.111**, 3.114			
	Sch.8 para.17A **3.112**, 3.115			
	Sch.8 para.42 .... **3.113**, 3.116			
1996	Social Security Benefit (Computation of Earnings) Regulations (SI 1996/2745)			reg.2 .... 3.011, 3.078
				reg.12(5) 3.030
			2000	Immigration (European Economic Area) Regulations (SI 2000/2326) 3.018
	reg.3 .... 2.013			
	Sch.1 .... 2.014			
1996	Fostering of Children (Scotland) Regulations (SI 1996/3263)			reg.5(2)(a) 3.013
				reg.5(2)(b) 3.013
				reg.6(1)(a) 3.018
	reg.9 .... 3.053, 3.106			reg.14 .... 3.018
1998	Education (Student Support) (Northern Ireland) Order (SI 1998/1760)			reg.14(4) 3.018
			2001	Social Security (Contributions) Regulations (SI 2001/1004)
	art.3 .... 3.028, 3.087			
1998	Civil Procedure Rules (SI 1998/3132)			Sch.3 Part 5 .... 3.019, 3.080
				Sch.6 .... 3.049, 3.050, 3.075, 3.101, 3.102, 3.103
	r.21.11(1) 3.060, 3.113, 3.125			
				Sch.6 Part I 3.072
1999	Social Security and Child Support (Decisions and Appeals) Regulations (SI 1999/991) 2.049, 2.050		2001	Social Security (Jobcentre Plus Interviews) Regulations (SI 2001/3210)
				reg.2 .... 4.042, 4.044
				reg.4 .... 4.044
	reg.1(3) 4.027			reg.16 .... 4.043
	reg.2 .... 4.028		2002	State Pension Credit Regulations (SI 2002/1792) 6.006, 6.007
	reg.6 .... 4.005, 4.029			
	reg.6(2)(a)(i) 4.029			
	reg.6(5) 4.005			reg.2 .... 3.116, **3.117**, 3.118
	reg.7(2) 4.030			reg.2(4)(a)–(e) 1.003, 3.117
	reg.7(2)(bc) **4.030**			reg.2(4)(h) 3.117
	reg.7A 4.031			reg.2(4)(hh) 3.117
	reg.10 .... 4.011			reg.2(4)(k) 3.117
	reg.26 .... 4.005, 4.032			reg.4 .... 3.119
	reg.30 ....4.032a			reg.5 .... 3.119
	reg.30(2)(a) 4.032a			reg.5(1A) **3.119**
	reg.31(4) 4.033, 4.034, 4.036			reg.10 .... 3.120
	reg.32(4) 4.034			reg.18 .... 3.121
	reg.39 .... 4.035			reg.18(1)–(1D) **3.121**
	reg.46 .... 4.036			reg.18(9),(10) **3.121**
	reg.49(1) 4.037			Sch.II 3.048, 3.124, 4.024
	reg.51 .... 4.038			Sch.II para.13 .... 3.122
	reg.53(1) 4.038a			Sch.II para.14 .... 3.123
	reg.53(4) 4.039			Sch.II para.14(7)(dd) **3.123**
	reg.55(1) 4.039a			Sch.V para.16(2) 3.125
	reg.57(1) 4.040			Sch.V para.16(2)(a) **3.125**
	Sch.3A para.3 .... 4.041			Sch.V para.16(2)(b) 3.125
	Sch.3A para.3(h) 4.041			

xxxiii

Table of Statutory Instruments

2002 Working Tax Credit (Entitlement and Maximum Rate) Regulations (SI 2002/2005)
  reg.4(1) 5.032
  reg.4(3)–(5) 5.032
  regs 5–8 .... 5.032
  reg.9(1)(a) 5.032
  reg.10(1) 5.032
  reg.10(2)(c) 5.032
  reg.10(2)(d) 5.032
  reg.11(2)(c) 5.032
  reg.13(1) 5.032
  reg.14 .... 5.023
  reg.14(2)(c) 5.023
  reg.16(1)(b) 5.032
  reg.18(3)(c) 5.032

2002 Tax Credits (Definition and Calculation of Income) Regulations (SI 2002/2006)
  reg.2 .... 5.024
  reg.3 .... 5.025
  reg.3(7)(b)–(d) **5.025**
  reg.5 .... 5.026, 5.027
  reg.5(1)(d),(e) **5.026**
  reg.5(1)(k) **5.026**
  reg.19 .... 5.028

2002 Child Tax Credit Regulations (SI 2002/2007)
  reg.3 .... 5.029, 5.030
  reg.3, Case F **5.029**
  reg.8 .... 3.042

2002 Tax Credits (Claims and Notifications) Regulations (SI 2002/2014)
  reg.5(2) 5.030a
  reg.5(2)(b) 5.014
  reg.7 .... 5.031
  reg.21 .... 5.013. 5.032, 5.033, 6.003
  reg.21(1A) 5.032
  reg.21(2) **5.032**
  reg.21(3) **5.032**, 6.003
  reg.22 .... 5.034
  reg.27 .... 5.035
  reg.27(2B) 5.032, **5.035**

2002 Statutory Paternity Pay and Statutory Adoption Pay (Weekly Rates) Regulations (SI 2002/2818)
  reg.2(a) 5.044
  reg.2(b) 5.044
  reg.3(a) 5.044
  reg.3(b) 5.044
  reg.4 .... **5.044**
  reg.21 .... 5.045
  reg.27A **5.046**
  reg.32 .... 5.047
  reg.32(1A) 5.047
  reg.39 .... 5.048

2002 Education (Student Support)(No.2) Regulations (SI 2002/3200)
  reg.15(7) 3.025, 3.084

2003 Tax Credits (Approval of Home Child Care Providers) Scheme (SI 2003/463) 5.036

2003 Tax Credits Act 2002 (Commencement No. 4, Transitional Provisions and Savings) Order (SI 2003/962) 3.010

2003 Social Security (Incapacity Benefit Work-focused Interviews) Regulations (SI 2003/2439) 6.004

2004 Social Security (Working Neighbourhoods) Regulations (SI 2004/959) 4.046
  reg.22 .... 4.046
  reg.24 .... 4.046
  reg.25(1) 4.046
  reg.25(2) 4.046
  reg.25(4) 4.046
  regs 25–27 .... 4.047
  reg.26(1) 4.046
  reg.26(3) 4.046

2004 Accession (Immigration and Worker Registration) Regulations (SI 2004/1219)
  reg.5 .... 3.017, 3.079, 3.117

2004 Social Security (Habitual Residence) Amendment Regulations (SI 2004/1232) 3.066
  reg.6 .... 1.004, 3.018

2004 Child Trust Funds Regulations (SI 2004/1450)
  reg.33 .... 5.049
  reg.33(3)(ea) **5.049**
  reg.33(4) 5.049
  reg.33A 5.050
  reg.33A(2) 5.050
  Sch. 5.051

2004 Community Care, Services for Carers and Children's Services (Direct Payments) (Wales) Regulations (SI 2004/1748)
  reg.12 .... 5.028
  Sch.2 para.3 .... 5.028

2005 Social Security (Incapacity Benefit Work-focused Interviews) (Amendment) Regulations (SI 2005/3) 6.004

Table of Statutory Instruments

2005 Education (Student Support Regulations (SI 2005/52)
    reg.3 .... 3.025, 3.084
    reg.19 .... 3.025, 3.084
    Sch.1 .... 3.025, 3.084

2005 Tax Credits (Approval of Home Care Providers) Scheme (SI 2005/93) 5.023, 5.036

2005 Social Security (Graduated Retirement Benefit) Regulations (SI 2005/454)
    Sch.1 .... 3.121

2005 Tax Credits Act 2002 (Transitional Provisions) Order (SI 2005/773) 3.010

2005 Tax Credits Act 2002 (Transitional Provisions) (No.2) Order (SI 2005/776) 3.010

2005 Tax Credits Act 2002 (Commencement No. 4, Transitional Provisions and Savings) (Amendment) Order (SI 2005/1106) 3.010

2005 Social Fund Maternity and Funeral Expenses (General) Regulations (SI 2005/3061)
    reg.7(10) 1.003
    reg.8 .... 3.131

2005 Tax and Civil Partnership Regulations (SI 2005/3229)
    reg.186 .... 5.020

2005 Social Security (Hospital In-Patients) Regulations (SI 2005/3360)
    reg.2(4) 3.011, 3.078
    reg.2(5) 3.011, 3.078

2006 Tax Credits (Approval of Home Care Providers) Scheme (Northern Ireland) (SR 2006/64) 5.023

2006 Housing Benefit (Persons who have attained the qualifying age for state pension credit) Regulations (SI 2006/214)
    reg.55 .... 3.123

2006 Child Benefit (General) Regulations (SI 2006/223)
    reg.1(3) 5.029

2006 Taxation of Pension Schemes (Consequential Amendments) Order (SI 2006/745)
    art.26(2)(a) 5.024
    art.26(2)(b) 5.024
    art.26(2)(c) 5.024
    art.26(2)(d) 5.024
    art.26(3) 5.025
    art.26(4)(a) 5.026
    art.26(4)(b) 5.026
    art.26(4)(c) 5.026
    art.26(4)(d) 5.027

2006 Social Security (Miscellaneous Amendments) (No.2) Regulations (SI 2006/832) 4.014, 4–015, 4–016

2006 Social Security (Working Neighbourhoods) Miscellaneous Amendments Regulations (SI 2006/909) 4.042, 4.043
    reg.22 .... 4.046
    reg.2 .... 4.044, 4.046
    reg.2(1) 3.076
    reg.3(2) 4.046
    reg.4 .... **3.076**, 4.046

2006 Immigration (European Economic Area) Regulations (SI 2006/1003) 3.018, 4.051
    reg.6(1) 3.017, 3.079, 3.117,
    reg.7 .... 3.017, 3.117
    reg.13 .... 3.017, 3.018, 3.079, 3.117
    reg.14 .... 3.017, 3.117

2006 Social Security (Persons from Abroad) Amendment Regulations (SI 2006/1026) **1.001**
    reg.1 .... **1.002**
    regs 2–5 .... 1.002
    reg.6 .... 3.066
    reg.6(2) 3.011
    reg.6(3) 3.017
    regs 6–9 .... 1.002
    reg.7(2) 3.078
    reg.7(3) 3.079
    reg.8(2) 3.128
    reg.8(3) 3.129
    reg.9 .... 3.117
    reg.10 .... **1.003**
    reg.10(e) 3.018
    reg.10(g) 3.130
    reg.10(h) 3.117
    reg.11 .... **1.004**
    reg.11(1)(a) 3.064, 3.066
    reg.11(2)(a) 3.065
    reg.11(2)(b) 3.018, 3.066

Table of Statutory Instruments

2006	Employment Equality (Age) Regulations (SI 2006/1031)	
	s.49(1) 5.007, 5.010, 5.011, 5.037, 5.038, 5.041, 5.042, 5.047, 5.048	
	Sch.8 Part 1 para.11(2)	5.007
	Sch.8 Part 1 para.11(3)	5.007
	Sch.8 Part 1 para.11(4)	5.007
	Sch.8 Part 1 para.12(2)	5.010
	Sch.8 Part 1 para.12(3)	5.010
	Sch.8 Part 1 para.12(4)	5.010
	Sch.8 Part 1 para.13(1)	5.011
	Sch.8 Part 1 para.13(2),(3)	**5.011**
	Sch.8 Part 1 para.17	5.011
	Sch.8 Part 2 para.50(2)	5.037
	Sch.8 Part 2 para.50(3) 5.037,	5.047
	Sch.8 Part 2 para.51	5.038
	Sch.8 Part 2 para.53	5.042
	Sch.8 Part 2 para.53(2)	5.041
	Sch.8 Part 2 para.53(3)	5.041
	Sch.8 Part 2 para.60	5.047
	Sch.8 Part 2 para.61	5.048
2006	Social Security (PPF Payments and FAS Payments) (Consequential Amendments) Regulations (SI 2006/1069) 2.015,	2.016
	reg.2	2.015
	reg.3	2.033
2006	Civil Partnership Act 2004 (Relationships Arising Through Civil Partnership) Order 2006 (SI 2006/1121)	4.013
2006	Child Tax Credit (Amendment No.2) Regulations (SI 2006/1163)	
	reg.2(2)	5.029
2006	Social Security (Income Support and Jobseeker's Allowance) Amendment Regulations (SI 2006/1402)	
	reg.2(2)	3.068
	reg.2(3)	3.070
	reg.2(4)	3.073
	reg.2(5)	3.074

2006	Social Security (Income Support and Jobseeker's Allowance) Amendment Regulations—*cont.*	
	reg.2(6)	3.089
	reg.3	3.032
2006	Work and Families Act 2006 (Commencement No.1) Order (SI 2006/1682)	6.002
2006	Social Security (Students and Income-related Benefits) Amendment Regulations (SI 2006/1752)	
	reg.4(2)(a) 3.024,	3.027
	reg.4(2)(b) 3.024,	3.027
	reg.4(3) 3.024,	3.025
	reg.4(4)	3.028
	reg.5(2)(a) 3.083,	3.086
	reg.5(2)(b) 3.083,	3.086
	reg.5(3) 3.083,	3.084
	reg.5(4)	3.087
	reg.6 .... 3.024, 3.025, 3.083,	3.084
2006	Taxation of Pension Schemes (Consequential Amendments)(No.2) Order (SI 2006/1963)	
	art.4	5.002
2006	Social Security (Lebanon) Amendment Regulations (SI 2006/1981)	3.018
	reg.2	3.017
	reg.3	3.079
	reg.4	3.117
2006	National Minimum Wage Regulations 1999 (Amendment) Regulations (SI 2006/2001)	3.002
2006	Adoption and Children Act 2002 (Consequential Amendment to Statutory Adoption Pay) Order (SI 2006/2012)	
	art.3(a)	5.008
2006	Vaccine Damage Payments (Specified Disease) Order (SI 2006/2066) **1.005**,	2.001
	art.1	**1.006**
	art.2	**1.007**
2006	Social Security (Adult Learning Option) Amendment Regulations 2006 (SI 2006/2144)	2.028
	reg.2	3.006

Table of Statutory Instruments

2006	Work and Families Act 2006 (Commencement No.2) Order (SI 2006/2232) 6.002	2006	Social Security (Miscellaneous Amendment)(No.4) Regulations—*cont.*
			reg.11(2) 2.051
2006	Statutory Paternity Pay and Statutory Pay and Statutory Adoption Pay (General and the Statutory Paternity Pay and Statutory Adoption Pay (Weekly Rates)(Amendment) Regulations (SI 2006/2236)		reg.11(3) 2.052
			reg.12(2) 2.034
			reg.12(3) 2.035, 3.005
			reg.12(4) 2.037
			reg.12(5) 3.005
			reg.13(1) 3.067
			reg.13(3) 3.075
			reg.13(3)(a) 3.072
			reg.13(3)(c) 3.101, 3.102
	reg.2 .... 5.044, 5.045, 5.046		reg.13(3)(d) 3.103
	reg.4 .... 5.044, 5.045		reg.13(4) 3.077
	reg.5 .... 5.046		reg.13(5) 3.080
2006	Social Security Act 1998 (Commencement No.14) Order (SI 2006/2376) 2.003		reg.13(6) 3.081
			reg.13(7) 3.085
			reg.13(10) 3.090, 3.091, 3.092
2006	Social Security (Miscellaneous Amendments) (No.3) Regulations (SI 2006/2377) 4–017, 4–014, 4.022, 4.024		reg.13(10)(b) 3.095
			reg.13(11)(a) 3.093
			reg.13(11)(b) 3.094
			reg.13(11)(c) 3.096
			reg.13(12)(a)(i) 3.104
	reg.3(2) 4.030		reg.13(12)(a)(ii) 3.104
	reg.3(3) 4.041		reg.13(12)(a)(iii) 3.104
2006	Social Security (Miscellaneous Amendment)(No.4) Regulations (SI 2006/2378) 2.018, 2.032, 4.025, 4.041a		reg.13(12)(b) 3.105
			reg.13(12)(c) 3.106
			reg.13(12)(d) 3.107
			reg.13(12)(e) 3.108
	reg.2 .... 2.026		reg.13(13)(a) 3.111
	reg.5(2) 3.009		reg.13(13)(b) 3.112
	reg.5(3) 3.019		reg.13(13)(c) 3.113
	reg.5(4) 3.021		reg.14(2) 3.119
	reg.5(5) 3.026		reg.14(3) 3.120
	reg.5(6) 3.031		reg.14(4)(a) 3.121
	reg.5(7) 3.035, 3.037		reg.14(4)(b) 3.121
	reg.5(7)(b) 3.039, 3.040		reg.14(5)(a) 3.122
	reg.5(8)(a) 3.037		reg.14(5)(b) 3.123
	reg.5(8)(b) 3.038		reg.14(6) 3.125
	reg.5(8)(c) 3.039	2006	Statutory Maternity Pay, Social Security (Maternity Allowance) and Social Security (Overlapping Benefits) (Amendment) Regulations (SI 2006/2379) 2.017
	reg.5(8)(d) 3.041		
	reg.5(9) 3.049, 3.050		
	reg.5(10)(a)(i) 3.051		
	reg.5(10)(a)(ii) 3.051		
	reg.5(10)(a)(iii) 3.051		
	reg.5(10)(b) 3.052		reg.3(2) 5.039
	reg.5(10)(c) 3.053		reg.3(3) 5.040
	reg.5(10)(d) 3.054		reg.3(4) 5.043
	reg.5(10)(e) 3.055		reg.4(2) 2.024
	reg.5(11)(a) 3.058		reg.4(3) 2.025
	reg.5(11)(b) 3.059	2006	Social Security (Persons from Abroad) Amendment (No.2) Regulations (SI 2006/2528)
	reg.5(11)(c) 3.060		
	reg.8 .... 2.020		
	reg.10(2) 2.029		
	reg.10(3) 2.030		reg.2 .... 3.017
	reg.10(4) 2.031		reg.4 .... 3.079, 3.117

xxxvii

Table of Statutory Instruments

2006	Social Security Act 1998 (Prescribed Benefits) Regulations (SI 2006/2529)	**1.008**, 4.003, 4.004
	reg.1	**1.009**
	reg.2	**1.010**
2006	Social Security Act 1998 (Commencement Nos 9 and 11) (Amendment) Order (SI 2006/2540)	4.004
2006	Social Fund Cold Weather Payments (General) Amendment Regulations (SI 2006/2655)	
	reg.3	3.126
	reg.4	3.127
2006	Child Trust Funds (Amendment No.2) Regulations (SI 2006/2684)	
	reg.3	5.049
	reg.4	5.049
	reg.5	5.050
	reg.6	5.051
2006	Tax Credits (Claims and Notifications) (Amendment) Regulations (SI 2006/2689)	6.003
	reg.3	5.013, 5.032
	reg.4	5.032
	reg.5	5.032
2006	Tax Credits (Claims and Notifications) (Amendment) Regulations—*cont.*	
	reg.6	5.032, 6.003
	reg.7	5.035
2006	Social Security (Incapacity Benefit Work-focused Interviews) Amendment (No.2) Regulations (SI 2006/3088)	6.004
2006	Social Security (Claims and Payments) Amendment (No.2) Regulations (SI 2006/3188)	6.005
2006	Social Security (Miscellaneous Amendments) (No.5) Regulations (SI 2006/3274)	6.006
2006	Accession (Immigration and Worker Authorisation) Regulations (SI 2006/3317)	6.007
2006	Social Security (Bulgaria and Romania) Amendment Regulations (SI 2006/3341)	6.007
2006	Tax Credits Act 2002 (Commencement and Transitional Provisions) Order (SI 2006/3369)	
	art.2	3.010
	art.4	3.010

PART I

NEW LEGISLATION

NEW STATUTES

There are none for the period covered by this Supplement.

NEW REGULATIONS AND ORDERS

The Social Security (Persons from Abroad) Amendment Regulations 2006

(2006 No. 1026)

ARRANGEMENT OF REGULATIONS

1. Citation and commencement
2.–9. *[Omitted]*
10. Nationals of Norway, Iceland, Liechtenstein and Switzerland
11. Revocations and savings

Made by the Secretary of State under sections 123(1)(a), (d) and (e), 131(3)(b), 135(1) and (2), 137(1) and (2), 138(1)(a) and (4) and 175(1), (3) and (4) of the Social Security Contributions and Benefits Act 1992, sections 4(5) and (12), 35(1) and 36(2) and (4) of, and paragraph 11 of Schedule 1 to, the Jobseekers Act 1995 and sections 1(5)(a) and 17(1) of the State Pension Credit Act 2002, after agreement by the Social Security Advisory Committee that proposals to make these Regulations should not be referred to it;

In force   **30th April 2006**

Citation and commencement

1. These Regulations shall be cited as the Social Security (Persons from Abroad) Amendment Regulations 2006 and shall come into force on 30th April 2006.

[Regulations 2–5 omitted as relating solely to housing benefit and council tax benefit]

[Regulations 6–9 noted at the appropriate places in the noter-up]

1.001

1.002

The Social Security (Persons from Abroad) Amendment Regulations 2006

Nationals of Norway, Iceland, Liechtenstein and Switzerland

1.003   **10.** The following provisions shall apply in relation to a national of Norway, Iceland, Liechtenstein or Switzerland or a member of his family (within the meaning of Article 2 of Council Directive No. 2004/38/EC) as if such a national were a national of a member State—

(a)–(d) *[Omitted as relating solely to housing benefit and council tax benefit]*

(e) regulation 21AA(4)(a) to (e) of the Income Support (General) Regulations 1987;

(f) regulation 85A(4)(a) to (e) of the Jobseeker's Allowance Regulations 1996;

(g) regulation 7(10) of the Social Fund Maternity and Funeral Expenses (General) Regulations 2005; and

(h) regulation 2(4)(a) to (e) of the State Pension Credit Regulations 2002.

Revocations and savings

1.004   **11.**—(1) The following Regulations are revoked—

(a)–(d) *[Noted at the appropriate places in the main text]*

(2) Nothing in these Regulations shall affect the continued operation of the transitional arrangements and savings provided for in—

(a) regulation 12 of the Social Security (Persons From Abroad) Miscellaneous Amendments Regulations 1996;

(b) regulation 6 of the Social Security (Habitual Residence) Amendment Regulations 2004; or

(c) *[Omitted as applying solely to housing benefit and council tax benefit]*

(SI 2005 No. 2066)

The Vaccine Damage Payments (Specified Disease) Order 2006

(SI 2005 No. 2066)

ARRANGEMENT OF ORDER

1. Citation and commencement
2. Addition to the diseases to which the Vaccine Damage Payments Act 1979 applies

The Secretary of State for Work and Pensions makes the following Order in exercise of the power conferred by section 1(2)(i) of the Vaccine Damage Payments Act 1979.

In force   **September 4, 2006**

Citation and commencement

1. This Order may be cited as the Vaccine Damage Payments (Specified Disease) Order 2006 and shall come into force on 4th September 2006.

Addition to the diseases to which the Vaccine Damage Payments Act 1979 applies

2. Pneumococcal infection is specified as a disease to which the Vaccine Damage Payments Act 1979 applies.

The Social Security Act 1998 (Prescribed Benefits) Regulations 2006

(SI 2006/2529)

ARRANGEMENT OF REGULATIONS

1.008
1. Citation and commencement
2. Prescribed benefits

The Secretary of State for Work and Pensions makes the following Regulations in exercise of the powers conferred by sections 8(3)(h), 79(1) and 84 of the Social Security Act 1998.

In accordance with section 173(1)(b) of the Social Security Administration Act 1992, the Secretary of State has obtained the agreement of the Social Security Advisory Committee that proposals in respect of these Regulations need not be referred to it.

In force   **October 16, 2006**

Citation and commencement

1.009
1.—(1) These Regulations may be cited as the Social Security Act 1998 (Prescribed Benefits) Regulations 2006 and shall come into force on 16th October 2006.

Prescribed benefits

1.010
2. The benefits prescribed for the purposes of section 8(3)(h) of the Social Security Act 1998 (decisions by Secretary of State) are—
    (a) the following benefits under the Social Security Act 1975—
        (i) sickness benefit under section 14;
        (ii) unemployment benefit under section 14;
        (iii) invalidity pension under section 15;
        (iv) invalidity allowance under section 16;
        (v) attendance allowance under section 35; and
        (vi) mobility allowance under section 37A;
    (b) supplementary benefit under the Supplementary Benefit Act 1976.

GENERAL NOTE

1.011
Except for attendance allowance, the benefits listed are benefits that had been abolished before the Social Security Act 1998 Act came into force and are therefore not within the scope of s.8(3)(a) to (g) of that Act. Attendance allowance has presumably been included from an abundance of caution because it is

now payable only to people over the age of 65, whereas until 1992 it was payable to younger people. The need for this provision was revealed by *CDLA/2999/2004*, in which it was held that, because the transitional provision made when the 1998 Act came into force relies on the concept of a "relevant benefit" as defined by s.8(3), there was no power to make a supersession decision under s.10 of the 1998 Act in respect of mobility allowance, with the consequence that an overpayment of mobility allowance could not be recovered under s.71 of the Social Security Administration Act 1992. It is not entirely clear why the scope of s.8(3) of the 1998 Act has not been made precisely the same as the scope of s.71 of the 1992 Act (see para.4(1) of Sch.10 to the 1992 Act) but perhaps it was thought unlikely that any wider prescription would be required in practice. It is doubtful that the omission of the second "s" from the short title of the Supplementary Benefits Act 1976 is significant.

PART II

UPDATING MATERIAL
VOLUME I

NON MEANS TESTED BENEFITS

Non Means Tested Benefits

p.4, *annotation to the Vaccine Damage Payments Act 1979, s.1(2) (addition of a new disease)*

With effect from September 4, 2006 Pneumococcal infection is added to the list of diseases by the Vaccine Damage Payments (Specified Disease) Order 2006 (SI 2006/2066). For text of the Order see Part I (new Regulations and Orders), above.

2.001

pp.44–46, *annotation to the Social Security Contributions and Benefits Act 1992, s.30C (period of incapacity for work—the effect of Chief Adjudication Officer v Astle (1999))*

In *CIB/1635/2006*, Deputy Commissioner Mark dealt with a case where a claimant suffering from chronic fatigue syndrome had a work pattern of two days followed by five days of no work, and sought to claim for the days of no work, arguing that each period of four or more days of incapacity entitled him to make a fresh claim in respect of each such spell. The Commissioner found against the claimant by applying Incapacity for Work (General) Regulations 1995, reg.16 (see update to Vol I, p.688, below), but said this on the way in which the tribunal had applied *Astle* to reject the claimant's appeal:

2.002

> "The tribunal considered that it was bound to find against the claimant by reason of the decision in *Chief Adjudication Officer v. Astle*. I do not follow this reasoning. That case was only concerned with a claim in respect of the days when the claimant was capable of work which was sandwiched between two linked periods where he was not capable of work, where by reason of the linking the whole period was said to be one single period of disability. In this case the claimant is claiming in respect of days when he did not work" (para.6).

p.56, *amendments to the Social Security Contributions and Benefits Act 1992, s.35*

With effect from October 1, 2006, s.35(5) was amended by the Social Security Act 1998 (Commencement No. 14) Order 2006 (SI 2006/2376). This brought into force s.67 of the Social Security Act 1998 which provides for the daily rate of Maternity Allowance to be calculated at the rate of 1/7th of the weekly rate. This amount will apply to a woman whose date of confinement falls on or after April 1, 2007. A woman whose date of confinement is earlier will be covered by the earlier version of s.35 which provided for a Sunday to be disregarded as a day of entitlement, and any other day to be paid at a rate of 1/6th of the weekly rate. (For the original version of s.35 see earlier editions of the main volume of this work).

2.003

p.60, *annotation to the Social Security Contributions and Benefits Act 1992, s.36: entitlement to bereavement payment*

The Commissioner's decision in *CG/2054/2004* (to be reported as *R(G)1/06*), confirms the effect of s.36(1) to the effect that the claimant

2.004

11

cannot succeed in a claim for a bereavement payment if they are over retirement age and entitled to a Category A Retirement Pension. This is because the benefit, like Widows Allowance that preceded it, was intended only for the loss of a breadwinner who was still in work and whose spouse would still have been dependent on the deceased as a source of their income. The decision also holds that this section is not in breach of the claimant's Convention Rights and that, under the Human Rights Act, it could not be interpreted in any other way.

p.87, *correction to the Social Security Contributions and Benefits Act 1992, s.44*

2.005   In subs.(5A)(a), before the words "that year" insert [, with footnote number 8. The words that follow those brackets are to be read as a part of paragraph (c).

In both versions of subs.(6) the words "Subject to subsection (7A) below" should be enclosed in square brackets with footnote number 5.

p.89, *annotation to the Social Security Contributions and Benefits Act 1992, s.44*

2.006   The final paragraph of this commentary should be substituted as follows:

"There are two versions of both subsection (5) and subsection (6) of this section. In the case of subsection (5) the second version is titled (5A); in the case of subsection (6) both versions appear with the same title. In each case the second version applies to someone who reaches pensionable age, or dies, after April 5, 2000, and to someone whose entitlement is derived from such a person (see s.128(4)–(6) Pensions Act 1995). The first version is retained for those reaching that age, or dying, before that date."

p.131, *annotations to the Social Security Contributions and Benefits Act 1992, s.72: meaning of "bodily functions"*

2.007   The concept of "bodily functions" has been examined by a tribunal of Commissioners in *CSDLA/133/2005* (to be reported as *R (DLA) 1/07*). The case concerned a child claimant whose mother described her as having behavioural problems, memory loss, difficulty concentrating and other problems, as well as being hyperactive. It was clear that at school she required special attention to motivate her and to aid in integrating with her peers, while at home her mother said she had to be with her all the time to control her behaviour and to ensure her safety. While there was no medical diagnosis of the condition a report by a paediatric neuropsychologist described her as "having significant learning difficulties with prominent language processing disorder and associated behavioural problems". The claimant's need for attention could probably be summed up as requiring help with motivation, communication and social integration. Her claim for the mobility component of DLA at the lower rate, and for care component at the middle rate, was refused and her appeal to a tribunal dismissed on the ground that the assistance she needed was not help in relation to her bodily functions.

The Tribunal of Commissioners allowed an appeal. They begin their reasons by facing the issue squarely and deciding that the functions of the brain are included within the term 'bodily functions'". They found authority for that in a series of cases including *Packer's Case, Mallinson, Cockburn and Fairey*. In accepting that cognitive functioning (thinking) can be a bodily function they expressly overrule a line of cases (*CSDLA/867/1997, CSDLA/867/1997, CSDLA/832/1999* and *CSDLA/860/2000*) asserting that it was not. The Commissioners also refer to *R (DLA) 3/03*, which had been relied on by the appeal tribunal, but they distinguished it as deciding only that the claimant there did not need the assistance for which he was claiming—the evidence suggested that he was able to communicate adequately without assistance—and did not decide that communication could never be a bodily function. The Commissioners in the present case made no reference to *CDLA/2974/2004*, a decision of Mr Commissioner Rowland, in which he accepted that the defective cognitive processes of a 16 year old autistic boy could amount to a defective bodily function.

The problem that the Commissioners then faced in their decision was to make any distinction between what have been known as activities and bodily functions. Here they break new ground by suggesting that what may be regarded as activities should be broken down into the parts that are contributed by individual organs of the body. If such organs are defective so as to need assistance in achieving that activity then that may be help in connection with a bodily function for the purposes of a claim to DLA. The Tribunal express their reasons for this as follows:

"33. As identified by Dunn LJ in *Packer's Case*, a 'bodily function' primarily refers to the normal action of any organ of the body. For example, the function or a function of the lower jaw is to move up and down, i.e. its normal action. By way of extension, we consider it quite appropriate to extend this reference to the organ's immediate purpose: in our example, the purpose of the lower jaw moving up and down is to masticate food, and we do not consider it would not (sic) be incorrect to refer to such mastication as a 'bodily function', i.e. a function of the lower jaw. It appears to us that the term is sufficiently wide to cover this extension.

34. Such functions might be voluntarily controlled (e.g. the lower jaw, as in our example), or involuntary (e.g. it is the function of the kidneys to filter waste products from the blood, which it does without any voluntary instigating action).

35. Furthermore, as Dunn LJ indicated in *Packer's Case* (see paragraph 30 above), 'bodily functions' includes not only the action of one organ of the body, but also those of any set of such organs in concert. Therefore, when the lower jaw is looked at with the mouth and various internal organs including the stomach and alimentary tract, it can properly be said of that set of organs of which the jaw is a part that the bodily function (in the sense of purpose as described above) is eating.

We see no inconsistency between the proposition that it is a function of the lower jaw to move up and down and masticate food, and, as part of a set of organs, its function is also eating. Indeed, far from there being a strict dichotomy between 'microfunctions' and 'macrofunctions'—and to be fair to Mr Collins he did not submit that there was such a clear and absolute dichotomy—in terms of the organs of the body, there is complex web of functionality that requires acknowledgment.

36. However, of course, there are limits. Not every activity performed by the body is a 'bodily function', because it cannot properly be said that that activity is either a normal action or purpose of that organ or set of organs. Shopping is one example which falls clearly on the wrong side of the line: whilst no doubt involving various functions of the body, shopping could not properly be said itself to be a function (in terms of either simple actions or purpose) of any organ or set of organs of the body. Similarly, it was not suggested by any of the judges in *Packer's Case* that cooking could itself be a 'bodily function'. There may be difficult, borderline cases; but, like Lord Slynn (and with respect to Lord Denning's obiter dicta in *Packer's Case* and those of subsequent judges, to which we have referred: see paragraph 31 above), we do not consider that getting in and out of bed, or dressing and undressing, are "bodily functions", because (in our respectful view) it cannot properly be said that it is the normal action or purpose of any organ or sets of organs to perform these exercises. These are not functions of organs of the body, but merely things which a body can do if the relevant bodily functions (e.g. movement of the limbs) are working normally.

37. However, given that activities such as shopping, dressing and undressing, getting in and out of bed necessarily involve bodily functions of one sort or another (which can be specifically identified, if necessary), why does the relevant 'bodily function' matter in any specific case? The answer to this lies in looking at the wording of the statutory provisions as a whole, as has been urged by the House of Lords (see paragraph 16 above) and in the approach to those provisions of Lord Woolf in *Mallinson* and the tribunal of Commissioners in R(DLA) 3/06. As already indicated (paragraphs 8–11), the focus of these provisions is on the disablement (i.e. functional deficiency) of the claimant. Even where such a disablement is shown, the relevant attention is that *reasonably required* by virtue of that functional deficiency. On the issue of relevant attention, it may therefore be necessary to focus upon the functional deficiency with some particularity. It may not be crucial whether the bodily function impaired in someone who cannot move his legs and consequently walk is looked at as (i) movement of the legs, or (ii) walking. We consider both have equal validity for the reasons we give above. However the function is viewed, the necessary attention to address the claimant's reasonable care requirements will be the same. But in other cases it may be of importance, because it will be necessary to identify the bodily function that is impaired with some precision so that the attention reasonably

required to address the impairment can be properly identified and assessed.

38. For example, Mr Mallinson was blind, and was consequently unable to walk in unfamiliar surroundings because (as Lord Woolf put it, at page 639H) he did not know where to walk or (e.g. when crossing the road) when to walk. As Lord Woolf pointed out (at page 639G), to say whether the attention he received in the form of being guided was 'in connection with his bodily functions' (i.e. reasonably necessary as the result of an impairment to those functions), it was necessary to identify the bodily function or functions to which the attention relates. We consider that in substance this is no more than ensuring that the relevant attention is reasonably necessary—because, as indicated above (paragraphs 8–9), the severity of the functional disablement is in fact defined by that attention. Therefore, although in one sense it could be said that Mr Mallinson's ability to walk was impaired (in the ways identified by Lord Woolf), in considering this question, as Mr Mallinson's legs were working normally—but his eyesight was not—of the interwoven bodily functions involved, 'it is preferable to focus on that function [i.e. his deficient ability to see]' (per Lord Woolf at page 641A). The relevant 'bodily function' that is impaired (i.e. the disablement) must therefore be identified with sufficient particularity so that the assistance reasonably required can be identified and assessed; and this is why 'bodily function' cannot be given a definition so wide as to include all human activity or indeed any particularly complex activity. This is therefore another reflection of the close relationship between functional disablement and the assistance reasonably required to cope with that disablement referred to in paragraph 9 above of identifying the relevant bodily functions given above.

39. However, even where an activity is such that it cannot itself properly be described as a bodily function, that will not be the end of the matter—because recourse will then have to be had to the discrete bodily functions which are involved in the activity and the extent to which they are impaired, and particularly as to whether the functions or (sic) any of them are so impaired that assistance to the level of any of the provisions of section 72 is required in respect of the disablement. In these circumstances, the relevant discrete bodily functions will have to be identified and 'unbundled', considered and assessed. Indeed, given the purpose of identifying the relevant bodily functions given above (paragraphs 36–37), in functionally complex activities which may be borderline, we regard this 'unbundling' exercise as the correct approach in any event, and warn against the temptation of considering in very fine detail whether the complex activity can truly be described as a single bodily function or not. We consider the potential dangers of such an arid exercise are well illustrated in this very case. As the various House of Lords opinions referred to above (but notably that of Lord Slynn in *Cockburn*) make clear, in borderline cases it cannot be incorrect to unbundle functions in this way, and it is likely to be helpful in approaching the issue of assistance reasonably required."

The Commissioners then go on to point out that just identifying a bodily function that is deficient so as to need assistance, is not a sufficient condition to qualify for DLA. It will remain necessary, as well, to show that the assistance has the requisite degree of intimacy, and also that it satisfies one of the tests as to frequency, constancy, etc.

Applying all this to the facts of the present case the Commissioners found it to be an error of law to say that communication was not a bodily function. It was necessary, they say, to "unbundle" that word and examine what the claimant's difficulty in communicating was caused by. Clearly elements such as hearing, seeing and speaking can qualify for assistance and now we can say also, in the light of their decision above, comprehending, thinking and concentrating. Cases that have held to the contrary were disapproved. Similarly, social integration needed to be unbundled so as to analyse the parts with which the claimant required assistance. Where these could be identified as requiring assistance in the form of close personal care and attention to particular mental processes the claimant may be regarded as requiring assistance with bodily functions. The case was referred to a fresh tribunal for further consideration of the evidence.

But this is unlikely to be the last word on these matters. Dyslexia has also produced a crop of disputed cases in recent years. In *CDLA/395/2005* Commissioner Williams refers to *CDLA/1420/2004* and *CDLA/2680/2001* (neither of which is available on the database) and in both of which it was held that assistance to cope with dyslexia could qualify for DLA.

In the case of *CDLA/395/2005* itself, the Commissioner dismissed the claimant's appeal because the tribunal had found as a fact that the claimant did not need such assistance. However, as both parties had submitted arguments on whether assistance to deal with dyslexia could qualify, he went on to hold that it could, though subject to the warning that dyslexia is a label that covers a variety of conditions affecting the ability to communicate. In the language of the decision above it will be necessary to unbundle the deficiency and see what particular brain function is affected.

A contrary conclusion has, however, been reached by Commissioner May in *CSDLA/427/2006*. There, a claim was made on behalf of an eight year old boy on the basis of the extra attention he required when learning at school and for help at home with his homework. The claim was refused and an appeal failed. The further appeal to the Commissioner was also dismissed. The Commissioner found that the help required by the claimant was assistance with his education and, as such, could not be attention in connection with a bodily function. In particular, the Commissioner compares the claimant's inability to read, to his own inability to read Japanese. He can, he says, see the script, but he cannot understand it because he has not learned that language. This is right. But the Commissioner's inability derives from a lack of knowledge, whereas the claimant's inability to read (or at least difficulty in acquiring the skill to do so), derives from a brain malfunction in being unable to remember the shapes or arrangements of letters. In other words the activity of reading needs to be unbundled to examine whether any organ of the body is dysfunctional.

The decision makes no reference to *CSDLA/133/2005*, because that case was decided only a few days earlier, and so this part of the decision may require reconsideration in the light of that decision.

But another argument is more problematic. It appears that the initial refusal of benefit may have included the reason that DLA could not be available for assistance with "educational activities" and that reason was also part of the appeal tribunal's conclusion. The Commissioner agreed. As he rightly points out, such assistance, at least in a state school, would be provided from public funding and to say that it qualified, as well, for entitlement to DLA would mean that the public purse was paying for the same service twice over. That can hardly, he suggests, have been the intention of Parliament in creating this benefit. Yet the section makes no reference to the source of funding for any assistance and it must be common place for some of the assistance received by DLA claimants to come from care workers who are publicly funded. The source of funding for the provision of care is accounted for in one sense in the DLA Regulations (reg.8), but that is only where the claimant is provided for in certain defined accommodation. This issue has been raised before (in *R (DLA) 1/04*) but, as Commissioner May observed, that point was not dealt with at all by the Court of Appeal in that case.

p.159, *annotation to the Social Security Contributions and Benefits Act 1992, s.73; ability to benefit from enhanced facilities for locomotion: s.73(8)*

In *CDLA/2142/2005* the Commissioner agrees with the decision in *CSDLA/12/2003* that the claimant (for lower rate mobility component), who was agoraphobic, must be willing to make use of the assistance by walking out of doors so as to show that she would benefit from enhanced locomotion. But he returned the case to a new tribunal with the suggestion to consider whether walking within the confines of the claimant's own back garden, which was all that she could be persuaded to do, could satisfy that test if it were beneficial to the health, both mental and physical, of the claimant.

2.008

In *CDLA/1639/2006* the Commissioner held that a tribunal which allowed a claim for higher rate mobility component in respect of a claimant suffering from severe attacks of migraine had erred in law by overlooking the effects of s.73(8). As the commissioner pointed out the only time that the claimant would have had any need for attention was during the time he was suffering a migraine attack; at that same time however, on his own evidence, he was compelled to sit or to lie down, so no amount of assistance could aid his mobility. (Though see also the annotation to p.533 below.)

p.160 *annotation to the Social Security Contributions and Benefit Act 1992, s.73(12): mobility component for the terminally ill*

The decision in *CDLA/845/2005*, (to be reported as *R(DLA) 7/06)*, confirms the view expressed in the note to subs.(12) that the only effect of the "terminally ill" provisions so far as the mobility component is

2.009

concerned, is to remove the need to satisfy the three month qualifying period and to extend that period of qualification to the time of death where appropriate. But it remains necessary for the claimant to show that one or other of the qualifying conditions for mobility component applies to them. In reaching this conclusion the deputy Commissioner rejects the view expressed in *CDLA/1804/1999* which appeared to suggest that a person who was terminally ill was deemed to satisfy conditions not only for the highest rate of the care component, but for the higher rate of mobility component as well.

pp.190–192, *annotation to the Social Security Contributions and Benefits Act 1992, s.94: meaning of "accident" and its coverage of stress-related illness*

2.010   In *CI/142/2006*, Commissioner Bano dealt with a claimant who worked as a civilian clerk in the intelligence department of a police force. She attributed her depression and chronic anxiety, which prevented her working, to a particular unexpected interview with the Sergeant in the unit about new shift patterns. She claimed that in that interview he told her that he had disclosed to the personnel office confidential personal information she had relayed to him and also that not changing to his preferred pattern would put her post in the unit at risk. She said she had felt threatened in the interview and so upset that she had to leave it. The tribunal could not find in the material any evidence of an untoward event describable as an "accident". Commissioner Bano disagreed and remitted the case to another tribunal. He drew on the Commissioners' decisions noted in the annotation and stated that the focus had to be on the manner and context of the interview. He continued:

> "As Miss Commissioner Fellner pointed out in CI/3511/2002, stress illnesses are more likely to result from a process rather than from a single event or series of events, but in those exceptional cases where depressive illness can be attributed to one or more specific incidents, it may be necessary to carry out a careful investigation of the context of the incidents in order to decide whether injury has been caused by accident.
>
> The tribunal in this case expressly declined to make any findings on whether Sergeant T's conversation with the claimant was a proper conversation. However, large employers, such as police forces, have detailed procedures precisely in order to give employees a measure of protection in relation to matters such as changes in their working hours. Employees in such organisations are entitled to expect that those procedures will be followed and may feel vulnerable if they are disregarded. The issue of whether the meeting on 12 May should have been conducted in the presence of a personnel officer needed to be determined in order to decide whether it was an unexpected event, so that even in terms of the basic definition of 'accident' in *Fenton v Thorley* the tribunal's failure to investigate that matter and its self-direction that there was no evidence of any untoward event were in error of law. The claimant contended that she did not expect to have the question of her working hours re-opened, or to discover that

Sergeant T had passed on information given to him into confidence, and findings on those matters were also necessary in order to decide whether the interview could be regarded as untoward. Those matters may at first sight appear relatively trivial, but it has not been disputed that the claimant was extremely distressed by the interview, and the tribunal itself appears to have accepted that the claimant's illness stemmed entirely from that event. Although the tribunal found that what was said at the interview caused depression 'in the entirely personal and private context of (the claimant's) reasons for not wanting to change her shift pattern' I can find no evidential basis for that conclusion and, in any case, without investigating the claimant's complaints about the interview, the tribunal was not in a position to decide whether it was the change in the claimant's working hours or the interview which caused her depression. The tribunal's finding that the depression resulted from the change in the claimant's working hours, which was the foundation of the Secretary of State's case, therefore cannot be sustained.

I therefore uphold the argument, ably advanced by the claimant's husband at the hearing before me, that the tribunal erred in law in failing to consider matters relevant to the issues which they had to decide. Accordingly, I allow the appeal and set aside the tribunal's decision. I have come to the conclusion that I cannot decide the claimant's entitlement to a declaration of an industrial accident on the papers, and that the case must therefore be referred for rehearing to a differently constituted tribunal.

The new tribunal will need to decide whether the interview on 12 May constituted an accident in accordance with the principles which I have set out and, if so, whether the claimant's depressive illness resulted from that interview or, as she originally asserted, was the result of a process. Although I have not had to comment on the claimant's complaints about the physical conditions in which the interview on 12 May took place, those matters may have relevance to the question of whether the interview was the cause of the claimant's depression, and may therefore need to be considered in detail by the new tribunal" (paras 16–19).

pp.216–219, *annotation to Social Security Contributions and Benefits Act 1992, s.103 (disablement pension) (a useful checklist of questions)*

In *CI/2930/2005*, Commissioner Williams considered a long-running appeal dealing with a claimant who had been disabled by two industrial accidents but as regards whose mental impairment there were also pre-existing causes. He applied a key statement (definitions and cautions) of Lord Simon in *Jones v Secretary of State for Social Services* [1972] AC 944, at p.1019:

2.011

"although in particular cases the concepts may overlap, the statute envisages them as separate—in order for 'disablement' benefit to be payable, the 'accident' must result in 'injury', which must result in 'loss of faculty', which must result in 'disability' . . . my understanding of the terminology is as follows: . . . 'injury' is hurt to body or mind . . . 'loss of faculty' is impairment of the proper functioning of part of the body or mind . . . 'disability' is partial or total failure of power to perform normal bodily or mental processes . . . 'disablement' is the sum of disabilities which, by contrast with the powers of a normal person, can be expressed as a percentage."

He also stressed (as had the Commissioner in *CI/34/1993*) the need to keep separate the underlying condition and the disabilities, the former being a cause of the latter (para.34). He then laid out in para.36 of his decision an extremely valuable framework on questions to be answered and the order of the rules to be applied to deal with the relevant issues:

"Reading that vocabulary into the statutory issues that I must consider, the questions to be answered are:
 (a) Did the claimant 'suffer personal injury ['hurt to body or mind'] caused' by the relevant accident?
Social Security Contributions and Benefits Act 1992 ('1992 Act'), section 94(1)
 (b) If so, did the claimant 'suffer as a result of the relevant accident from loss of physical or mental faculty' ['impairment of the proper functioning of part of the body or mind'] during the period relevant to this assessment?
1992 Act, section 103(1)
 (c) If so, what were 'the disabilities ['the partial or total failure of power to perform normal bodily or mental functions'] incurred by the claimant as a result of the relevant loss of faculty ['impairment of the proper functioning']'?
1992 Act, Schedule 6, paragraph 1. Paragraph 1(a) requires that 'the disabilities to be taken into account shall be all disabilities so incurred (whether or not involving loss of earning power or additional expense) to which the claimant may be expected, having regard to his physical and mental condition at the date of the assessment, to be subject during the period taken into account by the assessment as compared with a person of the same age and sex whose physical and mental condition is normal'
 (d) Do those disabilities ['failure of power to perform . . . '] take into account 'disabilities which, though resulting from the relevant loss of faculty ['impairment of the proper functioning . . . '], also result, or without the relevant accident might be expected to result, from a cause other than the relevant accident', if there are any?
This is required by 1992 Act, Schedule 6, paragraph 1(b) and Social Security (General Benefit) Regulations 1982 (SI 1982 No 1408 as amended) ('1982 Regulations'), regulation 11.
 (e) What is the total percentage of the 'assessed extent of the resulting disablement' ['the sum of disabilities', or of 'failure of power to perform . . . ']—
  (i) by reference to those disabilities ['failure of power to perform . . . '] without reference to the particular circumstances of the claimant other than age, sex and physical and mental condition, and

Non Means Tested Benefits

(ii) adding 'to the percentage of the disablement ['the sum of disabilities . . . '] . . . the assessed percentage of any present disablement' of the claimant resulting from any other industrial accident or any prescribed disease?
1992 Act, section 103(1), (2), and Schedule 6, paragraph 1(c).

(f) If the answers to (d) and (e) include disabilities ['failure of power to perform . . . '] resulting from the loss of faculty ['impairment of the proper functioning . . . '] both from the relevant accident and from any effective cause other than the relevant accident (whether congenital defect, injury or disease) that predate the accident, then what is the extent of disablement ['the sum of disabilities'] 'to which the claimant would have been subject . . . if the relevant accident had not occurred'?
1992 Act, Schedule 6, paragraph 1(c) and 1982 Regulations, regulation 11(3). Regulation 11(5) requires that where there are two or more industrial accidents (or disease) then the disablement resulting from both or all 'shall only be taken into account in assessing the extent of disablement resulting from . . . the one which occurred or developed last in point of time'.

(g) If the answers to (d) and (e) include disabilities ['failure of power to perform . . . '] resulting from the loss of faculty ['impairment of the proper functioning . . . '] both from the relevant accident and from any effective cause that postdates the accident and are not directly attributable to it, then what is the extent of disablement if that other effective cause had not arisen?
1982 Regulations, regulation 11(4). That requires that if the answer to (g) is not less than 11 per cent, then the answer to (e) 'shall also take account of any disablement to which the claimant may be subject as a result of that other effective cause except to the extent to which the claimant would have been subject thereto in the relevant accident had not occurred'. See also regulation 11(5) noted to question (f)."

pp.217–218, *annotation to Social Security Contributions and Benefits Act 1992, s.103 (disablement pension) (aggregation of assessments)*

Following *R(I)4/03*, Commissioner Rowland in *CI/954/2006* agreed that aggregation is a mere alternative to a separate award of disablement pension (para.16). It can be set in motion by an application for supersession.

2.012

p.404, *annotation to Computation of Earnings Regulations 1996, reg.3*

Secretary of State for Work and Pensions v Doyle is reported as *R(IB) 1/06.*

2.013

p.419, *annotation to Computation of Earnings Regulations 1996, Sch.1*

In *CG/1752/2006*, the Commissioner considered the proper interpretation of the word "temporarily" in para.7. Following *CIS/17020/1996* (which was about a paragraph in the same terms in the Income Support General Regulations), the Commissioner concluded

2.014

Non Means Tested Benefits

that "an arrangement which is not permanent is not necessarily temporary". In defining the term "temporarily" as meaning "not permanent", the tribunal had erred in law.

p.440, *amendment to the Dependency Regulations 1997, reg.9A*

2.015   With effect from May 5, 2006, the Social Security (PPF Payments and FAS Payments) (Consequential Amendments) Regulations 2006 (SI 2006/1069) amended reg.9A to read as follows:

> "9A.—[² For the purposes of section 89(1) of, and paragraph 7(1) of Schedule 7 to, the Contributions and benefits Act, where payment by way of occupational or personal pension, or for the purposes of section 89(1A) of that Act by way of PPF periodic payment,] is for any period made otherwise than weekly, the amount of any such payment for any week in that period shall be determined—
> (a) where payment is made for a year, by dividing the total by 52;
> (b) where payment is made for three months, by multiplying the total by 13;
> (c) where payment is made for a month, by multiplying the total by 12 and dividing the result by 52;
> (d) where payment is made for two or more months, otherwise than for a year or for three months, by dividing the total by the number of months, multiplying the result by 12 and dividing the result of that multiplication by 52; or
> (e) in any other case, by dividing the amount of the payment by the number of days in the period for which it is made and multiplying the result by 7."

AMENDMENTS

Regulation 9A was inserted by The Social Security Benefit (Dependency) Amendment Regulations 1989 (SI 1989/523), reg.5 (April 11, 1989).
1. The Social Security (Miscellaneous Provisions) Amendment Regulations 1992 (SI 1992/247), reg.4(2) (March 9, 1992). This amendment is superseded by the amendment listed below.
2. The Social Security (PPF Payments and FAS Payments) (Consequential Amendments) Regulations 2006 (SI 2006/1069), reg.2 (May 5, 2006).

p.447, *amendment to the Dependency Regulations 1996, Sch.2, para.9(1)*

2.016   With effect from May 5, 2006, The Social Security (PPF Payments and FAS Payments) (Consequential Amendments) Regulations 2006 (SI 2006/1069) amend para.9(1) by inserting the words "or PPF periodic payment" after the words "occupational or personal pension".

p.465, *amendment to the Overlapping Benefits Regulations 1979, reg.14*

2.017   With effect from October 1, 2006, the Statutory Maternity Pay, Social Security (Maternity Allowance) and Social Security (Overlapping Benefits) (Amendment) Regulations 2006, (SI 2006/2379) substituted the following for reg.14(1):

Non Means Tested Benefits

"**14.**—(1) Where an adjustment falls to be made under these regulations for part of a week, benefit (whether under the Contributions and Benefits Act or otherwise) shall be deemed to be payable at a rate equal to one-seventh of the appropriate weekly rate for each day of the week in respect of any such benefit."

p.504, *amendment to the Attendance Allowance Regulations 1991, reg.2*

With effect from October 1, 2006, reg.7 of the Social Security (Miscellaneous Amendment) (No. 4) Regulations 2006 (SI 2006/2378) amended reg.2 by deleting para.(1)(b) together with the word "and" that precedes it, and by deleting para.(4).

2.018

p.508, *annotation to the Attendance Allowance Regulations 1991, reg.7: cost of accommodation from public funds*

In *CSA/469/2005*, (and in *CSA/164/2004* which preceded it) the Commissioner holds that the cost of accommodation in a private nursing home that is met by a payment made to the claimant for personal care allowances under the Community Care and Health (Scotland) Act 2002 is a payment that disqualifies the claimant from entitlement to Attendance Allowance under reg.7. This is so even though the same payment made to a claimant who was living in their own home would not disqualify them. The Commissioner finds that to be the inevitable outcome of legislation that has been enacted only for Scotland and without any amendment to the legislation for Attendance Allowance.

2.019

p.516, *amendment to the Disability Living Allowance Regulations 1991, reg.2*

With effect from October 1, 2006, reg.8 of the Social Security (Miscellaneous Amendment) (No. 4) Regulations 2006 (SI 2006/2378) amended reg.2 by deleting para.(1)(b) together with the word "and" that precedes it, and by deleting para.(3).

2.020

p.533, *annotation to the Disability Living Allowance Regulations 1991, reg.12(1); unable to walk, effect of migraine attacks*

In *CDLA/1639/2006* the claimant gave evidence that he suffered from severe attacks of migraine that caused pain, dizziness, and lack of vision. At such times—at least 80 hours a week—he could do nothing more than sit down or lie down. A tribunal, by a majority allowed his appeal, but the Commissioner held that in doing so their decision demonstrated an error of law. They had failed to examine sufficiently the way in which his headaches affected his ability to walk. The loss of vision, he says, is not relevant to a claim for higher rate mobility component because it relates only to the direction of walking and not to the ability to walk itself. Pain

2.021

(in the form of headaches), too, would not count as that had nothing to do with the physical process of walking, though it might clearly make the claimant disinclined to walk outside. Dizziness, or loss of balance, however, was relevant because it affects the manner of walking or even the ability to walk at all. The appeal was allowed and returned to a new tribunal to consider the extent of the element of dizziness and its effect. As the attack of migraine could happen suddenly when he was already out walking they were asked to consider whether the claimant should qualify for mobility at the lower rate, on the basis of his need for supervision in case of a sudden onset of a migraine attack.

p.535, *annotation to the Disability Living Allowance Regulations 1991, reg.12; Alzheimer's disease and virtual inability to walk*

2.022   The question of whether a claimant could qualify for mobility component, at the higher rate, on the basis of being "virtually unable to walk" under reg.12(1)(a)(ii) when, because of Alzheimer's disease, she could not progress effectively in her own was considered in *CSDLA/ 399/2005.*

The Commissioner concludes that no error of law had been shown in the decision of a tribunal that had dismissed the claimant's appeal against a refusal of benefit, but she does so on the ground that the appellant had failed at the original hearing to make out a sufficient factual basis for her claim. On the question of whether an Alzheimer's patient could be said to be suffering from a "physical disability" the Commissioner adopted the view expressed in *CDLA/156/1994* which was in favour of such a conclusion, but felt that the claimant may still need to produce evidence in the form of medical opinion to support that view—the time had not yet come, she thought, when a tribunal could take judicial notice of the aetiology of the condition. In the present case the report of the doctor had described the claimant's condition as "100% mental due to Alzheimer's disease" and while this statement could have contained some ambiguity it did mean that there was no evidence before the tribunal to suggest a physical disability.

p.542, *annotation to the Disability Living Allowance Regulations 1991, reg.12; exertion leading to serious deterioration in health*

2.023   The meaning of this phrase has been further considered in *CDLA/ 3941/2005.* The Commissioner allowed an appeal by a claimant who suffered from cartilage damage and arthritis in her knee. The effect of walking for extensive distances, which she had to do in taking her children to and from school, was said to be likely to result in more frequent arthroscopies (wash-out of the knee joint) and eventually would hasten the need for a knee replacement. This, the Commissioner thought, should satisfy the test in reg.(12)(1)(a)(iii). He gave his own decision that she was entitled to benefit.

Non Means Tested Benefits

p.569, *amendments to the Maternity Allowance Regulations 1987, reg.2*

With effect from October 1, 2006, reg.4(2) of the Statutory Maternity Pay, Social Security (Maternity Allowance) and Social Security (Overlapping Benefits) (Amendment) Regulations 2006 (SI 2006/2379) amended reg.2(1)(a) by substituting the following:

2.024

"(a) during the maternity allowance period she does any work in employment as an employed or self-employed earner, for more than 10 days, whether consecutive or not, falling within that period and the disqualification shall be for such part of the maternity allowance period as may be reasonable in the circumstances, provided that the disqualification shall, in any event, be for the number of days on which she so worked in excess of 10 days."

This amendment will apply only in respect of a woman whose expected week of confinement falls on or after April 1, 2007.

p.570, *amendment to the Maternity Allowance Regulations 1987, reg.3(2A)*

With effect from October 1, 2006, reg.4(3) of the Statutory Maternity Pay, Social Security (Maternity Allowance) and Social Security (Overlapping Benefits) (Amendment) Regulations 2006 (SI 2006/2379) amended reg.3(2A) by substituting for the words "26 weeks commencing with the week following that in which she stopped work" the words following:

2.025

"39 weeks commencing no earlier than the day she becomes entitled to maternity allowance and no later than the day following the day on which she is confined".

This amendment will apply only in respect of a woman whose expected week of confinement falls on or after April 1, 2007.

p.609, *amendment to the Widow's Benefit and Retirement Pensions Regulations 1979, reg.3A*

With effect from October 9, 2006 reg.2 of the Social Security (Miscellaneous Amendment) (No. 4) Regulations 2006 (SI 2006/2378) amended reg.3A by deleting "52 weeks" and substituting "104 weeks".

2.026–
2.027

p.634, *amendments to the Incapacity Benefit Regulations 1994, reg.4*

With effect from September 1, 2006, reg.3 of the Social Security (Adult Learning Option) Amendment Regulations 2006 (SI 2006/2144) amended reg.4 in two ways.

2.028

First, it inserted after para.(2)(c) a new subparagraph, numbered (2)(d). Paragraph (2) as amended now reads:

"(2) Paragraph (1)(c) shall not apply—
  (a) for the purposes of any claim for incapacity benefit for a period commencing after a person ceased attending such a training course; or
  (b) in calculating a period of continuous incapacity for work for the purposes of regulation 2 of the Social Security Benefit (Persons Abroad) Regulations 1975;
  (c) where, such payment as is made, is for the sole purpose of travelling or meal expenses incurred or to be incurred under the arrangement made under section 2(1) of the Employment and Training Act 1973 or section 2(3) of the Enterprise and New Towns (Scotland) Act 1990 [; or
  (d) to any part of such a payment made—
    (i) as a consequence of the person taking part in the scheme known as the Adult Learning Option (which is provided in pursuance of arrangements made by or on behalf of the Secretary of State under section 2 of the Employment and Training Act 1973), and
    (ii) which is not intended to meet the cost of living expenses to which paragraph (3) applies.]"

Secondly, it inserted after para.(2) a new paragraph numbered (3) to read:

"(3) This paragraph applies to living expenses which relate to—
  (a) food,
  (b) ordinary clothing or footwear,
  (c) household fuel,
  (d) rent for which housing benefit is payable,
  (e) any housing costs (to the extent that they are met under regulation 83(f) or 84(1)(g) of the Jobseeker's Allowance Regulations 1996 or regulation 17(1)(e) or 18(1)(f) of the Income Support (General) Regulations 1987 (housing costs)) of the claimant or, where the claimant is a member of the family, any other member of his family, or
  (f) any council tax or water charges for which that claimant or member is liable."

pp.635–636, *amendment to the Incapacity Benefit Regulations 1994, reg.5A*

2.029 With effect from October 1, 2006, reg.10(2) of the Social Security (Miscellaneous Amendments) (No. 4) Regulations 2006 (SI 2006/2378) amended reg.5A by substituting "104 weeks" for "52 weeks".

p.639, *amendment to the Incapacity Benefit Regulations 1994, reg.8*

2.030 With effect from October 1, 2006, reg.10(3) of the Social Security (Miscellaneous Amendments) (No. 4) Regulations 2006 (SI 2006/2378) amended reg.8 so as to increase the prescribed amount of councillor's allowance from £81.00 to £86.00.

Non Means Tested Benefits

pp.644–645, *amendment to the Incapacity Benefit Regulations 1994, reg.16*

With effect from October 1, 2006, reg.10(4) of the Social Security (Miscellaneous Amendments) (No. 4) Regulations 2006 (SI 2006/2378) amended reg.16 by omitting paras (2) and (3) from the regulation.

2.031

p.660, *amendment to the Incapacity Benefit—Increases for Dependants Regulations 1994, reg.9*

With effect from October 1, 2006, The Social Security (Miscellaneous Amendments) (No. 4) Regulations 2006, (SI 2006/2378) amended reg.9 by adding new paragraphs after para.(2A) as follows:

2.032

"(2B) For the purposes of paragraph (1)(c) a beneficiary shall be treated as if he were entitled to child benefit in respect of a child or qualifying young person for any period throughout which—
(a) child benefit has been awarded to a parent of that child or qualifying young person with whom that child or qualifying young person is living and with whom the beneficiary is residing and either—
   (i) the child or qualifying young person is being wholly or mainly maintained by the beneficiary; or
   (ii) the beneficiary is also a parent of the child or qualifying young person; or
(b) (i) the beneficiary;
   (ii) his spouse or civil partner with whom he is residing; or
   (iii) a parent (other than the beneficiary) to whom sub-paragraph (a) would refer if that parent were entitled to child benefit,
would have been entitled to child benefit in respect of that child had the child been born at the end of the week immediately preceding the week in which the birth occurred.
(2C) Where for any period a person who is in Great Britain could have been entitled to an increase of incapacity benefit pursuant to paragraph (1)(c) but for the fact that in pursuance of any agreement with the government of a country outside the United Kingdom—
(a) he;
(b) his spouse or civil partner who is residing with him; or
(c) a parent (other than the beneficiary) to whom paragraph (2B)(a) would refer if that parent were entitled to child benefit,
is entitled in respect of the child or qualifying young person in question to the family benefits of that country and is not entitled to child benefit, he shall for the purposes of entitlement to the increase be treated as if he were entitled to child benefit for the period in question.
(2D) For the purposes of paragraphs (2B) and (2C)—
(a) 'week' means a period of 7 days beginning with a Monday; and
(b) a child or qualifying young person shall not be regarded as living with a person unless he can be so regarded for the purposes of

Non Means Tested Benefits

section 143 (meaning of 'person responsible for child or qualifying young person')."

p.662, *amendment to the Incapacity Benefit—Increases for Dependants Regulations 1994, reg.11 (apportionment of payments by way of occupational or personal pension made otherwise then weekly)*

2.033   With effect from May 5, 2006, reg.3 of the Social Security (PPF Payments and FAS Payments) (Consequential Amendments) Regulations 2006 (SI 2006/1069) amended reg.11 to read as follows:

"**11.**—For the purpose of section 89 (earnings to include occupational or personal pension [or PPF periodic payment] for certain purposes) in so far as it relates to incapacity benefit, where payment by way of occupational or personal pension [or PPF periodic payment] is for any period made otherwise than weekly, the amount of any such payment for any week in that period shall be determined—
  (a) where payment is made for a year, by dividing the total by 52;
  (b) where payment is made for three months, by dividing the total by 13;
  (c) where payment is made for a month, by multiplying the total by 12 and dividing the result by 52;
  (d) where payment is made for two or more months, otherwise than for a year or for three months, by dividing the total by the number of months, multiplying the result by 12 and dividing the result of that multiplication by 52; or
  (e) in any other case, by dividing the amount of the payment by the number of days in the period for which it is made and multiplying the result by 7."

pp.679–680, *substitution of a new Incapacity for Work (General) Regulations 1995, reg.11 (person with an infectious or contagious disease)*

2.034   With effect from October 1, 2006, reg.12(2) of the Social Security (Miscellaneous Amendments) (No. 4) Regulations 2006 (SI 2006/2378) substituted for the current text a new reg.11 reading as follows:

"Person with an infectious or contagious disease

[**11.**—(1) A person shall be treated as incapable of work on any day in respect of which he is—
  (a) excluded or abstains from work pursuant to a request or notice in writing lawfully made under an enactment; or
  (b) otherwise prevented from working pursuant to an enactment, by reason of his being a carrier, or having been in contact with a case, of a relevant disease.
  (2) For the purposes of paragraph (1)—
'enactment' means an enactment comprised in, or in an instrument made under
  (a) an Act; or

(b) an Act of the Scottish Parliament; and
'relevant disease' means—
(a) in England and Wales, any disease, food poisoning, infection, infectious disease or notifiable disease—
  (i) to which section 20(1) of the Public Health (Control of Disease) Act 1984 (stopping of work to prevent spread of disease) applies; or
  (ii) to which—
    (aa) regulation 3 (public health enactments applied to certain diseases) of, and Schedule 1 to,
    (bb) regulation 9(1) (provisions for preventing the spread of typhus and relapsing fever) of, and Schedule 3 to, or
    (cc) regulation 9(2) (provisions for preventing the spread of food poisoning and food borne infections) of, and Schedule 4 to,
    the Public Health (Infectious Diseases) Regulations 1988 apply; or
  (iii) to which regulations 8 and 9 (examination, etc. of the persons on aircraft and powers in respect of persons leaving aircraft) of the Public Health (Aircraft) Regulations 1979 apply; or
  (iv) to which regulations 9 and 10 (examination, etc. of the persons on ships and powers in respect of certain persons on ships) of the Public Health (Ships) Regulations 1979 apply; and
(b) in Scotland, any food poisoning or infectious disease—
  (i) to which section 71(1) of the Health Services and Public Health Act 1968 (compensation for stopping employment to prevent spread of disease in Scotland) applies;
  (ii) to which—
    (aa) regulations 8 and 9 (examination, etc. of persons on aircraft and powers in respect of persons leaving aircraft) of the Public Health (Aircraft) (Scotland) Regulations 1971; or
    (bb) regulations 9 and 10 (examination, etc. of persons on ships and powers in respect of persons on ships) of the Public Health (Ships) (Scotland) Regulations 1971,
    apply.]"

DEFINITIONS

"enactment": see para.(2).
"relevant disease": see para.(2).

GENERAL NOTE

This regulation is designed to help those who are excluded from or abstain from work pursuant to a request or notice in writing lawfully made under an

Non Means Tested Benefits

enactment or who is otherwise prevented from working pursuant to an enactment, by reason of his being a carrier, or having been in contact with a case, of a relevant disease. An enactment is any Act of the Westminster Parliament or of the Scottish Parliament. A "relevant disease" is defined differently in England and Wales, on the one hand, and in Scotland, on the other. As regards England and Wales it covers any disease, food poisoning, infection, infectious disease or notifiable disease to which there applies a variety of public health legislation specified in sub-paras (i)–(iv) of head (a) in the definition in para.(2). In Scotland it covers food poisoning or any infectious disease to which there applies the legislation in head (b) of the definition in para.(2). The help given is that the person covered is treated as being incapable of work.

pp.681–683, *amendment to the Incapacity for Work (General) Regulations 1995, reg.13A (welfare to work beneficiary)*

2.035   With effect from October 1, 2006, reg.12(3) of the Social Security (Miscellaneous Amendments) (No. 4) Regulations 2006 (SI 2006/2378) effected a number of amendments to reg.13A(1).

Firstly, at the end of para.(1)(b) it inserted "and". Secondly, it substituted "one month" for "one week" in para.(1)(b). Thirdly, it omits from the regulation both para.(1)(d) and the "and" at the end of para.(1)(c).

From the same date, it also substituted a new para.(3) and inserted immediately after it a new paragraph numbered (3A):

> "(3) A person is not a welfare to work beneficiary under paragraph (1) if his immediate past period of incapacity for work was ended by a determination, other than a determination in the circumstances set out in paragraph (1) or (3A), that he was, or was treated as, capable of work.
>
> (3A) The circumstances are that the person had successfully appealed against a determination made in respect of the personal capability assessment or the own occupation test in relation to his immediate past period of incapacity for work."

In para.(4) from the same date, it also replaced "52 weeks" in the definition of "linking term" with "104 weeks", and amended the definition of "immediate past period of incapacity for work" to read:

> "'immediate past period of incapacity for work' means [the most recent of]
>   (i) a period of incapacity for work under section 30C(1) of the Contributions and Benefits Act,
>   (ii) a period of incapacity for work under section 152 of the Contributions and Benefits Act, or
>   (iii) a term composed of a period of incapacity for work under section 30C(1) and a period of incapacity for work under section 152 and includes any two such periods of incapacity for work which are separated by a period of not more than 8 weeks."

p.688, *annotation to the Incapacity for Work (General) Regulations 1995, reg.16(5) (partial relief from the rule that a person who works is to be treated as incapable of work throughout the week in which the day(s) fall)*

In *CIB/1635/2006*, dealing with the identically worded predecessor of this provision (then in reg.16(3)), Deputy Commissioner Mark considered the case of a claimant suffering from chronic fatigue syndrome who had five days of no work between his two days of work as a lecturer each week. He rejected the claimant's argument that this provision entitled him to make weekly claims so that the days were not caught by the general rule in reg.16(1) because for each new claim this relieving provision applied. The Commissioner did so because on proper construction the provision's twofold reference to "in any period" could only be referring to "period of incapacity for work", so that the provision could apply only at the beginning and end of a single period of incapacity for work. The "spells" of no work were not each separate periods of incapacity for work. Rather, each of the "spells" of no work for which the claimant claimed incapacity benefit were forged by the "continuity" and "linking" rules into a single period of incapacity for work (see SSCBA 1992, s.30C and commentary). The Commissioner further stated: 2.036

"The claimant has contended that this would leave regulation 16(3) empty of effect. I do not consider that to be the case. Any claimant who becomes sick will inevitably have a first week in which he becomes entitled to benefit, and in that week, regulation 16(3)(a) will apply. If he recovers, there will come a week in the course of which he goes back to work. In that week regulation 16(3)(b) will, on the face of it, apply.

There is a problem if the claimant becomes sick again within the 8 weeks period, so that the linking provisions apply, because although it may have appeared at the time that the week the claimant went back to work was the last week in any period in which he was incapable of work, subsequent events will have shown that not to be so. In my judgment, that is an evidential issue. A decision maker could defer making a decision on the last few days of benefit until it can be seen whether the claimant falls ill again within the linking period, or whether the period of incapacity has indeed come to an end" (paras 14, 15).

pp.690–691, *amendment to the Incapacity for Work (General) Regulations 1995, reg.17 (exempt work earnings limit)*

With effect from October 1, 2006, reg.12(4) of the Social Security (Miscellaneous Amendments) (No. 4) Regulations 2006 (SI 2006/2378) substituted "£86.00" for "£81.00" in paras (3) and (4). 2.037

p.694, *annotation to the Incapacity for Work (General) Regulations 1995, reg.17 (the earnings limit—Computation of Earnings Regs applicable)*

Secretary of State v Doyle is also reported as *R(IB) 1/06*. 2.038

pp.705–708, *annotation to the Incapacity for Work (General) Regulations 1995, reg.24 (dealing with the evidence, in particular with differing medical opinions and reports)*

2.039   In *CIB/3108/2005* (to be reported as *R(IB) 2/06*) Commissioner Rowland held that a tribunal medical member is not precluded by virtue of the SSA 1998, s.20(3)(a) from looking at X Rays put in evidence. That provision only precludes "physical examination" of the claimant. But a tribunal is not bound to look at such X Rays:

> "In this case, both members of the tribunal have referred to the medically qualified panel member's lack of expertise in analysing X-rays. If a tribunal is presented with X-rays that it cannot analyse, there must arise the question whether it should adjourn the proceedings so as to enable the parties to obtain a report from the relevant expert from among those treating the claimant. A failure to adjourn where a claimant has brought evidence that he not unreasonably thought the tribunal would be able to understand may amount to a breach of the rules of natural justice because the claimant is effectively being denied the opportunity to put his or her case properly. Deciding whether or not to adjourn will involve consideration of the relevance of the X-rays and the likelihood of them being helpful in relation to a live issue in the case. Where a person complains of back pain, it is usually accepted that he or she suffers from some such pain. The question are usually: how much and how disabling is it? If an X-ray is unlikely to give much indication as to how disabling the condition is, except in the most serious cases, there may well be little to gain from adjourning, and a tribunal may properly refuse to do so. However, if asked for a statement of reasons, it should explain what its approach was. Whenever a tribunal declines to consider evidence, that should ideally be recorded in the record of proceedings, together with a note of the reason that will usually have been given orally to the parties. Whether or not that is done, a reference to the refusal to consider the evidence is usually to be expected in the statement of reasons particularly where, as in this case, the claimant's application for a statement of reasons specifically stated that he wanted to know why his X-rays were not looked at" (para.10).

p.712, *annotation to Incapacity for Work (General) Regulations 1995, reg.25(3): the need properly to characterise a particular condition so that the appropriate set(s) of descriptors are considered*

2.040   It is clear that this key tribunal task must be executed with considerable care. As noted in the annotation, in *CIB/6244/1997*, considering a case of chronic fatigue syndrome, Commissioner Jacobs sent the case back to another tribunal to consider whether the claimant's condition was entirely physical, entirely mental, or partly physical or mental in origin. In *CIB/2357/2006*, Commissioner Rowland held that a tribunal erred by ignoring physical descriptors in any detail in a case of chronic fatigue syndrome simply because the claimant had not identified any problems with the physical activities on her IB50 form. She had characterised herself as "ill" rather than disabled, but had also stated that she was often so exhausted that she was unable to do anything except retire to bed. The tribunal itself had also noted her claim that after getting up there was only a "5 hour window" in which she could function relatively normally. Commissioner Rowland held that this put the tribunal on notice that the claimant's condition manifested itself in physical signs and symptoms. It seemed to Commissioner Rowland that "she was therefore in fact claiming to be physically disabled during much of the day" (para.3), thus putting in issue matters of whether she could "normally" perform certain activities as and when called upon to do so and whether it could be done on a repeated basis (*ibid.*).

pp.718–720, *annotation to Incapacity for Work (General) Regulations 1995, reg.27: the "old" head (b) as modified by Moule ("substantial risk to mental or physical health of any person if he were found capable of work")*

In *CIB/1064/2006*, Deputy Commissioner Ovey, having considered the authorities noted in the annotation, encapsulated her task thus: 2.041

"I must consider whether there is evidence that a job of the kind which it is likely the claimant would be required to be available for would result in consequences for his health which, although not necessarily life-threatening, would be substantial having regard to both likelihood of occurrence and degree of harm" (para.20).

Here the claimant had been a chauffeur, a job he had lost because of his dermatitis. The Deputy Commissioner concluded that the evidence before the tribunal was capable of putting the provision in issue. The claimant, to a degree supported by his doctor, stated that his removal from that working environment, in which friction and repeated activities would cause flare ups of his dermatitis, had improved matters. Where the Deputy Commissioner parted company with the tribunal was in its failure adequately to explain its confinement of the work the claimant should be measured against to driving (his previous job) and why it thought the risk to the claimant to be "substantial". The tribunal in this way had erred in law and the Deputy Commissioner remitted the matter to another tribunal.

pp.731–735, *annotation to Incapacity for Work (General) Regulations 1995, Sch.1: An Important Note on Amendments and Possible Invalidity: the decision of the Tribunal of Commissioners resolving the conflict of authorities*

In their decision on two appeals heard jointly, a Tribunal of Commissioners (Commissioner Rowland, Commissioner Parker and Deputy Commissioner Sir Crispin Agnew of Lochnaw BT Q.C.) has in *CSIB/803/2005 and CSIB/2005* resolved the conflict of authorities. To hold invalid on *Howker* procedural impropriety grounds any of the January 1997 changes to the Incapacity for Work Regulations, it must be established both that the Department's presentation to the SSAC of the 2.042

change in question as neutral was inaccurate and that the SSAC was misled by that characterisation into not requiring the change to be the subject of a formal reference to it.

> "In practice, we suggest, a party seeking to show that a regulation is invalid on the grounds that the Committee was given misleading information must show both that there is a real possibility that the information might have misled the Committee as to the effect that the proposed regulation would have and that there is a real possibility that, had the Committee been aware of its true effect, it would have wished to have the proposed regulation formally referred to it" (para.37).

This will require examination of "all of the material placed before the SSAC to consider whether the overall effect was misleading since only then will the Secretary of State be in breach of his duty under s.170(4) of the Social Security Administration Act 1992 to provide information to enable the Committee properly to carry out its functions so that there was [as in *Howker*] no "informed agreement" by the SSAC not to require a formal reference of the proposed change (para.35). It is not enough merely to consider whether applying the label "neutral" to the change was correct, since sometimes an incorrect application may have negligible impact because the further description of the change in explanatory material makes its effect sufficiently clear (para.35).

The matters of validity and the proper construction of the proposed change are intertwined, since something that might be invalid on one construction might on another albeit strained construction be found valid, and wherever possible "a provision should be construed so that it is valid" (para.38).

With respect to the change in wording to Activity 14, the Tribunal of Commissioners found that the SSAC was not misled. The Commissioners stressed that although an omission to mention other possible cases that might be affected may have a misleading effect, care had to be taken before finding that the SSAC was misled. Members of the Committee have considerable expertise. They are neither naive nor passive. They will probably have done preparatory work before a meeting and so "have a broad understanding of the context in which new regulations are proposed, and are likely to understand the significance of most proposed regulations notwithstanding minor inaccuracies or omissions in the information provided" (para.51). If in doubt they can and are likely to ask questions (*ibid.*).

Applying this to the changes to Activity 14, the Tribunal of Commissioners considered the situation clearly distinguishable from that in *Howker*. There was in that case a clear misrepresentation of the difference between the old regulation and the proposed new one, only discoverable by careful study of them side by side, something which the commentary accompanying the proposed text implied was not necessary. The case before the Tribunal of Commissioners was different:

> "What is important in this instance is that, from the terms of the draft amendment itself and from the commentary, the Committee could see for themselves that only those who suffered from seizures would be

within the scope of Activity 14 when the amendment came into force. The commentary was plainly not intended to be a detailed policy document dealing with all possible issues and it had to be read with the draft regulation. When the two documents are read together, it is impossible to say that the Secretary of State misled the Committee or was in breach of his duty to furnish the Committee with such information as it might reasonably require, provided that the word "seizures" was not intended to be understood only in its technical sense. The point that there might be some people who would suffer from a condition causing them to lose consciousness without experiencing a seizure and that those people would be excluded from the scope of Activity 14 was implicit in the material before the Committee and members could have asked about it had they wished. If they overlooked the point, that was not, in our judgment, because they were misled by the information in the commentary.

... Here, the fact that people who did not suffer seizures were to be omitted from the scope of the amended Activity 14 was abundantly clear from the material provided to the Committee as was the fact that there were at least different views as to whether such people were anyway outside the scope of the original version" (paras 52, 53).

The Tribunal of Commissioners thus endorses the approach taken by Commissioner May in *CSIB/0148/2005 and CSIB/196/2005* and rejects that of Commissioner Jacobs in *R(IB)3/04*.

pp.757–758, *annotation to the Incapacity for Work (General) Regulations 1995, Sch.1, Pt I, Physical Disabilities, Activity 8: "lifting and carrying"*

Since the wording of the descriptor stipulates "by the use of the upper body and arms", that legal test "permits a tribunal to take account of a claimant's back pain", and a tribunal which refuses to do so misdirects itself in law. Commissioner Jacobs so held in *CIB/0960/2006* (para.15). However, a mere misdirection which did not affect the outcome is not an error of law (*R (Iran) v Secretary of State for the Home Department* [2005] EWCA Civ 982). Accordingly, since the claimant could only have scored eight points, the mistake did not affect the outcome of the appeal to the tribunal and its decision was thus not erroneous in law.

2.043

pp.768–772, *annotation to the Incapacity for Work (General) Regulations 1995, Sch.1, Pt I, Physical Disabilities, Activity 14 "remaining conscious without having epileptic or similar seizures during waking moments": validity and meaning of this change*

As noted in the update to pp.731–735, above, a Tribunal of Commissioners has in *CSIB/803/2005 and CSIB/2005* resolved the conflict of authorities on the approach to invalidity on *Howker* procedural impropriety grounds. It has upheld the validity of the January 1997 change of wording. It has also considered the meaning of that wording, and the interpretation proffered in the cases noted in the annotation need to be considered in the light of what the Tribunal of Commissioners said:

2.044

"the word 'seizures' is to be construed as meaning episodes that are involuntary, overwhelming and sudden and the phrase 'similar seizures' is to be construed by reference to the similarity of the *effects* of the seizures to epileptic seizures, including the degree of suddenness of the loss or alteration of consciousness but without consideration of whether the seizures are characterised by the discharge of cerebral neurones, the amendment to Activity 14 is not invalid on procedural grounds. . . . [D]rawing a distinction between events characterised by electrical activity in the brain and other sudden losses or alterations of consciousness makes little sense" (para.56).

pp.770–772, *annotation to the Incapacity for Work (General) Regulations 1995, Sch.1, Pt I, Physical Disabilities, Activity 14 descriptors: "altered consciousness"*

2.045   In the Tribunal of Commissioners decision in *CSIB/803/2005 and CSIB/2005*, noted in the update immediately above, the Commissioners in para.69 noted that mere sleepiness or doziness is not "altered consciousness". But a person who regularly feels sleepy during the day due to his medication will, during periods when he actually falls asleep, suffer episodes of "lost consciousness".

p.775, *annotation to the Incapacity for Work (General) Regulations 1995, Sch.1, Pt II, Mental Disabilities, Activity 16: daily living: descriptor (e) "sleeping problems interfere with daytime activities"*

2.046   While a tribunal should be cautious in awarding points about sleep patterns without corroborative evidence about mental disorder, where there is such evidence which clearly points to an interconnection between the mental health problem and the daytime sleepiness a point should be awarded under the descriptor (*CIB/1374/2006, para.10, per* Commissioner Williams).

p.777, *new entry in annotation to the Incapacity for Work (General) Regulations 1995, Sch.1, Pt II, Mental Disabilities, Activity 17: coping with pressure; descriptor (c) "avoids carrying out routine activities because he is convinced they will prove too tiring or stressful"*

2.047   In *CIB/1374/2006*, Commissioner Williams commented:

"This descriptor clearly requires (a) a finding whether the claimant 'avoids carrying out routine activities', and (b) a finding whether 'this is because he is convinced that they will prove too tiring or stressful'. It does not require that the claimant *cannot* do these things. That would be in part a physical descriptor. It requires the claimant's approach to be as stated. As with problems with sleep, the general requirement is that this arises because of the mental health problems. There is evidence of (a) in this case from the past medical assessments, the approved doctor's IB85 (where there is also evidence of the opposite) and the claimant. As to (b), the tribunal found that the inactivity was of his own choosing. That misses the point. Why did he choose that? Was he convinced that they would prove too tiring or stressful? The secretary of state's representative submits that the evidence indicates that the claimant was so convinced. I accept that, and award 1 point" (para.12).

p.778, *annotation to the Incapacity for Work (General) Regulations 1995, Sch.1, Pt II, Mental Disabilities, Activity 18: descriptors (b) ("gets upset by ordinary events and this results in disruptive behavioural problems") and (d) ("gets irritated by things that would not have bothered him before he became ill")*

In *CIB/1374/2006*, Commissioner Williams agreed with Commissioner Parker's view in *CSIB/1521/2001* that these two descriptors overlap and that "disruptive behaviour" is not limited to aggressive behaviour. Applying this to the case before him, he considered that these: 2.048

"two descriptors are in ordinary English that do not warrant further definitions. 'Upset' and 'irritated' are widely drawn and overlapping terms. The phrase used by the claimant in his appeal notice was 'I get stressed'. That overlaps with both. The focus is on any upset or irritation arising from the mental health problems, in this case the claimant's anxiety problems. I agree with both parties that the two descriptors should be looked at together, with any relevant evidence assessed under both descriptors. On that basis, I am unable to accept the tribunal's 'no evidence approach'. Given the evidence before it, I fail to see how it reached the conclusion it did. My view might have been different had it taken a 'balance of evidence' approach, but its decision as it stands is either wrong or inadequate. Again on the evidence, and applying the test from CSIB 1521 2001, I accept the secretary of state's representative's submission that both descriptors are met. That scores 3 points" (para.12).

p.788, *amendment to the Incapacity Benefit (Transitional) Regulations 1995, reg.11*

With effect from October 16, 2006, art.2(3)(b) amended art.3 of the Social Security Act 1998 (Commencement No. 9, and Savings and Consequential and Transitional Provisions) Order 1999 (SI 1999/2422) (as amended) so as to add to it new paras (15) and (16). The effect of this is to insert into reg.11 from October 16, 2006 a new para.(6) reading as follows: 2.049

"(6) The transitional award under paragraph (1) is treated as a decision of the Secretary of State under section 8(1) of the Social Security Act 1998 (decisions by Secretary of State) and as an incapacity decision for the purposes of the Social Security and Child Support (Decisions and Appeals) Regulations 1999."

Non Means Tested Benefits

p.794, *amendment to the Incapacity Benefit (Transitional) Regulations 1995, reg.17*

2.050 With effect from October 16, 2006, art.2(3)(b) amended art.3 of the Social Security Act 1998 (Commencement No. 9, and Savings and Consequential and Transitional Provisions) Order 1999 (SI 1999/2422) (as amended) so as to add to it new paras (15) and (16). The effect of this is to insert into reg.17 from October 16, 2006 a new para.(5) reading as follows:

> "(5) The transitional award under paragraph (1) is treated as a decision of the Secretary of State under section 8(1) of the Social Security Act 1998 (decision by Secretary of State) and as an incapacity decision for the purposes of the Social Security and Child Support (Decisions and Appeals) Regulations 1999."

p.796, *amendment to the Incapacity Benefit (Transitional) Regulations 1995, reg.17B*

2.051 With effect from October 1, 2006, reg.11(2) of the Social Security (Miscellaneous Amendments) (No. 4) Regulations 2006 (SI 2006/2378) amended reg.17B by substituting "104 weeks" for "52 weeks".

p.802, *amendment to the Incapacity Benefit (Transitional) Regulations 1995, reg.23(2)*

2.052 With effect from October 1, 2006, reg.11(3) of the Social Security (Miscellaneous Amendments) (No. 4) Regulations 2006 (SI 2006/2378) amended reg.23(2) by substituting "104 weeks" for "52 weeks".

pp.857–862, *annotation to the Social Security (General Benefit) Regulations 1982, reg.11 (assessment of disablement in multi-cause situations)*

2.053 For an illustration of the operation of these rules and a framework of questions for approaching these matters, see the decision of Commissioner Williams in *CI/2930/2005*, noted in the update to pp.216–219, above (disablement pension).

pp.923–925, *annotation to Prescribed Diseases Regulations 1985, Sch.1, PD A11 (vibration white finger)*

2.054 In *CI/421/2006*, Commissioner Turnbull held that a claimant refused permission to stand outside the tribunal for a short while in cold weather the better to support his claim that he suffered from vibration white finger was denied natural justice. The Commissioner also suggested that since this claimant had also requested that the last tribunal conduct a Cold Water Provocation Test, it might be wise to offer one at the new hearing. Although a negative result from such a test did not disprove vibration white finger, a positive result could assist a claimant whose history or symptoms were inconclusive (citing *R (on the application of*

NACODS) v Secretary of State for Work and Pensions [2003] EWHC 607, paras 41, 43). The result of any diagnostic test, however, had to be considered in the light of the history and clinical findings in the case.

p.928, *annotation to Prescribed Diseases Regulations 1985, Sch.1, PD A11 (vibration white finger)*

Secretary of State v Westgate is also reported as *R(I) 1/06*.   2.055

pp.937–938, *annotation to Prescribed Diseases Regulations 1985, Sch.1, PD D7 (occupational asthma)*

In *CI/3565/2004*, Commissioner Levenson dealt with an appeal by a claimant midwife in respect of occupational asthma said to be brought on by exposure to latex in the course of her work, but prior to the specific prescription of latex products in D7(wa) from March 14, 2005. He held that on the balance of probabilities it was the latex allergy which caused the asthma and that latex constituted "any other sensitising agent" and fell within D7(x).   2.056

PART III

UPDATING MATERIAL
VOLUME II

INCOME SUPPORT, JOBSEEKER'S ALLOWANCE, STATE PENSION CREDIT AND THE SOCIAL FUND

Income Support, Jobseekers' Allowance, etc.

pp.91–94, annotation to the Jobseekers Act 1995, s.19(3), (4)

In *CJSA/1703/2006*, Commissioner Levenson considered the case of a claimant who had voluntarily left his employment because travelling costs in relation to his wage made seeking more local employment a better prospect. He had not before leaving attempted to find such employment. The Commissioner held that he did not have just cause for leaving his employment voluntarily, but did allow his appeal on the period of preclusion, substituting four weeks for the 20 weeks initially imposed and upheld by the tribunal. In so doing, Commissioner Levenson referred to Jobseeker's Allowance Regulations 1996, reg.70, stressing that all the circumstances of the case had to be taken into account in fixing the appropriate period of preclusion:

3.001

"In addition to the matters specified by statute or regulations, and without prejudice to any other considerations, the tribunal must take account of the reasons given for leaving the employment, any attempts to find other employment, the prospects of so doing, whether leaving the employment created any particular problems for the employer, the claimant's fellow workers, or the employer's customers and, in the light of the working conditions (including travel to and from work) the length of time the claimant had been in the employment" (para.17).

He held that one relevant factor of public interest to be taken into account was how close the leaving was to the end of the exempting trial period protection afforded by Jobseekers Act 1995, s.20(3) and Jobseeker's Allowance Regulations 1996, reg.74. Here the leaving was within two weeks of the end of that period. If he had left two weeks earlier there would have been no preclusion of benefit, so the public interest was here "better served by the claimant working for those two weeks than by him leaving at the earlier date and claiming JSA" (para.18).

In addition, Commissioner Levenson stressed that an appeal to a tribunal is by way of rehearing. It should not simply record that the 20 week period imposed by the Secretary of State was "reasonable in all the circumstances". Rather it is required to make a judicial decision, its own decision on the matters under appeal and issue reasons from which an intelligent reader can understand how and why each conclusion has been reached, otherwise it will err in law.

In fixing the period, it is not appropriate to start with the 26 week period and allow some deduction by way of mitigation, as the Secretary of State and the tribunal may have done.

"The 26 week period is not a starting point. It is the maximum. It seems to me that wording of the statute requires that one week be taken as the starting point and then that it be adjusted by reference to any aggravating and mitigating factors. I am not suggesting that a rigid or formulaic or mathematical approach be taken, but that relevant considerations must be taken into account in fixing the appropriate period. It must also be remembered that, unlike the previous provisions that were replaced by the introduction of JSA, what is provided here is a total and permanent loss of JSA for the relevant number of weeks, rather than a deferral or postponement (CJSA/3304/1999). This is a real (and in some circumstances harsh) penalty" (para.16).

p.113, *annotation to the Jobseekers Act 1995, s.19(9) (national minimum wage rates)*

3.002 With effect from October 1, 2006, the hourly rates become £5.35 for those 22 and over; £4.45 for those aged 18–21; and £3.30 for those workers under 18 who have ceased be of compulsory school age. The change in rates was effected by the National Minimum Wage Regulations 1999 (Amendment) Regulations 2006 (SI 2006/2001).

p.154, *annotation to the State Pension Credit Act 2002, s.7: fixing of claimant's retirement provision for assessed income period*

3.003 The minister's statement to the Standing Committee about the lottery winner was considered by Mr Commissioner Levenson in *CPC/0206/2005*. The claimant made a claim for state pension credit (SPC), reporting that she had rented sheltered accommodation, but not yet moved in, and disclosing that she had savings of some £19,500 and that her own house, in which she was still living, had been put up for sale for some £85,000. An official decided that the value of her home should be disregarded for the time being but noted that this decision would change in the event of sale. The Secretary of State then awarded SPC by way of savings credit for a five year assessed income period. Four months later the claimant reported that the sale of her home had just taken placed, resulting in net proceeds of over £73,000. Mr Commissioner Levenson observed that the minister's statement did not cover a case such as this, where the issue was "what the Secretary of State should do if it is known that a large amount of capital is likely to be on its way" (para.10). The Commissioner held that the original decision awarding SPC subject to a five year assessed income period should be revised for official error and replaced with a decision awarding SPC without specifying an assessed income period (AIP). That decision was then subject to supersession for the change of circumstances in the receipt of the proceeds of sale. According to the Commissioner:

"23. It seems to me that the concept of 'error' involves more than merely taking a decision that another decision maker with the same information would not take, but is not limited to (although it includes, subject to the statutory exceptions) a public law or any other error of law. Other than that it is not helpful (and could be misleading) to go beyond the words of the regulation. On the facts of the present case, though, I take the view that no Secretary of State or decision maker acting reasonably could have imposed a 5 year AIP. It was already known that number 8 was up for sale and that it would realise a sum of several tens of thousands of pounds (even if the exact amount was not known) and a view had already been taken that the progress of the sale should be monitored. In these respects the position was very different from that of a lottery winner who, at the time of the decision on the claim, had done no more than buy a ticket."

Income Support, Jobseekers' Allowance, etc.

See also the decision of Mr Commissioner Rowland in *CPC/1928/2005*, discussed in the note to p.156 below.

p.156, *annotation to the State Pension Credit Act 2002, s.9: duration of assessed income period*

In *CPC/1928/2005* the claimant applied for state pension credit (SPC) in December 2003, having moved into rented property with her husband and having put their own house up for sale. The claimant was awarded SPC on April 1, 2004, without taking account of the capital value of their former home, and with an assessed income period of October 6, 2003 to March 9, 2010. On April 22, 2004 the claimant's husband moved permanently to a care home. On May 19, 2004 the couple received the proceeds of sale in respect of their former home, amounting to over £95,000. The Secretary of State became aware of these facts in September 2004, and in October 2004 made a decision superseding the decision of April 1, 2004 on the basis that the claimant should be treated as a single person from April 22, 2004 and should be regarded as having additional capital representing half the proceeds of sale as from May 19, 2004. The tribunal disallowed the claimant's appeal. Mr Commissioner Rowland, dismissing the claimant's further appeal, held that the tribunal had reached the correct conclusion, albeit for the wrong reasons. On these facts, with sale to be anticipated within a few months, no assessed income period should have been set from April 22, 2004. Moreover, "Where a substantial sum is expected on an uncertain date, not setting an assessed income period will generally be preferable to setting a short one, in the absence of other considerations such as likely minor variations of other income that the decision-maker considers should be ignored" (para.11). 3.004

See also the decision of Mr Commissioner Levenson in *CPC/0206/2005*, discussed in the note to p.154 above.

p.225, *annotation to the Income Support (General) Regulations 1987, reg.2: definition of "welfare to work beneficiary"*

With effect from October 9, 2006, reg.13A of the Social Security (Incapacity for Work) (General) Regulations 1995 (which sets out the conditions for a person to be a "welfare to work beneficiary") has been amended by reg.12(3) and (5) of the Social Security (Miscellaneous Amendments) (No. 4) Regulations 2006 (SI 2006/2378). The effect of those amendments is that: (i) it will no longer be necessary for the claimant to notify the Secretary of State that he has started work or training; (ii) the work or training can start within one month of benefit ending (rather than one week); (iii) the requirement for the last period of incapacity for work to have ended 28 weeks or more after the end of any earlier linking term has been removed, i.e. if a person claims benefit again and qualifies for the linking protection, there is no longer a requirement to spend a further 28 weeks on benefit before he can take advantage of the linking rules again; and (iv) the linking period is extended from 52 to 104 weeks. It is specifically provided that these amendments 3.005

Income Support, Jobseekers' Allowance, etc.

to reg.13A apply whether the person's last period of incapacity for work ended before or after October 9, 2006.

p.235, *amendment to the Income Support (General) Regulations 1987, reg.4ZA (Prescribed categories of person)*

3.006   With effect from September 1, 2006, reg.2 of the Social Security (Adult Learning Option) Amendment Regulations 2006 (SI 2006/2144) inserted the word "; or" at the end of sub-para.(c) of reg.4ZA(3) followed by the following sub-paragraph:

"(d) he is taking part in the scheme known as the Adult Learning Option (which is provided in pursuance of arrangements made by or on behalf of the Secretary of State under section 2 of the Employment and Training Act 1973)."

p.237, *annotation to the Income Support (General) Regulations 1987, reg.4ZA*

3.007   The Adult Learning Option is part of the "New Deal for Skills", under which claimants can remain entitled to benefit while studying full-time for a "Level 2" qualification (i.e. any qualification that is equivalent to five GCSEs at A*–C or a National Vocational Qualification (NVQ)). It is being introduced on a pilot basis in certain areas of England. Participants continue to receive their existing benefit, plus a training premium paid under s.2 of the Employment and Training Act 1973 (see para.13 of Sch.9 to the Income Support Regulations for the disregard of such a premium). However, because they will be studying full-time, they would, unless exempted, count as students and be excluded from income support (see reg.4ZA(2)). The new reg.4ZA(3)(d) therefore adds a person who is taking part in the Adult Learning Option scheme to the list of students who are not excluded from entitlement to income support.

p.264, *annotation to the Income Support (General) Regulations 1987, reg.15(1) (Circumstances in which a person is to be treated as responsible or not responsible for another)*

3.008   In *CIS/2317/2006*, Mr Commissioner Jacobs confirmed that the person who is "receiving child benefit" for the purposes of para.(1) is the person who claimed and was awarded that benefit even when that person subsequently paid over a sum equal to the amount of that benefit to another person.

p.266, *amendment to the Income Support (General) Regulations 1987, reg.16 (Circumstances in which a person is treated as being or not being a member of the household)*

3.009   With effect from October 2, 2006, reg.5(2) of the Social Security (Miscellaneous Amendments) (No. 4) Regulations 2006 (SI 2006/2378) amended head (a) of para.(3) by substituting for "special hospitals" the words "high security psychiatric services".

Income Support, Jobseekers' Allowance, etc.

p.274, *annotation to the Income Support (General) Regulations 1987, reg.17 (Applicable amounts): migration of child elements to child tax credit*

The process of migrating "transitional cases" (i.e. recipients of IS and JSA who still retain an entitlement to what the Main Volume calls the "child elements") to child tax credit is to be postponed. Again. The migration will not now commence until at least 2008. A written statement to Parliament by the Paymaster General on December 6, 2006 announced that:

3.010

"The Government will continue to make improvements to the tax credit system, including those announced in the 2005 pre-Budget report, while minimising the risk of disruption to claimants. To minimise those risks and ensure that some of the most vulnerable families are protected, the Government will not begin migration of the remaining IS/JSA recipients with children to the child tax credit in 2007. In addition, HMRC is putting in place special arrangements for a small proportion of claimants who may experience disruption in their payments following the processing of changes in their circumstances, and will update the IT system in April 2007 to prevent this."

The postponement has been achieved by the Tax Credits Act 2002 (Commencement and Transitional Provisions) Order 2006 (SI 2006/3369). Article 2 of that Order amends SI 2003/962 by substituting "31st December 2008" for "31st December 2006" as the date on which s.1(3)(d) of the Tax Credits Act 2002 will come into force (see para.2.127 of the Main Work). Article 4 makes the same substitution for the end date of the transitional provision made by SI 2005/773 (see para. 2.132). SI 2005/776 and SI 2005/1106 have been revoked.

pp.279–280, *Income Support (General) Regulations 1987, reg.21(3)–(3G) (Special cases)*

With effect from April 30, 2006, reg.6(2) of the Social Security (Persons from Abroad) Amendment Regulations 2006 (SI 2006/1026) amended para.(3) to read as follows:

3.011

"(3) [In Schedule 7]—
'partner of a person subject to immigration control' means a person—
    (i) who is not subject to immigration control within the meaning of section 115(9) of the Immigration and Asylum Act; or
    (ii) to whom section 115 of that Act does not apply by virtue of regulation 2 of the Social Security (Immigration and Asylum) Consequential Amendments Regulations 2000; and
    (iii) who is a member of a couple and the member's partner is subject to immigration control within the meaning of section 115(9) of that Act and section 115 of that Act applies to the partner for the purposes of exclusion from entitlement to income support;

['person from abroad' has the meaning given in regulation 21AA;]
'patient' means a person (other than a prisoner) who is regarded as receiving free in-patient treatment within the meaning of regulation 2(4) and (5) of the Social Security (Hospital In-Patients) Regulations 2005;
'prisoner' means a person who—
- (a) is detained in custody pending trial or sentence upon conviction or under a sentence imposed by a court; or
- (b) is on temporary release in accordance with the provisions of the Prison Act 1952 or the Prisons (Scotland) Act 1989,

other than a person who is detained in hospital under the provisions of the Mental Health Act 1983, or, in Scotland, under the provisions of the Mental Health (Care and Treatment) (Scotland) Act 2003 or the Criminal Procedure (Scotland) Act 1995;"

and revoked paras (3F) and (3G).

p.282, *annotation to the Income Support (General) Regulations 1987, reg.21(1) (Special cases)*

3.012 The claimant in *R(RJM) v Secretary of State for Work and Pensions* has been given leave to appeal to the Court of Appeal against the decision of the High Court that the refusal of premiums to a person without accommodation did not infringe his Convention Rights under ECHR, Art.14 and Art.1 of the First Protocol.

p.300, *annotation to the Income Support (General) Regulations 1987, reg.21(1) (Special cases): Right to reside—Workers*

3.013 In *CIS/3182/2005*, Mr Commissioner Rowland held that the phrase "temporarily incapable of work as a result of illness or accident" in reg.5(2)(a) of the Immigration (European Economic Area) Regulations 2000 referred to the illness of the worker herself and not, for example, the illness of a dependent child.

In *CIS/3315/2005*, Mr Rowland considered the position of a Dutch national who had worked in the UK for a period of slightly less than three months and who had subsequently claimed IS as a lone parent. The issue was whether she continued to be a "worker" by virtue of reg.5(2)(b) of the 2000 Regulations. To succeed, the claimant had to show both that she was "involuntarily unemployed" and that "that fact is duly recorded by the relevant employment office".

On the first point, the Commissioner (following Mr Commissioner Mesher in *R(IS)12/98*) held that the concept of "involuntary unemployment" "must be regarded as focussing upon the question whether the claimant was still in the labour market rather than on the circumstances in which she ceased to be employed," although those circumstances may be relevant as evidence on the former issue. Whether the claimant was still in the labour market depended upon whether she was seeking work that was "genuine and effective" and had reasonable prospects of securing such work. In the case before the Commissioner, there was no doubt that the work being sought by the claimant was "genuine". In order to be "effective" the hours during which she was prepared to work and her likely earnings had to be sufficient to avoid her being a "burden on the social assistance scheme of the United Kingdom". This meant that her likely earnings had to be sufficient to remove entitlement to IS or income-based JSA and to pay those housing costs that would be covered by housing benefit (i.e. the "eligible rent" calculated in accordance with the determinations made by the Rent Officer). Applying that test it was just possible to regard the work for which the claimant was applying as effective. However, she had restricted the hours during which she was available to such an extent that she did not have reasonable prospects of employment.

On the second issue, the Secretary of State having originally taken the point that a person who claimed IS as a lone parent could not be treated as a work-seeker, conceded that "a person could be a work-seeker notwithstanding that he or she was claiming income support rather than jobseeker's allowance" and that the requirement for registration of that fact was met "if the claimant claimed income support and declared that he or she was a work-seeker". The commissioner left open the possibility (at para.13) that there might be cases where the requirement was satisfied even if a claimant had answered "No" to the relevant question on the Right to Reside Stencil as long as there was compelling evidence that the claimant was actually looking for work. The concession by the Secretary of State is important as it affects the law before April 30, 2006. For the position after that date see the General Note to the new reg.21AA of the Income Support Regulations (below).

p.301, *annotation to the Income Support (General) Regulations 1987, reg.21(1) (Special cases): Right to reside—Providers of, and recipients of services.*

In *CIS3875/2005*, Mr Commissioner Rowland held that a French national with paranoid schizophrenia who was receiving support from the workers in the hostel in which he lived and medical treatment from the NHS did not have a right to reside as a recipient of services. Although the provision of accommodation, social services and medical services are capable of being "services" within the scope of Art.50 of the EC Treaty, that was only the case if they were "normally provided for remuneration". In addition, C.–196/87 *Steymann v Staatssecretaris van Justitie* and C.–70/95 *Sodemare S.A. v Regione Lombardia* had held that the Treaty right to receive services "did not apply where a national of a Member State goes to the territory of another Member State and establishes his permanent residence there in order to provide or receive services there for an indefinite period". Finally, the tribunal had erred by failing to consider whether the claimant had come to the UK *for the purpose* of receiving those services.

In *CH/1400/2006*, Mr Commissioner Howell Q.C. held—applying the judgment of the ECJ in C.–109/92 *Wirth v Landeshauptstadt Hannover* —that a student attending a course at Kings College, London did not have a right to reside as a recipient of services under Directive

3.014

Income Support, Jobseekers' Allowance, etc.

73/148/EEC. The college was a charitable institution that received the bulk of its funding from public or endowment sources and could not engage in commercial activity. The services that the claimant received from the college were therefore insufficiently commercial in nature, even though she had paid a tuition fee in order to attend the course.

p.302, *annotation to the Income Support (General) Regulations 1987, reg.21(1) (Special cases): Right to reside—Students*

3.015　　For an example in which a claim by a student failed because of the absence of a declaration as to sufficient resources and of sickness insurance, see *CH/1400/2006*.

p.305, *annotation to the Income Support (General) Regulations 1987, reg.21(1) (Special cases): Right to reside—Compatibility of the right to reside test with EC law*

3.016　　In *CIS/3182/2005*, Mr Commissioner Rowland followed what was said by the Tribunal of Commissioners in *CIS/3573/2005* about the justification of indirect discrimination, subject to the proviso that the justification identified by the Tribunal may not apply in every case. It was also necessary to consider "whether the social policy [i.e. the policy relied upon by the State to establish justification] is proportionate having regard to the desirability of both that policy and the avoidance of covert discrimination". It was one thing to use the right to reside test to put pressure on people who have never been economically active and have only been in the UK a few months to leave but the position might be different where a person had been economically active in the past or had been established in the UK for many years but had for some reason not acquired a right of permanent residence.

p.308, *Income Support (General) Regulations 1987, reg.21(AA) (Special cases): supplemental—persons from abroad*

3.017　　With effect from April 30, 2006, reg.6(3) of the Social Security (Persons from Abroad) Amendment Regulations 2006 (SI 2006/1026) inserted a new reg.21AA. As further amended with effect from July 25, 2006 by the Social Security (Lebanon) Amendment Regulations 2006 (SI 2006/1981), reg.2 (adding a new reg.21AA(4)(k) and with effect from October 9, 2006 by the Social Security (Persons from Abroad) Amendment (No. 2) Regulations 2006 (SI 2006/2528), reg.2 (substituting a new reg.21AA(4)(h) and (hh)), reg.21AA now reads as follows:

"**Special cases: supplemental—persons from abroad**

21AA.—(1) 'Person from abroad' means, subject to the following provisions of this regulation, a claimant who is not habitually resident in the United Kingdom, the Channel Islands, the Isle of Man or the Republic of Ireland.

(2) No claimant shall be treated as habitually resident in the United Kingdom, the Channel Islands, the Isle of Man or the Republic of

Ireland unless he has a right to reside in (as the case may be) the United Kingdom, the Channel Islands, the Isle of Man or the Republic of Ireland other than a right to reside which falls within paragraph (3).

(3) A right to reside falls within this paragraph if it is one which exists by virtue of, or in accordance with, one or more of the following—
- (a) regulation 13 of the Immigration (European Economic Area) Regulations 2006;
- (b) regulation 14 of those Regulations, but only in a case where the right exists under that regulation because the claimant is—
  - (i) a jobseeker for the purpose of the definition of 'qualified person' in regulation 6(1) of those Regulations, or
  - (ii) a family member (within the meaning of regulation 7 of those Regulations) of such a jobseeker;
- (c) Article 6 of Council Directive No. 2004/38/EC ; or
- (d) Article 39 of the Treaty establishing the European Community (in a case where the claimant is a person seeking work in the United Kingdom, the Channel Islands, the Isle of Man or the Republic of Ireland).

(4) A claimant is not a person from abroad if he is—
- (a) a worker for the purposes of Council Directive No. 2004/38/EC;
- (b) a self-employed person for the purposes of that Directive;
- (c) a person who retains a status referred to in sub-paragraph (a) or (b) pursuant to Article 7(3) of that Directive;
- (d) a person who is a family member of a person referred to in sub-paragraph (a), (b) or (c) within the meaning of Article 2 of that Directive;
- (e) a person who has a right to reside permanently in the United Kingdom by virtue of Article 17 of that Directive;
- (f) a person who is an accession State worker requiring registration who is treated as a worker for the purpose of the definition of 'qualified person' in regulation 6(1) of the Immigration (European Economic Area) Regulations 2006 pursuant to regulation 5 of the Accession (Immigration and Worker Registration) Regulations 2004;
- (g) a refugee within the definition in Article 1 of the Convention relating to the Status of Refugees done at Geneva on 28th July 1951, as extended by Article 1(2) of the Protocol relating to the Status of Refugees done at New York on 31st January 1967;
- (h) a person who has exceptional leave to enter or remain in the United Kingdom granted outside the rules made under section 3(2) of the Immigration Act 1971;
- (hh) a person who has humanitarian protection granted under those rules;
- (i) a person who is not a person subject to immigration control within the meaning of section 115(9) of the Immigration and Asylum Act and who is in the United Kingdom as a result of

his deportation, expulsion or other removal by compulsion of law from another country to the United Kingdom; or

(j) a person in Great Britain who left the territory of Montserrat after 1st November 1995 because of the effect on that territory of a volcanic eruption.

(k) a person in Great Britain who left Lebanon on or after 12th July 2006 because of the armed conflict there."

GENERAL NOTE TO REG.21AA

3.018 The habitual residence test for income support (including the right to reside test) was removed from reg.21 with effect from April 30, 2006 and the law was recast as reg.21AA. The only changes to the previous law relate to the right to reside test and reflect the coming into force of Directive 2004/38/EC (the Citizenship Directive) and the repeal of Directives 64/221/EEC, 68/360/EEC, 72/194/EEC, 75/34/EEC, 75/35/EEC, 90/364/EEC, 90/365/EEC and 93/96/EEC on that date.

For the text of the Citizenship Directive, see pp.946 *et seq.* of Vol.3 of the Main Work and the updater to pp.950 and 953 of that Volume in this Supplement. The Directive is implemented in the UK by the Immigration (European Economic Area) Regulations 2006 (SI 2006/1003) ("the I(EEA) Regulations").

For income support, the important points to note in the new law are as follows:

- With two exceptions, any person who has a right to reside in the CTA under the Citizenship Directive will satisfy the right to reside test for income support. Those exceptions are set out in para.(3).
  - Under Art.6 of the Directive (implemented by reg.13 of the I(EEA) Regulations), any EU citizen and his or her family members have an initial right of residence "on the territory of another Member State for a period of up to three months without any conditions or formalities other than the requirement to hold a valid identity card or passport" or, in the case of family members, a valid passport. However, by virtue of the new reg.21AA(3)(a) and (c), any claimant whose *only* right to reside in the UK arises "by virtue of, or in accordance with," reg.13 of the I(EEA) Regulations or Art. 6 of the Citizenship Directive does not satisfy the right to reside test.
  - An important change from the Immigration (European Economic Area) Regulations 2000 (see p.300 of Vol.II of the Main Work) is that reg.6(1)(a) of the I(EEA) Regulations now includes "a jobseeker" in the definition of a "qualified person" (i.e. a person who has an extended right of residence after the initial three month period under reg.14). Regulation 14(4) defines a "jobseeker" as "a person who enters the United Kingdom in order to seek employment and can provide evidence that he is seeking employment and has a genuine chance of being engaged". However, by virtue of the new reg.21AA(3)(b) and (d), any claimant whose *only* right to reside in the UK arises "by virtue of, or in accordance with," reg.14 of the I(EEA) Regulations because the claimant is a jobseeker or the family member of a jobseeker, or under Art.39 of the EC Treaty (which also confers residence rights on jobseekers in certain circumstances) does not satisfy the right to reside test *for income support*. It is very important to note that the new reg.85A(3) of the Jobseeker's Allowance Regulations 1996 (below) does not contain provisions equivalent to reg.21AA(3)(b) and (d). The effect appears to be that, from April 30, 2006, any claimant seeking to establish a right to reside as a jobseeker for social security

Income Support, Jobseekers' Allowance, etc.

purposes *must* claim JSA rather than IS if his or her claim is not to be defeated by reg.21AA.
- From April 30, 2006 heads (a) to (e) of para.(4) apply to nationals of Norway, Iceland, Liechtenstein and Switzerland—and to members of their families as defined by Art.2 of the Rights of Residence Directive—as if those nationals were EU nationals (see reg.10(e) of SI 1026/2006). The effect of the change is substantially to reverse the decision of the Tribunal of Commissioners in *CPC/2920/2005*.
- The transitional protection in reg.6 of the Social Security (Habitual Residence) Amendment Regulations 2004 (see pp.305 and 683 of Vol.II) and is preserved by reg.11(2)(b) of SI 1026/2006 (see Part I of this Supplement).

Note finally that the amendment made by the Social Security (Lebanon) Amendment Regulations 2006 (SI 2006/1981) (i.e. the introduction of para.(k)) will cease to have effect on January 31, 2007.

p.334, *amendment to the Income Support (General) Regulations 1987, reg.35 (Earnings of employed earners)*

With effect from October 2, 2006, reg.5(3) of the Social Security (Miscellaneous Amendments) (No. 4) Regulations 2006 (SI 2006/2378) substituted the words "Part 5 of Schedule 3 to the Social Security (Contributions) Regulations 2001" for the words "regulation 18(22) to (25) of the Social Security (Contributions) Regulations 1979" in reg.35(1)(j).

3.019

p.375, *annotation to the Income Support (General) Regulations 1987, reg.42*

CSJSA/23/2006 concerned the application of the notional earnings rules in reg.105(13) and (13A) of the JSA Regulations (the equivalent of reg.42(6) and (6A)) in a case where the claimant was the sole director and majority shareholder of an unlimited company. The main activity of the company was that of chartered accountants. The claimant stated that he received no remuneration for his part-time work for the company. The Commissioner emphasizes that in deciding whether it was reasonable for the claimant to provide his services free of charge, all the circumstances, not just the means of the employer, must be considered. The claimant might be able to point to some other factor making it reasonable for him to undertake such gratuitous work, quite separate from the finances of the business. The Commissioner further holds that the tribunal had erred in simply adopting the decision-maker's use of the national minimum wage as the appropriate comparator for deciding the amount of the claimant's notional earnings. The test was what was paid for a comparable employment in the area and so relevant findings of fact needed to be made to establish local comparable earnings. In addition, in a case such as this where there was no actual or implied contract, the period over which the earnings were payable and when they were due to be paid also had to be established in accordance with what were the likely terms of employment in a similar job in the area. The Commissioner concluded by remitting the appeal to a new tribunal which she suggested

3.020

Income Support, Jobseekers' Allowance, etc.

should contain a financially-qualified panel member (which seems a wise suggestion in the circumstances).

p.387, *amendment to the Income Support (General) Regulations 1987, reg.48 (Income treated as capital)*

3.021   With effect from October 2, 2006, reg.5(4) of the Social Security (Miscellaneous Amendments) (No. 4) Regulations 2006 (SI 2006/2378) substituted ", 25 to 28, 44 or 45" for "or 25 to 28" in reg.48(4).

p.388, *annotation to the Income Support (General) Regulations 1987, reg.48*

3.022   The effect of the amendment to reg.48(4) is that income from funds held in court that derive from damages for personal injury, or compensation for the loss of a parent or parents where the person concerned is under 18, is no longer to be treated as capital but will count as income. It will thus be treated in the same way as income from personal injury awards held in trust or in an annuity or income paid by virtue of an agreement or court order made in consequence of personal injury to the claimant. But note also the amendment to para.15 of Sch.9 to the Income Support Regulations below. The consequence of that amendment is that income from such court funds will be totally disregarded.

p.398, *annotation to the Income Support (General) Regulations 1987, reg.51*

3.023   *CIS/1757/2006* (heard with *CIS/1807/2006* and *CH/1822/2006*) decides that the rule in reg.51(1) can apply to deprivations made by someone who only later becomes the claimant's partner. About a year before she became the claimant's partner Ms H, who was unemployed and who had been in receipt of jobseeker's allowance, sold her house. She used the proceeds of sale to, among other things, repay her daughter's debts of £30,000 (incurred when the daughter was a student) and to take all the members of her family on holiday to see her mother in the West Indies. The tribunal found that in disposing of her capital Ms H had acted with the significant operative purpose of securing entitlement to income support. The Commissioner did not consider that the tribunal had erred in law in so doing. He then went on to decide that the claimant was caught by the rule in reg.51(1) even though Ms H was not his partner at the time of the deprivation. He states:

> "The notional capital rule will only apply to a future partner where there has been conduct that is related to future entitlement to benefit either for the person alone or as a member of a family. That will limit the circumstances in which the rule applies and restrict it to those cases in which a course of conduct has been directed at future benefit entitlement."

Income Support, Jobseekers' Allowance, etc.

p.449, *amendment to the Income Support (General) Regulations 1987, reg.62 (Calculation of grant income)*

With effect from September 1, 2006 (or if the student's period of study begins between August 1 and August 31, 2006, the first day of the period), reg.4(2)(a) of the Social Security (Students and Income-related Benefits) Amendment Regulations 2006 (SI 2006/1752) substituted the sum "£285" for the sum "£280" in reg.62(2A)(a).

From the same date, reg.4(2)(b) of the same amending regulations substituted the sum "£361" for the sum "£352" in reg.62(2A)(b).

From the same date, reg.4(3) and reg.6 of the same amending regulations omitted reg.62(2B).

3.024

p.452, *annotation to the Income Support (General) Regulations 1987, reg.62*

With regard to the amendment made by reg.4(3) and reg.6 of the Social Security (Students and Income-related Benefits) Amendment Regulations 2006, see the note to reg.62 in the main volume. This explains that although reg.62(2B) was omitted with effect from September 1, 2005 (or if the student's period of study began between August 1, 2005 and August 31, 2005, the first day of the period), the previous form of reg.62(2B) remained in force for "transitional cases" (i.e. those cases in which the claimant is still receiving amounts for his children in his income support—see further the note to reg.17 of the Income Support Regulations in the main volume). However the effects of various amendments was that only sub-para.(e) of the previous form of reg.62(2B) continued to have effect. This had been introduced to provide a disregard of a grant paid under reg.15(7) of the Education (Student Support) (No. 2) Regulations 2002 (SI 2002/3200) known as a "parents' learning allowance". (Note that the 2002 regulations were revoked by reg.3 of and Sch.1 to the Education (Student Support) Regulations 2005 (SI 2005/52)—the parents' learning allowance was then provided for under reg.19 of those Regulations). As the disregard in reg.62(2)(i) covers the parents' learning allowance, the disregard sub-para.(e) of the previous form of reg.62(2B) is not required and so that provision has been omitted.

3.025

p.455, *amendment to the Income Support (General) Regulations 1987, reg.65*

With effect from October 2, 2006, the words from "and any other income" to the end of the regulation in reg.65 were omitted by reg.5(5) of the Social Security (Miscellaneous Amendments) (No. 4) Regulations 2006 (SI 2006/2378).

3.026

p.458, *amendment to the Income Support (General) Regulations 1987, reg.66A (Treatment of student loans)*

With effect from September 1, 2006 (or if the student's period of study begins between August 1 and August 31, 2006, the first day of the

3.027

Income Support, Jobseekers' Allowance, etc.

period), reg.4(2)(a) of the Social Security (Students and Income-related Benefits) Amendment Regulations 2006 (SI 2006/1752) substituted the sum "£285" for the sum "£280" in reg.66A(5)(a).

From the same date, reg.4(2)(b) of the same amending regulations substituted the sum "£361" for the sum "£352" in reg.66A(5)(b).

p.462, *Income Support (General) Regulations 1987, reg.66C (Treatment of fee loans)*

3.028   With effect from September 1, 2006 (or if the student's period of study begins between August 1 and August 31, 2006, the first day of the period), reg.4(4) of the Social Security (Students and Income-related Benefits) Amendment Regulations 2006 (SI 2006/1752) inserted the following new regulation:

"**Treatment of fee loans**

66C. A loan for fees, known as a fee loan or a fee contribution loan, made pursuant to regulations made under Article 3 of the Education (Student Support) (Northern Ireland) Order 1998, section 22 of the Teaching and Higher Education Act 1998 or section 73(f) of the Education (Scotland) Act 1980, shall be disregarded as income."

p.462, *annotation to the Income Support (General) Regulations 1987, reg.66C*

3.029   Fee loans and fee-contribution loans have been introduced as part of the student support system from the beginning of the academic year in 2006. Regulation 66C provides for a disregard of any such loan for tuition fees.

p.470, *annotation to the Income Support (General) Regulations 1987, reg.70 (Urgent cases): "Ceases to be an asylum seeker"*

3.030   In *CIS/176/2006*, Mr Commissioner Jacobs confirmed that under reg.12(5) of the Social Security (Immigration and Asylum) (Consequential Provisions) Regulations 2000, a person ceases to be an asylum seeker as soon as the first Home Office decision refusing his claim for asylum is sent to him and not when all subsequent appeals have been exhausted. This point had been conceded by the claimant in the *Anufrijeva* case and had therefore not been formally decided by the House of Lords in that case.

p.485, *amendment to the Income Support (General) Regulations 1987, Sch.1B (Prescribed categories of person), para.16 (Certain persons aged 50 who have not been in remunerative work for 10 years)*

3.031   With effect from October 7, 2006, para.16 of Sch.1B was omitted by reg.5(6) of the Social Security (Miscellaneous Amendments) (No. 4) Regulations 2006 (SI 2006/2378).

Income Support, Jobseekers' Allowance, etc.

p.485, *amendment to the Income Support (General) Regulations 1987, Sch.1B (Prescribed categories of person), para.19 (Persons required to attend court)*

With effect from May 30, 2006, reg.3 of the Social Security (Income Support and Jobseeker's Allowance) Amendment Regulations 2006 (SI 2006/1402) substituted the following paragraph for para.19:

3.032

"**Persons required to attend court or tribunal**

19.—(1) A person who is required to attend a court or tribunal as a justice of the peace, a party to any proceedings, a witness or a juror.

(2) In this paragraph, 'tribunal' means any tribunal listed in Schedule 1 to the Tribunals and Inquiries Act 1992."

p.494, *annotation to the Income Support (General) Regulations 1987, Sch.1B, para.16*

This paragraph has been revoked because it only applied to people who were aged 50 or over on October 6, 1996. By October 7, 2006 such a person will be 60 or over and therefore will have reached the qualifying age for state pension credit and so will no longer be entitled to income support.

3.033

p.494, *annotation to the Income Support (General) Regulations 1987, Sch.1B, para.19*

The previous form of para.19 only applied to a person who had to attend court as a justice of the peace, a party to any proceedings, a witness or a juror. From May 30, 2006 this has been extended so that para.19 now also applies where a person is required to attend a tribunal in a relevant capacity.

3.034

p.501, *Income Support (General) Regulations 1987, Sch.2, para.10 (Higher Pensioner Premium)*

With effect from October 1, 2006, reg.5(7) of the Social Security (Miscellaneous Amendments) (No. 4) Regulations 2006 (SI 2006/2378) amended sub-para.(4) by substituting for "52 weeks" the words "104 weeks".

3.035

p.502, *amendment to the Income Support (General) Regulations 1987, Sch.2, para.12 (Additional condition for the Higher Pensioner and Disability Premiums)*

With effect from October 1, 2006, reg.5(7) of the Social Security (Miscellaneous Amendments) (No. 4) Regulations 2006 (SI 2006/2378) amended sub-para.(1A) by substituting for "52 weeks" the words "104 weeks".

3.036

Income Support, Jobseekers' Allowance, etc.

p.519, *amendment to the Income Support (General) Regulations 1987, Sch.3 (Housing costs), para.1 (Housing costs)*

3.037　With effect from October 2, 2006, reg.5(8)(a) of the Social Security (Miscellaneous Amendments) (No. 4) Regulations 2006 (SI 2006/2378) inserted the following at the end of para.1(3)(b):

"; or
　　(c) who is disabled or severely disabled for the purposes of section 9(6) (maximum rate) of the Tax Credits Act 2002."

p.521, *amendment to the Income Support (General) Regulations 1987, Sch.3 (Housing costs), para.3 (Circumstances in which a person is to be treated as occupying a dwelling as his home)*

3.038　With effect from October 2, 2006, reg.5(8)(b) of the Social Security (Miscellaneous Amendments) (No. 4) Regulations 2006 (SI 2006/2378) substituted the following sub-head for sub-head (ii) in para.3(7)(c):

"(ii) the move was delayed pending the outcome of an application under Part 8 of the Contributions and Benefits Act for a social fund payment to meet a need arising out of the move or in connection with setting up the home in the dwelling, and—
　　(aa) a member of the claimant's family is aged five or under,
　　(bb) the claimant's applicable amount includes a premium under paragraph 9, 9A, 10, 11, 13 or 14 of Schedule 2 (applicable amounts), or
　　(cc) a child tax credit is paid for a member of the claimant's family who is disabled or severely disabled for the purposes of section 9(6) (maximum rate) of the Tax Credits Act 2002; or".

p.526, *amendment to the Income Support (General) Regulations 1987, Sch.3 (Housing costs), para.7 (Transitional protection)*

3.039　With effect from October 2, 2006, reg.5(8)(c) of the Social Security (Miscellaneous Amendments) (No. 4) Regulations 2006 (SI 2006/2378) inserted the following sub-paragraph after sub-para.(4) in para.7:

"(4A) For the purposes of sub-paragraphs (3) and (4), there is an increase in the amount of existing housing costs where in any benefit week, those costs are higher than they were in the previous benefit week (whether or not those costs are higher than they were in the second benefit week)."

With effect from October 9, 2006, reg.5(7)(b) of the same amending regulations substituted "104 weeks" for "52 weeks" in sub-para.(10) of para.7.

pp.531–532, *amendment to the Income Support (General) Regulations 1987, Sch.3 (Housing costs), para.14 (Linking rule)*

3.040　With effect from October 9, 2006, reg.5(7)(b) of the Social Security (Miscellaneous Amendments) (No. 4) Regulations 2006 (SI 2006/2378)

Income Support, Jobseekers' Allowance, etc.

substituted "104 weeks" for "52 weeks" in both para.14(3AA)(b) and para.14(10).

p.533, *amendment to the Income Support (General) Regulations 1987, Sch.3 (Housing costs), para.17 (Other housing costs)*

With effect from October 2, 2006, the words "and, in Scotland, payments by way of feu duty" in para.17(1)(a) were omitted by reg.5(8)(d) of the Social Security (Miscellaneous Amendments) (No. 4) Regulations 2006 (SI 2006/2378).

3.041

pp.539–540, *annotation to the Income Support (General) Regulations 1987, Sch.3, para.1*

In para.1a a person is defined as a "disabled person" for the purposes of Sch.3 if his income support, or the income support of a person living with him, includes (or would include if there was entitlement to income support) one of the listed premiums, among them the disabled child premium. However the transfer to tax credits of financial support for children and the consequential abolition of the "child elements" in income support (including the disabled child premium) means that the definition has had to be updated so that it also covers a person who satisfies the conditions for the disabled or severely disabled child elements of child tax credit (for these conditions see reg.8 of the Child Tax Credit Regulations 2002 (SI 2002/2008) in Vol.IV of this series).

3.042

p.544, *annotation to the Income Support (General) Regulations 1987, Sch.3, para.3*

Paragraph 3(7)(c)(ii) has been amended with effect from October 2, 2006 so that it also applies where child tax credit is being paid for a member of the claimant's family who satisfies the conditions for the disabled or severely disabled child elements of child tax credit. This amendment is needed because of the transfer to tax credits of financial support for children. See further the note to para.1 of Sch.3 above.

3.043

p.547, *annotation to the Income Support (General) Regulations 1987, Sch.3, para.4*

Paragraph 4(12) reads "The following provisions of this Schedule shall have effect subject to the provisions of this paragraph". *CIS/ 933/2006*, to be reported as *R(IS) 2/07*, confirms that this does not have the effect that the restrictions on meeting housing costs contained in subsequent paragraphs of Sch.3, e.g. the £100,000 ceiling in para.11(5), do not apply in a case where the claimant falls within any of the provisions in para.4(8) to (11). As *CIS/5327/1998* had explained, those subparagraphs contain exceptions to the normal exclusion under para.4(2) of loans taken out by a person while entitled to income support or caught by the linking rule. They are not concerned with defining or quantifying the amount of housing costs to be met in those special cases, which is

3.044

Income Support, Jobseekers' Allowance, etc.

dealt with under the normal rules for computation to be found elsewhere in the Schedule. That is made clear by the reference in para.4(7) (which introduces the provisions in para.4(8) to (11)) to "additional limitations". In other words, any special limitations imposed by para.4(8) to (11) are to be in addition to whatever limitations otherwise apply in any case in determining the amount of housing costs allowable.

p.554, *annotation to the Income Support (General) Regulations 1987, Sch.3, para.7*

3.045 *Sub-para.(4A)*

This new sub-paragraph has been inserted to overturn the effect of the Court of Appeal's decision in *Arathoon* (for a discussion of that decision see the main volume) and to restore the original policy intention that the add back should be reduced by *any* increase in the claimant's existing housing costs "whether or not those costs are higher than they were in the second benefit week".

Amendment to para.7(10)

As part of the Government's strategy to encourage claimants receiving benefit on the ground of incapacity for work to try out work, there are special, more generous, linking rules for "welfare to work beneficiaries" (broadly claimants who have been incapable of work for a period of 196 days or more and who start work or a training course—see further the note to the definition of "welfare to work beneficiary" in reg.2 of the Income Support Regulations in the main volume). These linking rules affect, among other things, entitlement to housing costs. With effect from October 9, 2006 the linking period for such welfare to work beneficiaries has been increased from 52 to 104 weeks. This has necessitated the amendment to para.7(10).

p.561, *annotation to the Income Support (General) Regulations 1987, Sch.3, para.12*

3.046 From September 10, 2006 the standard rate for interest on eligible loans has been 6.33 per cent.

pp.564–568, *annotation to the Income Support (General) Regulations 1987, Sch.3, para.14*

3.047 With effect from October 9, 2006, the linking period for a "welfare to work beneficiary" has been extended from 52 to 104 weeks. See further the note to the amendment to para.7(10) of Sch.3 above.

p.577, *annotation to the Income Support (General) Regulations 1987, Sch.3, para.17*

3.048 The reference to feu duty has been removed to reflect the fact that feu duty has been abolished since November 28, 2004.

Income Support, Jobseekers' Allowance, etc.

On service charges, see *CPC/1820/2005* and *CPC/2574/2005*, to be reported as *R(PC) 1/07*, which concerns the evidence required to establish the eligible proportion of the costs of a warden. The decision is discussed in more detail in the annotation to Sch.II to the State Pension Credit Regulations below.

CIS/2901/2004 discussed in the main volume is to be reported as *R(IS) 3/07*.

p.588, *amendment to the Income Support (General) Regulations 1987, Sch.8 (Sums to be disregarded in the calculation of earnings), para.7*

With effect from October 2, 2006, reg.5(9) of the Social Security (Miscellaneous Amendments) (No. 4) Regulations 2006 (SI 2006/2378) substituted the words "Schedule 6 to the Social Security (Contributions) Regulations 2001" for the words "Schedule 3 to the Social Security (Contributions) Regulations 1979" in para.7(1)(d). 3.049

p.589, *amendment to the Income Support (General) Regulations 1987, Sch.8 (Sums to be disregarded in the calculation of earnings), para.15A*

With effect from October 2, 2006, reg.5(9) of the Social Security (Miscellaneous Amendments) (No. 4) Regulations 2006 (SI 2006/2378) substituted the words "Schedule 6 to the Social Security (Contributions) Regulations 2001" for the words "Schedule 3 to the Social Security (Contributions) Regulations 1979" in para.15A(a). 3.050

p.595, *amendment to the Income Support (General) Regulations 1987, Sch.9 (Sums to be disregarded in the calculation of income other than earnings), para.15*

With effect from October 2, 2006, reg.5(10)(a)(i) of the Social Security (Miscellaneous Amendments) (No. 4) Regulations 2006 (SI 2006/2378) substituted the following sub-paragraph for sub-para.(1) of para.15: 3.051

"(1) Subject to sub-paragraph (3) and paragraph 39, any relevant payment made or due to be made at regular intervals."

From the same date, reg.5(10)(a)(ii) of the same amending regulations substituted the words "Sub-paragraph (1)" for the words "Sub-paragraphs (1) and (2)" in sub-para.(3) of para.15.

From the same date, sub-paras (2), (4) and (5) of para.15 were omitted by reg.5(10)(a)(iii) of the same amending regulations.

p.595, *amendment to the Income Support (General) Regulations 1987, Sch.9 (Sums to be disregarded in the calculation of income other than earnings), para.15A*

With effect from October 2, 2006, para.15A is omitted by reg.5(10)(b) of the Social Security (Miscellaneous Amendments) (No. 4) Regulations 2006 (SI 2006/2378). 3.052

Income Support, Jobseekers' Allowance, etc.

p.598, *amendment to the Income Support (General) Regulations 1987, Sch.9 (Sums to be disregarded in the calculation of income other than earnings), para.26*

3.053   With effect from October 2, 2006, reg.5(10)(c) of the Social Security (Miscellaneous Amendments) (No. 4) Regulations 2006 (SI 2006/2378) substituted the words "local authority under regulation 9 of the Fostering of Children (Scotland) Regulations 1996 (payment of allowances)" for the words from "care authority" to the end of the paragraph in para.26.

p.599, *amendment to the Income Support (General) Regulations 1987, Sch.9 (Sums to be disregarded in the calculation of income other than earnings), para.30A*

3.054   With effect from October 2, 2006, the words "but not a payment to which paragraph 15A applies" in para.30A were omitted by reg.5(10)(d) of the Social Security (Miscellaneous Amendments) (No. 4) Regulations 2006 (SI 2006/2378).

p.599, *amendment to the Income Support (General) Regulations 1987, Sch.9 (Sums to be disregarded in the calculation of income other than earnings), para.36*

3.055   With effect from October 2, 2006, reg.5(10)(e) of the Social Security (Miscellaneous Amendments) (No. 4) Regulations 2006 (SI 2006/2378) substituted the words "paragraph 16" for the words "paragraphs 15(1) and 16" in para.36.

pp.611–614, *annotation to the Income Support (General) Regulations 1987, Sch.9, para.15*

3.056   The effect of the amendments to para.15 in force from October 2, 2006 is to replace the current disregard of regular payments that are charitable or voluntary or made from funds that are derived from a personal injury award to the claimant with a total disregard of such payments. See also below for the amendment to para.12 of Sch.10 to the Income Support Regulations (which provides for a capital disregard of personal injury awards placed on trust) and the further capital disregard of personal injury awards that has been introduced by the new para.12A of Sch.10. The amendment to para.12 of Sch.10 applies the disregard to a payment made in consequence of a personal injury to *either* the claimant *or* the claimant's partner (similarly under para.12A the disregard applies whether the injury was to the claimant or the claimant's partner). However the disregard in para.15 has not been similarly extended to include payments in respect of an injury to the claimant's partner. It is not clear why this is the case.

Note too the amendment made to reg.48(4) of the Income Support Regulations, also with effect from October 2, 2006 (see above). The effect of that amendment is that income from funds held in court that

Income Support, Jobseekers' Allowance, etc.

derive from damages for personal injury, or compensation for the loss of a parent or parents where the person concerned is under 18, is no longer to be treated as capital but will count as income. However, such income will attract the disregard in para.15.

p.614, *annotation to the Income Support (General) Regulations 1987, Sch.9, para.15A*

In view of the amendments to para.15 the disregard in this paragraph is no longer needed. 3.057

p.626, *amendment to the Income Support (General) Regulations 1987, Sch.10 (Capital to be disregarded), para.12*

With effect from October 2, 2006, reg.5(11)(a) of the Social Security (Miscellaneous Amendments) (No. 4) Regulations 2006 (SI 2006/2378) inserted the words "or the claimant's partner" after the word "claimant" in para.12. 3.058

p.626, *Income Support (General) Regulations 1987, Sch.10 (Capital to be disregarded), para.12A*

With effect from October 2, 2006, reg.5(11)(b) of the Social Security (Miscellaneous Amendments) (No. 4) Regulations 2006 (SI 2006/2378) inserted the following new paragraph after para.12: 3.059

"12A.—(1) Any payment made to the claimant or the claimant's partner in consequence of any personal injury to the claimant or, as the case may be, the claimant's partner.
  (2) But sub-paragraph (1)—
  (a) applies only for the period of 52 weeks beginning with the day on which the claimant first receives any payment in consequence of that personal injury;
  (b) does not apply to any subsequent payment made to him in consequence of that injury (whether it is made by the same person or another);
  (c) ceases to apply to the payment or any part of the payment from the day on which the claimant no longer possesses it;
  (d) does not apply to any payment from a trust where the funds of the trust are derived from a payment made in consequence of any personal injury to the claimant.
  (3) For the purposes of sub-paragraph (2)(c), the circumstances in which a claimant no longer possesses a payment or a part of it include where the claimant has used a payment or part of it to purchase an asset.
  (4) References in sub-paragraphs (2) and (3) to the claimant are to be construed as including references to his partner (where applicable)."

Income Support, Jobseekers' Allowance, etc.

p.628, *amendment to the Income Support (General) Regulations 1987, Sch.10 (Capital to be disregarded), para.44*

3.060   With effect from October 2, 2006, reg.5(11)(c) of the Social Security (Miscellaneous Amendments) (No. 4) Regulations 2006 (SI 2006/2378) substituted the following paragraph for para.44:

"**44.**—(1) Any sum of capital to which sub-paragraph (2) applies and—
   (a) which is administered on behalf of a person by the High Court or the County Court under Rule 21.11(1) of the Civil Procedure Rules 1998 or by the Court of Protection;
   (b) which can only be disposed of by order or direction of any such court; or
   (c) where the person concerned is under the age of 18, which can only be disposed of by order or direction prior to that person attaining age 18.

(2) This sub-paragraph applies to a sum of capital which is derived from—
   (a) an award of damages for a personal injury to that person; or
   (b) compensation for the death of one or both parents where the person concerned is under the age of 18."

p.642, *annotation to the Income Support (General) Regulations 1987, Sch.10, para.12*

3.061   The amendment to para.12 means that the disregard of trust funds of personal injury payments now also applies where the injury was to the claimant's partner.

p.642, *annotation to the Income Support (General) Regulations 1987, Sch.10, para.12A*

3.062   Paragraph 12A provides for a new general capital disregard of payments for personal injury (for the disregard where the payment has been placed on trust see para.12 or where it is being administered by a court see paras 44 and 45). The disregard applies to a payment made in consequence of a personal injury to *either* the claimant *or* the claimant's partner. It does not apply to payments from a trust fund. But note that the disregard only applies for 52 weeks from the date that the claimant *first* receives any payment in respect of the injury; it does not apply to any subsequent payment (even if made by another person). This is because the purpose of the disregard is to introduce a "grace period" during which a trust fund can be set up or an annuity purchased (or the money spent). The disregard will cease to apply to the payment or any part of it when the claimant no longer possesses it, e.g. because he has used it to purchase an asset. Unless any of the other disregards in Sch.10 apply, it will then be taken into account as capital.

Income Support, Jobseekers' Allowance, etc.

p.648, *annotation to the Income Support (General) Regulations 1987, Sch.10, para.44*

Paragraph 44 has been amended so that it applies not only to capital administered by a court but also to capital "which can only be disposed of by order or direction of [a] court". According to the Explanatory Memorandum which accompanies this SI, this amendment is to allow for the contracting-out of administering court funds to the private sector, which the DCA is apparently contemplating.

3.063

p.656, *Income-related Benefits Schemes (Miscellaneous Amendments) (No. 3) Regulations 1994*

With effect from April 30, 2006, these regulations were revoked by reg.11(1)(a) of the Social Security (Persons from Abroad) Amendment Regulations 2006 (SI 2006/1026).

3.064

p.662, *annotation to the Social Security (Persons from Abroad) Miscellaneous Amendments Regulations 1996, reg.12 (Saving)*

The transitional protection established by reg.12 is unaffected by anything in the Social Security (Persons from Abroad) Amendment Regulations 2006 (SI 2006/1026)—see reg.11(2)(a) of SI 2006/1026.

3.065

p.683, *Social Security (Habitual Residence) Amendment Regulations 2004*

With effect from April 30, 2006, these regulations were revoked by reg.11(1)(a) of the Social Security (Persons from Abroad) Amendment Regulations 2006 (SI 2006/1026), except for the transitional arrangements and savings in reg.6 which are continued in force by reg.11(2)(b) of the same amending regulations.

3.066

p.768, *amendment to the Jobseeker's Allowance Regulations 1996, reg.1(3) (definition of "benefit week")*

With effect from October 2, 2006, reg.13(1) of the Social Security (Miscellaneous Amendments) (No. 4) Regulations 2006 (SI 2006/2378) amended the definition of "benefit week" in reg.1(3) by inserting after "regulation 23" each time it appears the words "or regulation 23A".

3.067

p.792, *amendment to the Jobseeker's Allowance Regulations 1996, reg.5(1) (exceptions to requirement to be available immediately)*

With effect from May 30, 2006, reg.2(2) of the Social Security (Income Support and Jobseeker's Allowance) Amendment Regulations 2006 (SI 2006/1402) amended reg.5(1) to read:

3.068

"**5.**—(1) In order to be regarded as available for employment—
  (a) [*Omitted*];

Income Support, Jobseekers' Allowance, etc.

(b) a person who is engaged in voluntary work [or who has caring responsibilities] is not required to be able to take up employment immediately, providing he is willing and able—
   (i) to take up employment on being given one week's notice; and
   (ii) to attend for interview in connection with the opportunity of any such employment on being given 48 hours' notice."

p.794, *annotation to the Jobseeker's Allowance Regulations 1996, reg.5 (Carers) (paras (1), (5))*

3.069 The effect of the amendment from May 30, 2006, noted in the update immediately above is that a carer (someone "who has caring responsibilities" defined later in the annotation) benefits from an enhanced relaxation of the rules on immediate availability. Such a person is from that date exempt from the requirement to be immediately available provided that he is willing and able to take up employed earner's employment on being given one weeks' notice (rather than just 48 hours) so long as he is also willing and able to attend for interview in connection with the opportunity of any such employment on being given 48 hours' notice.

pp.810–813, *amendments to the Jobseeker's Allowance Regulations 1996, reg.14 (circumstances in which a person is to be treated as available)*

3.070 With effect from May 30, 2006, reg.2(3) of the Social Security (Income Support and Jobseeker's Allowance) Amendment Regulations 2006 (SI 2006/1402) amended reg.14 in a number of ways.

First of all, it inserted in line one of para.(1) ", (bc)" after the phrase "to whom regulation 15(a), (b)".

Secondly, it inserted the following sub-paragraphs after para.(1)(q):

"(r) if he is required to attend a court or tribunal as a justice of the peace, a party to any proceedings, a witness or a juror;
(s) if, for a maximum of 96 hours before being released, he is in—
   (i) police detention within the meaning in section 118(2) of the Police and Criminal Evidence Act 1984 (general interpretation), or
   (ii) legal custody within the meaning in section 295 of the Criminal Procedure (Scotland) Act 1995 (legal custody in Scotland) but is not a prisoner as defined by regulation 85(4) (special cases)."

Thirdly, it inserted after para.(2A) a new paragraph numbered (2B) to read as follows:

"(2B) A person shall not be treated as available for employment under paragraph (1)(r)—
   (a) for more than eight weeks,
   (b) where he does not, before the period during which he is required to attend the court or tribunal, give an employment

officer notice, in writing where requested by the employment officer, that he is so required, or

(c) where he is a prisoner as defined by regulation 85(4) (special cases)."

Finally, it inserted after para.(6) a new paragraph numbered (7) to read as follows:

"(7) In this regulation, 'tribunal' means any tribunal listed in Schedule 1 to the Tribunals and Inquiries Act 1992."

p.814, *annotation to the Jobseeker's Allowance Regulations 1996, reg.14*

Substitute the following paragraph (embodying the amendments in the update immediately above) for the first paragraph of the annotation:

3.071

"Like its predecessors under the unemployment benefit regime (USI Regs, regs 9–12A), this regulation sets out in paras (1) and (2) a range of situations in which, for the periods specified therein, someone is to be treated as available for employment even though, were it applied to him, he might fail to satisfy the test of availability for work set out in s.6(1) of the Jobseekers Act 1995 as modified by regs 5–17. Generally someone falling within reg.15 (a), (b), (bc) or (c)—which require full-time students, prisoners on temporary release, men in receipt of paternity allowance, and women in receipt of maternity allowance to be treated as not available for employment—cannot avail himself of the protection afforded by this regulation. But paras (1)(a) and (k) provide exceptions in respect of the summer vacation in the situation in which both members of a couple are full-time students and one is treated as responsible for a child or young person (see further annotation to reg.15(a)). Paragraph (3) concerns the situation in which para.(1) protections (other than those in sub-paras (i) and (j)) and para.(2) protections apply only in respect of part of a benefit week (generally the period of seven days ending with the day corresponding to the claimant's 'signing'/attendance day; see regs 4, 1(3)). The protection offended by para.(1)(i) only extends to claimants meeting the conditions in para.(2A). The protection offended by para.(1)(r) only extends to claimants meeting the conditions in para.(2B). The remainder of the regulation contains relevant definitions."

p.825, *amendment to the Jobseeker's Allowance Regulations 1996, reg.18 (steps to be taken by persons actively seeking employment)*

With effect from October 2, 2006, reg.13(3)(a) of the Social Security (Miscellaneous Amendments) (No. 4) Regulations 2006 (SI 2006/2378) amended reg.18(3)(f)(v) to read:

3.072

"(v) engaged in duties as a member of any territorial or reserve force prescribed in Part I of [Schedule 6 to the Social Security (Contributions) Regulations 2001]."

pp.830–832, *amendments to the Jobseeker's Allowance Regulations 1996, reg.19 (circumstances in which a person is to be treated as actively seeking employment)*

3.073   With effect from May 30, 2006, reg.2(4) of the Social Security (Income Support and Jobseeker's Allowance) Amendment Regulations 2006 (SI 2006/1402) amended reg.19 in a number of ways.

First of all, in line two of para.(1), for "paragraph (2)" it substituted "paragraphs (2) and (2A)".

Secondly, after para.(1)(u), it inserted insert the following sub-paragraphs—

> "(v) in any week during which he is, for not less than three days, required to attend a court or tribunal as a justice of the peace, a party to any proceedings, a witness or a juror;
> (w) if, for a maximum of 96 hours before being released, he is in—
>> (i) police detention within the meaning in section 118(2) of the Police and Criminal Evidence Act 1984 (general interpretation), or
>> (ii) legal custody within the meaning in section 295 of the Criminal Procedure (Scotland) Act 1995 (legal custody in Scotland) but is not a prisoner as defined by regulation 85(4) (special cases).";

Thirdly, after para.(2), it inserted a new paragraph numbered (2A) to read as follows:

> "(2A) A person shall not be treated as actively seeking employment under paragraph (1)(v)—
> (a) for more than eight weeks,
> (b) where he does not, before the period during which he is required to attend the court or tribunal, give an employment officer notice, in writing where requested by the employment officer, that he is so required, or
> (c) where he is a prisoner as defined by regulation 85(4) (special cases)."

Finally, it inserted in para.(3), between the definitional entry for "treatment" and that for "urban development corporation", the following definition:

> " 'tribunal' means any tribunal listed in Schedule 1 to the Tribunals and Inquiries Act 1992;".

p.845, *amendments to the Jobseeker's Allowance Regulations 1996, reg.30 (good cause for failure to comply with a notification)*

3.074   With effect from May 30, 2006, reg.2(5) of the Social Security (Income Support and Jobseeker's Allowance) Amendment Regulations 2006 (SI 2006/1402) amended reg.30 in two ways.

Firstly, it deleted "(a) or" from para.(a).

Secondly, it inserted ", (r) or (s)" after "(k)–(n)".

Income Support, Jobseekers' Allowance, etc.

p.868, *amendment to the Jobseeker's Allowance Regulations 1996, reg.53 (Persons treated as not engaged in remunerative work)*

With effect from October 2, 2006, reg.13(3) of the Social Security (Miscellaneous Amendments) (No. 4) Regulations 2006 (SI 2006/2378) amended the definition of "benefit week" by substituting for the words "Schedule 3 to the Social Security (Contributions) Regulations 1979" the words "Schedule 6 to the Social Security (Contributions) Regulations 2001". 3.075

p.913, *amendment to the Jobseeker's Allowance Regulations 1996, reg.75(1)(a)(iii) ("Interpretation")*

With effect from April 24, 2006, reg.2(1) of the Social Security (Working Neighbourhoods) Miscellaneous Amendments Regulations 2006 (SI 2006/909) amended para.(1)(a)(iii) by omitting the words "or the Social Security (Working Neighbourhoods) Regulations 2004". The amendment is, however, subject to the transitional provision in reg.4 of those amending regulations. It reads (so far as relevant for this update): 3.076

"Transitional provisions for employment zones

4.—(1) The provisions listed in paragraph (2) shall continue to apply as if these Regulations had not been made—
   (a) in the case of a person falling within paragraph (3), and
   (b) for the period specified in paragraph (4).
(2) [see updates to Working neighbourhoods Regulations in Vol. III].
(3) A person falls within this paragraph if immediately before these Regulations come into force, he is participating in an employment zone programme following a direction given under regulation 17 or 18 of the principal Regulations.
(4) The period specified in this paragraph begins on 24th April 2006 and ends on—
   (a) the date the person ceases to participate in that employment zone programme by virtue of regulation 19 or 21 of the principal Regulations, or
   (b) 31st October 2006,
whichever is the earlier."

p.919, *amendment to the Jobseeker's Allowance Regulations 1996, reg.78 (Circumstances in which a person is treated as being or not being a member of the household)*

With effect from October 2, 2006, reg.13(4) of the Social Security (Miscellaneous Amendments) (No. 4) Regulations 2006 (SI 2006/2378) amended head (a) of para.(3) by substituting for "special hospitals" the words "high security psychiatric services". 3.077

Income Support, Jobseekers' Allowance, etc.

p.930, *amendment to the Jobseeker's Allowance Regulations 1996, reg.85(4)–(4B) (Special cases)*

3.078 With effect from April 30, 2006, reg.7(2) of the Social Security (Persons from Abroad) Amendment Regulations 2006 (SI 2006/1026) amended para.(4) to read as follows:

"(4) [In this regulation] and subject to Schedule 5—
'partner of a person subject to immigration control' means a person—
  (i) who is not subject to immigration control within the meaning of section 115(9) of the Immigration and Asylum Act; or
  (ii) to whom section 115 of that Act does not apply by virtue of regulation 2 of the Social Security (Immigration and Asylum) Consequential Amendments Regulations 2000; and
  (iii) who is a member of a couple and the member's partner is subject to immigration control within the meaning of section 115(9) of that Act and section 115 of that Act applies to the partner for the purposes of exclusion from entitlement to jobseeker's allowance;
['person from abroad' has the meaning given in regulation 85A;]
'patient' means a person (other than a prisoner) who is regarded as receiving free in-patient treatment within the meaning of regulation 2(4) and (5) of the Social Security (Hospital In-Patients) Regulations 2005;
'prisoner' means a person who—
  (a) is detained in custody pending trial or sentence upon conviction or under a sentence imposed by a court; or
  (b) is on temporary release in accordance with the provisions of the Prison Act 1952 or the Prisons (Scotland) Act 1989,
other than a person who is detained in hospital under the provisions of the Mental Health Act 1983, or, in Scotland, under the provisions of the Mental Health (Care and Treatment) (Scotland) Act 2003 or the Criminal Procedure (Scotland) Act 1995;"

and revoked paras (4A) and (4B).

p.935, *Jobseeker's Allowance Regulations 1996, reg.85(A) (Special cases: supplemental—persons from abroad)*

3.079 With effect from April 30, 2006, reg.7(3) of the Social Security (Persons from Abroad) Amendment Regulations 2006 (SI 2006/1026) inserted a new reg.85A. As further amended with effect from July 25, 2006 by the Social Security (Lebanon) Amendment Regulations 2006 (SI 2006/1981), reg.3 (adding a new reg.85A(4)(k) and with effect from October 9, 2006 by the Social Security (Persons from Abroad) Amendment (No. 2) Regulations 2006 (SI 2006/2528), reg.4 (substituting a new reg.85A(4)(h) and (hh)), reg.85A now reads as follows:

"Special cases: supplemental—persons from abroad

85A.—(1) 'Person from abroad' means, subject to the following provisions of this regulation, a claimant who is not habitually resident in the United Kingdom, the Channel Islands, the Isle of Man or the Republic of Ireland.

(2) No claimant shall be treated as habitually resident in the United Kingdom, the Channel Islands, the Isle of Man or the Republic of Ireland unless he has a right to reside in (as the case may be) the United Kingdom, the Channel Islands, the Isle of Man or the Republic of Ireland other than a right to reside which falls within paragraph (3).

(3) A right to reside falls within this paragraph if it is one which exists by virtue of, or in accordance with, one or more of the following—

- (a) regulation 13 of the Immigration (European Economic Area) Regulations 2006;
- (b) Article 6 of Council Directive No. 2004/38/EC; or

(4) A claimant is not a person from abroad if he is—

- (a) a worker for the purposes of Council Directive No. 2004/38/EC;
- (b) a self-employed person for the purposes of that Directive;
- (c) a person who retains a status referred to in sub-paragraph (a) or (b) pursuant to Article 7(3) of that Directive;
- (d) a person who is a family member of a person referred to in sub-paragraph (a), (b) or (c) within the meaning of Article 2 of that Directive;
- (e) a person who has a right to reside permanently in the United Kingdom by virtue of Article 17 of that Directive;
- (f) a person who is an accession State worker requiring registration who is treated as a worker for the purpose of the definition of "qualified person" in regulation 6(1) of the Immigration (European Economic Area) Regulations 2006 pursuant to regulation 5 of the Accession (Immigration and Worker Registration) Regulations 2004;
- (g) a refugee within the definition in Article 1 of the Convention relating to the Status of Refugees done at Geneva on 28th July 1951, as extended by Article 1(2) of the Protocol relating to the Status of Refugees done at New York on 31st January 1967;
- (h) a person who has exceptional leave to enter or remain in the United Kingdom granted outside the rules made under section 3(2) of the Immigration Act 1971;
- (hh) a person who has humanitarian protection granted under those rules;
- (i) a person who is not a person subject to immigration control within the meaning of section 115(9) of the Immigration and

Income Support, Jobseekers' Allowance, etc.

Asylum Act and who is in the United Kingdom as a result of his deportation, expulsion or other removal by compulsion of law from another country to the United Kingdom; or

(j) a person in Great Britain who left the territory of Montserrat after 1st November 1995 because of the effect on that territory of a volcanic eruption.

(k) a person in Great Britain who left Lebanon on or after 12th July 2006 because of the armed conflict there."

GENERAL NOTE TO REG.85A

See the commentary to reg.21AA of the IS regulations. Note, in particular, the difference in wording between reg.21AA(3) and reg.85A(3), with the apparent effect that from April 30, 2006, any claimant seeking to establish a right to reside as a jobseeker for social security purposes *must* claim JSA rather than IS if his or her claim is not to be defeated by reg.21AA.

p.951, *amendment to the Jobseeker's Allowance Regulations 1996, reg.98 (Earnings of employed earners)*

3.080   With effect from October 2, 2006, reg.13(5) of the Social Security (Miscellaneous Amendments) (No. 4) Regulations 2006 (SI 2006/2378) substituted the words "Part 5 of Schedule 3 to the Social Security (Contributions) Regulations 2001" for the words "regulation 18(22) to (25) of the Social Security (Contributions) Regulations 1979" in reg.98(1)(h).

p.973, *amendment to the Jobseeker's Allowance Regulations 1996, reg.110 (Income treated as capital)*

3.081   With effect from October 2, 2006, reg.13(6) of the Social Security (Miscellaneous Amendments) (No. 4) Regulations 2006 (SI 2006/2378) substituted ", 17, 42 or 43" for "or 17" in reg.110(4).

p.974, *annotation to the Jobseeker's Allowance Regulations 1996, reg.110*

3.082   See the note to reg.48 of the Income Support Regulations above.

p.996, *amendment to the Jobseeker's Allowance Regulations 1996, reg.131 (Calculation of grant income)*

3.083   With effect from September 1, 2006 (or if the student's period of study begins between August 1 and August 31, 2006, the first day of the period), reg.5(2)(a) of the Social Security (Students and Income-related Benefits) Amendment Regulations 2006 (SI 2006/1752) substituted the sum "£285" for the sum "£280" in reg.131(3)(a).

From the same date, reg.5(2)(b) of the same amending regulations substituted the sum "£361" for the sum "£352" in reg.131(3)(b).

From the same date, reg.5(3) and reg.6 of the same amending regulations omitted reg.131(3A).

Income Support, Jobseekers' Allowance, etc.

p.997, *annotation to the Jobseeker's Allowance Regulations 1996, reg.131*

With regard to the amendment made by reg.5(3) and reg.6 of the Social Security (Students and Income-related Benefits) Amendment Regulations 2006, see the note to reg.131 in the main volume. This explains that although reg.131(3A) was omitted with effect from September 1, 2005 (or if the student's period of study began between August 1, 2005 and August 31, 2005, the first day of the period), the previous form of reg.131(3A) remained in force for "transitional cases" (i.e. those cases in which the claimant is still receiving amounts for his children in his income-based JSA—see further the note to reg.83 of the Jobseeker's Allowance Regulations and reg.17 of the Income Support Regulations in the main volume). However the effects of various amendments was that only sub-para.(e) of the previous form of reg.131(3A) continued to have effect. This had been introduced to provide a disregard of a grant paid under reg.15(7) of the Education (Student Support) (No. 2) Regulations 2002 (SI 2002/3200) known as a "parents' learning allowance". (Note that the 2002 Regulations were revoked by reg.3 of and Sch.1 to the Education (Student Support) Regulations 2005 (SI 2005/52)—the parents' learning allowance was then provided for under reg.19 of those Regulations). As the disregard in reg.131(2)(h) covers the parents' learning allowance, the disregard in sub-para.(e) of the previous form of reg.131(3A) is not required and so that provision has been omitted.

3.084

p.999, *amendment to the Jobseeker's Allowance Regulations 1996, reg.134 (Relationship with amounts to be disregarded under Sch.7)*

With effect from October 2, 2006, the words from "and any other income" to the end of the regulation in reg.134 are omitted by reg.13(7) of the Social Security (Miscellaneous Amendments) (No. 4) Regulations 2006 (SI 2006/2378).

3.085

p.1002, *amendment to the Jobseeker's Allowance Regulations 1996, reg.136 (Treatment of student loans)*

With effect from September 1, 2006 (or if the student's period of study begins between August 1 and August 31, 2006, the first day of the period), reg.5(2)(a) of the Social Security (Students and Income-related Benefits) Amendment Regulations 2006 (SI 2006/1752) substituted the sum "£285" for the sum "£280" in reg.136(5)(a).

From the same date, reg.5(2)(b) of the same amending regulations substituted the sum "£361" for the sum "£352" in reg.136(5)(b).

3.086

p.1003, *Jobseeker's Allowance Regulations 1996, reg.136B (Treatment of fee loans)*

With effect from September 1, 2006 (or if the student's period of study begins between August 1 and August 31, 2006, the first day of the period), reg.5(4) of the Social Security (Students and Income-related

3.087

Income Support, Jobseekers' Allowance, etc.

Benefits) Amendment Regulations 2006 (SI 2006/1752) inserted the following new regulation:

"Treatment of fee loans

136B. A loan for fees, known as a fee loan or a fee contribution loan, made pursuant to regulations made under Article 3 of the Education (Student Support) (Northern Ireland) Order 1998, section 22 of the Teaching and Higher Education Act 1998 or section 73(f) of the Education (Scotland) Act 1980, shall be disregarded as income."

p.1003, *annotation to the Jobseeker's Allowance Regulations 1996, reg.136B*

3.088   Fee loans and fee-contribution loans have been introduced as part of the student support system from the beginning of the academic year in 2006. Regulation 136B provides for a disregard of any such loan for tuition fees.

p.1038, *amendment to the Jobseeker's Allowance Regulations 1996, Sch.A1 (Categories of members of a joint-claim couple who are not required to satisfy the conditions in s.1(2B)(b)), para.15 (members required to attend court)*

3.089   With effect from May 30, 2006, reg.2(6) of the Social Security (Income Support and Jobseeker's Allowance) Amendment Regulations 2006 (SI 2006/1402) substituted the following paragraph for para.15:

"Members required to attend a court or tribunal

15.—(1) A member who is required to attend a court or tribunal as a justice of the peace, a party to any proceedings, a witness or a juror.

(2) In this paragraph, 'tribunal' means any tribunal listed in Schedule 1 to the Tribunals and Inquiries Act 1992."

p.1043, *amendment to the Jobseeker's Allowance Regulations 1996, Sch.1, para.12 (Higher pensioner premium)*

3.090   With effect from October 1, 2006, reg.13(10) of the Social Security (Miscellaneous Amendments) (No. 4) Regulations 2006 (SI 2006/2378) amended sub-para.(3) by substituting for "52 weeks" the words "104 weeks".

p.1048, *amendment to the Jobseeker's Allowance Regulations 1996, Sch.1, para.20F (Higher pensioner premium)*

3.091   With effect from October 1, 2006, reg.13(10) of the Social Security (Miscellaneous Amendments) (No. 4) Regulations 2006 (SI 2006/2378) amended sub-para.(3) by substituting for "52 weeks" the words "104 weeks".

Income Support, Jobseekers' Allowance, etc.

p.1049, *amendment to Jobseeker's Allowance Regulations 1996, Sch.1, para.20H (Additional conditions for higher pensioner and disability premiums)*

With effect from October 1, 2006, reg.13(10) of the Social Security (Miscellaneous Amendments) (No. 4) Regulations 2006 (SI 2006/2378) amended sub-para.(2) by substituting for "52 weeks" the words "104 weeks".

3.092

p.1055, *amendment to the Jobseeker's Allowance Regulations 1996, Sch.2 (Housing costs), para.1 (Housing costs)*

With effect from October 2, 2006, reg.13(11)(a) of the Social Security (Miscellaneous Amendments) (No. 4) Regulations 2006 (SI 2006/2378) inserted the following at the end of para.1(3)(c):

3.093

"; or
  (d) who is disabled or severely disabled for the purposes of section 9(6) (maximum rate) of the Tax Credits Act 2002."

p.1057, *amendment to the Jobseeker's Allowance Regulations 1996, Sch.2 (Housing costs), para.3 (Circumstances in which a person is to be treated as occupying a dwelling as his home)*

With effect from October 2, 2006, reg.13(11)(b) of the Social Security (Miscellaneous Amendments) (No. 4) Regulations 2006 (SI 2006/2378) substituted the following sub-head for sub-head (ii) in para.3(7)(c):

3.094

"(ii) the move was delayed pending the outcome of an application under Part 8 of the Benefits Act for a social fund payment to meet a need arising out of the move or in connection with setting up the home in the dwelling, and—
  (aa) a member of the claimant's family is aged five or under,
  (bb) the claimant's applicable amount includes a premium under paragraph 10, 11, 12, 13, 15 or 16 of Schedule 1 (applicable amounts), or
  (cc) a child tax credit is paid for a member of the claimant's family who is disabled or severely disabled for the purposes of section 9(6) (maximum rate) of the Tax Credits Act 2002; or".

p.1066, *amendment to the Jobseeker's Allowance Regulations 1996, Sch.2 (Housing costs), para.13*

With effect from October 9, 2006, reg.13(10)(b) of the Social Security (Miscellaneous Amendments) (No. 4) Regulations 2006 (SI 2006/2378) substituted "104 weeks" for "52 weeks" in both para.13(4A)(b) and para.13(12).

3.095

Income Support, Jobseekers' Allowance, etc.

p.1068, *amendment to the Jobseeker's Allowance Regulations 1996, Sch.2 (Housing costs), para.16 (Other housing costs)*

3.096   With effect from October 2, 2006, the words "and, in Scotland, payments by way of feu duty" in para.16(1)(a) were omitted by reg.13(11)(c) of the Social Security (Miscellaneous Amendments) (No. 4) Regulations 2006 (SI 2006/2378).

p.1073, *annotation to the Jobseeker's Allowance Regulations 1996, Sch.2, para.1*

3.097   See the note to para.1 of Sch.3 to the Income Support Regulations above.

p.1073, *annotation to the Jobseeker's Allowance Regulations 1996, Sch.2, para.3*

3.098   See the note to para.3 of Sch.3 to the Income Support Regulations above.

p.1073, *annotation to the Jobseeker's Allowance Regulations 1996, Sch.2, para.13*

3.099   See the note to para.14 of Sch.3 to the Income Support Regulations above.

p.1073, *annotation to the Jobseeker's Allowance Regulations 1996, Sch.2, para.16*

3.100   See the note to para.17 of Sch.3 to the Income Support Regulations above.

p.1084, *amendment to the Jobseeker's Allowance Regulations 1996, Sch.6 (Sums to be disregarded in the calculation of earnings), para.9*

3.101   With effect from October 2, 2006, reg.13(3)(c) of the Social Security (Miscellaneous Amendments) (No. 4) Regulations 2006 (SI 2006/2378) substituted the words "Schedule 6 to the Social Security (Contributions) Regulations 2001" for the words "Schedule 3 to the Social Security (Contributions) Regulations 1979" in para.9(d).

p.1085, *amendment to the Jobseeker's Allowance Regulations 1996, Sch.6 (Sums to be disregarded in the calculation of earnings), para.19*

3.102   With effect from October 2, 2006, reg.13(3)(c) of the Social Security (Miscellaneous Amendments) (No. 4) Regulations 2006 (SI 2006/2378) substituted the words "Schedule 6 to the Social Security (Contributions) Regulations 2001" for the words "Schedule 3 to the Social Security (Contributions) Regulations 1979" in para.19(a).

Income Support, Jobseekers' Allowance, etc.

p.1090, *amendment to the Jobseeker's Allowance Regulations 1996, Sch.6A (Sums to be disregarded in the calculation of earnings of members of joint-claim couples), para.5*

With effect from October 2, 2006, reg.13(3)(d) of the Social Security (Miscellaneous Amendments) (No. 4) Regulations 2006 (SI 2006/2378) substituted the words "Schedule 6 to the Social Security (Contributions) Regulations 2001" for the words "Schedule 3 to the Social Security (Contributions) Regulations 1979" in para.5(a).

3.103

p.1092, *amendment to the Jobseeker's Allowance Regulations 1996, Sch.7 (Sums to be disregarded in the calculation of income other than earnings), para.15*

With effect from October 2, 2006, reg.13(12)(a)(i) of the Social Security (Miscellaneous Amendments) (No. 4) Regulations 2006 (SI 2006/2378) substituted the following sub-paragraph for sub-para.(1) of para.15:

3.104

"(1) Subject to sub-paragraph (3) and paragraph 41, any relevant payment made or due to be made at regular intervals."

From the same date, reg.13(12)(a)(ii) of the same amending regulations substituted the words "Sub-paragraph (1)" for the words "Sub-paragraphs (1) and (2)" in sub-para.(3) of para.15.

From the same date, sub-paras (2), (4) and (5) of para.15 were omitted by reg.13(12)(a)(iii) of the same amending regulations.

p.1092, *amendment to the Jobseeker's Allowance Regulations 1996, Sch.7 (Sums to be disregarded in the calculation of income other than earnings), para.16*

With effect from October 2, 2006, para.16 is omitted by reg.13(12)(b) of the Social Security (Miscellaneous Amendments) (No. 4) Regulations 2006 (SI 2006/2378).

3.105

p.1095, *amendment to the Jobseeker's Allowance Regulations 1996, Sch.7 (Sums to be disregarded in the calculation of income other than earnings), para.27*

With effect from October 2, 2006, reg.13(12)(c) of the Social Security (Miscellaneous Amendments) (No. 4) Regulations 2006 (SI 2006/2378) substituted the words "local authority under regulation 9 of the Fostering of Children (Scotland) Regulations 1996 (payment of allowances)" for the words from "care authority" to the end of the paragraph in para.27.

3.106

p.1096, *amendment to the Jobseeker's Allowance Regulations 1996, Sch.7 (Sums to be disregarded in the calculation of income other than earnings), para.32*

With effect from October 2, 2006, the words "but not a payment to which paragraph 16 applies" in para.32(1) were omitted by

3.107

Income Support, Jobseekers' Allowance, etc.

reg.13(12)(d) of the Social Security (Miscellaneous Amendments) (No. 4) Regulations 2006 (SI 2006/2378).

p.1096, *amendment to the Jobseeker's Allowance Regulations 1996, Sch.7 (Sums to be disregarded in the calculation of income other than earnings), para.38*

3.108 With effect from October 2, 2006, reg.13(12)(e) of the Social Security (Miscellaneous Amendments) (No. 4) Regulations 2006 (SI 2006/2378) substituted the words "paragraph 17" for the words "paragraphs 15(1) and 17" in para.38.

p.1103, *annotation to the Jobseeker's Allowance Regulations 1996, Sch.7, para.15*

3.109 See the note to para.15 of Sch.9 to the Income Support Regulations above.

p.1103, *annotation to the Jobseeker's Allowance Regulations 1996, Sch.7, para.16*

3.110 See the note to para.15A of Sch.9 to the Income Support Regulations above.

p.1105, *amendment to the Jobseeker's Allowance Regulations 1996, Sch.8 (Capital to be disregarded), para.17*

3.111 With effect from October 2, 2006, reg.13(13)(a) of the Social Security (Miscellaneous Amendments) (No. 4) Regulations 2006 (SI 2006/2378) inserted the words "or the claimant's partner" after the word "claimant" in para.17.

p.1105, *Jobseeker's Allowance Regulations 1996, Sch.8 (Capital to be disregarded), para.17A*

3.112 With effect from October 2, 2006, reg.13(13)(b) of the Social Security (Miscellaneous Amendments) (No. 4) Regulations 2006 (SI 2006/2378) inserted the following new paragraph after para.17:

"**17A.**—(1) Any payment made to the claimant or the claimant's partner in consequence of any personal injury to the claimant or, as the case may be, the claimant's partner.
　(2) But sub-paragraph (1)—
　　(a) applies only for the period of 52 weeks beginning with the day on which the claimant first receives any payment in consequence of that personal injury;
　　(b) does not apply to any subsequent payment made to him in consequence of that injury (whether it is made by the same person or another);
　　(c) ceases to apply to the payment or any part of the payment from the day on which the claimant no longer possesses it;

Income Support, Jobseekers' Allowance, etc.

(d) does not apply to any payment from a trust where the funds of the trust are derived from a payment made in consequence of any personal injury to the claimant.

(3) For the purposes of sub-paragraph (2)(c), the circumstances in which a claimant no longer possesses a payment or a part of it include where the claimant has used a payment or part of it to purchase an asset.

(4) References in sub-paragraphs (2) and (3) to the claimant are to be construed as including references to his partner (where applicable)."

p.1108, *amendment to the Jobseeker's Allowance Regulations 1996, Sch.8 (Capital to be disregarded), para.42*

With effect from October 2, 2006, reg.13(13)(c) of the Social Security (Miscellaneous Amendments) (No. 4) Regulations 2006 (SI 2006/2378) substituted the following paragraph for para.42:   3.113

"**42.**—(1) Any sum of capital to which sub-paragraph (2) applies and—
  (a) which is administered on behalf of a person by the High Court or the County Court under Rule 21.11(1) of the Civil Procedure Rules 1998 or by the Court of Protection;
  (b) which can only be disposed of by order or direction of any such court; or
  (c) where the person concerned is under the age of 18, which can only be disposed of by order or direction prior to that person attaining age 18.
(2) This sub-paragraph applies to a sum of capital which is derived from—
  (a) an award of damages for a personal injury to that person; or
  (b) compensation for the death of one or both parents where the person concerned is under the age of 18."

pp.1112–1113, *annotation to the Jobseeker's Allowance Regulations 1996, Sch.8, para.17*

See the note to para.12 of Sch.10 to the Income Support Regulations above.   3.114

pp.1112–1113, *annotation to the Jobseeker's Allowance Regulations 1996, Sch.8, para.17A*

See the note to para.12A of Sch.10 to the Income Support Regulations above.   3.115

pp.1112–1113, *annotation to the Jobseeker's Allowance Regulations 1996, Sch.8, para.42*

See the note to para.44 of Sch.10 to the Income Support Regulations above.   3.116

Income Support, Jobseekers' Allowance, etc.

p.1123, *amendment to the State Pension Credit Regulations 2002, reg.2 (Persons not in Great Britain)*

3.117   With effect from April 30, 2006, reg.9 of the Social Security (Persons from Abroad) Amendment Regulations 2006 (SI 2006/1026) substituted a new reg.2. As further amended with effect from July 25, 2006 by the Social Security (Lebanon) Amendment Regulations 2006 (SI 2006/1981), reg.4 (adding a new reg.2(4)(k)), and with effect from October 9, 2006 by the Social Security (Persons from Abroad) Amendment (No. 2) Regulations 2006 (SI 2006/2528), reg.4 (substituting a new reg.2(4)(h) and (hh)), reg.2 now reads as follows:

"**Persons not in Great Britain**

2.—(1) A person is to be treated as not in Great Britain if, subject to the following provisions of this regulation, he is not habitually resident in the United Kingdom, the Channel Islands, the Isle of Man or the Republic of Ireland.

(2) No person shall be treated as habitually resident in the United Kingdom, the Channel Islands, the Isle of Man or the Republic of Ireland unless he has a right to reside in (as the case may be) the United Kingdom, the Channel Islands, the Isle of Man or the Republic of Ireland other than a right to reside which falls within paragraph (3).

(3) A right to reside falls within this paragraph if it is one which exists by virtue of, or in accordance with, one or more of the following—

   (a) regulation 13 of the Immigration (European Economic Area) Regulations 2006;
   (b) regulation 14 of those Regulations, but only in a case where the right exists under that regulation because the person is—
      (i) a jobseeker for the purpose of the definition of 'qualified person' in regulation 6(1) of those Regulations, or
      (ii) a family member (within the meaning of regulation 7 of those Regulations) of such a jobseeker;
   (c) Article 6 of Council Directive No. 2004/38/EC; or
   (d) Article 39 of the Treaty establishing the European Community (in a case where the person is seeking work in the United Kingdom, the Channel Islands, the Isle of Man or the Republic of Ireland).

(4) A person is not to be treated as not in Great Britain if he is—
   (a) a worker for the purposes of Council Directive No. 2004/38/EC;
   (b) a self-employed person for the purposes of that Directive;
   (c) a person who retains a status referred to in sub-paragraph (a) or (b) pursuant to Article 7(3) of that Directive;
   (d) a person who is a family member of a person referred to in sub-paragraph (a), (b) or (c) within the meaning of Article 2 of that Directive;
   (e) a person who has a right to reside permanently in the United Kingdom by virtue of Article 17 of that Directive;

Income Support, Jobseekers' Allowance, etc.

(f) a person who is an accession State worker requiring registration who is treated as a worker for the purpose of the definition of 'qualified person' in regulation 6(1) of the Immigration (European Economic Area) Regulations 2006 pursuant to regulation 5 of the Accession (Immigration and Worker Registration) Regulations 2004;

(g) a refugee within the definition in Article 1 of the Convention relating to the Status of Refugees done at Geneva on 28th July 1951, as extended by Article 1(2) of the Protocol relating to the Status of Refugees done at New York on 31st January 1967;

(h) a person who has exceptional leave to enter or remain in the United Kingdom granted outside the rules made under section 3(2) of the Immigration Act 1971;

(hh) a person who has humanitarian protection granted under those rules;

(i) a person who is not a person subject to immigration control within the meaning of section 115(9) of the Immigration and Asylum Act 1999 and who is in the United Kingdom as a result of his deportation, expulsion or other removal by compulsion of law from another country to the United Kingdom;

(j) a person in Great Britain who left the territory of Montserrat after 1st November 1995 because of the effect on that territory of a volcanic eruption.

(k) a person in Great Britain who left Lebanon on or after 12th July 2006 because of the armed conflict there."

With effect from April 30, 2006, reg.10(h) of the Social Security (Persons from Abroad) Amendment Regulations 2006 (SI 2006/1026) provides that reg.2(4)(a)–(e) apply to a national of Norway, Iceland, Liechtenstein or Switzerland or a member of his family (within the meaning of Art.2 of Council Directive No. 2004/38/EC) as if such were a national of a Member State.

p.1124, *annotation to the State Pension Credit Regulations 2002, reg.2 (persons not in Great Britain)*

In *CPC/2920/2005* the claimant, a Norwegian aged 69 of Somali origin, arrived in the United Kingdom on April 20, 2004 and claimed state pension credit (SPC) on June 14, 2004. His claim was refused on the basis that he had no right to reside in the United Kingdom and so was not habitually resident. The Tribunal of Commissioners in *CPC/2920/2005*, dismissing the claimant's appeal, held that their reasoning on the impact of regs 21(3) and 21(3G) of the Income Support (General) Regulations 1987 (SI 1987/1967) in the context of income support applied equally to reg.2 as it relates to SPC. The Commissioners also held that:

3.118

"Directive 90/364 cannot found for citizens of Norway a right to reside in Great Britain other than to the limited extent set out in Article 32

Income Support, Jobseekers' Allowance, etc.

and Annex VIII, which do not apply to the claimant. He cannot, in these circumstances, rely on it or the anti-discrimination provision of the agreement as the Agreement has no application in the circumstances set out above" (para.20).

p.1127, *amendment to the State Pension Credit Regulations 2002, reg.5 (persons treated as being or not being members of the same household)*

3.119 With effect from October 2, 2006, reg.14(2) of the Social Security (Miscellaneous Amendments) (No. 4) Regulations 2006 (SI 2006/2378) amended reg.5 by omitting para.(1)(e) and inserting after para.(1) a new para.(1A) as follows:

"(1A) Paragraph (1)(d) and (f) shall not apply where a person is treated as being in Great Britain in accordance with regulation 4."

p.1133, *amendment to the State Pension Credit Regulations 2002, reg.10 (Assessed income period)*

3.120 With effect from October 2, 2006, reg.14(3) of the Social Security (Miscellaneous Amendments) (No. 4) Regulations 2006 (SI 2006/2378) amended reg.10 by omitting para.(8). See also the decision of Mr Commissioner Levenson in *CPC/0206/2005*, discussed in the note to p.154 above, and the decision of Mr Commissioner Rowland in *CPC/1928/2005*, discussed in the note to p.155 above.

p.1149, *amendment to the State Pension Credit Regulations 2002, reg.18 (Notional income)*

3.121 With effect from October 2, 2006, reg.14(4)(a) of the Social Security (Miscellaneous Amendments) (No. 4) Regulations 2006 (SI 2006/2378) amended reg.18(1) by substituting new paras (1)–(1D) as follows:

"(1) A claimant who has attained the qualifying age shall be treated as possessing the amount of any retirement pension income—
    (a) to which section 16(1)(a) to (e) applies,
    (b) for which no claim has been made, and
    (c) to which the claimant might expect to be entitled if a claim for it were made,
but only from the date on which that income could be expected to be acquired if a claim for it were made.
(1A) Paragraph (1) is subject to paragraphs (1B) and (1C).
(1B) Where a claimant—
    (a) has deferred entitlement to retirement pension income to which section 16(1)(a) to (c) applies for at least 12 months, and
    (b) would have been entitled to make an election under Schedule 5 or 5A to the 1992 Act or under Schedule 1 to the Graduated Retirement Benefit Regulations,
he shall be treated for the purposes of paragraph (1) as possessing the amount of retirement pension income to which he might expect to be entitled if he were to elect to receive a lump sum.
(1C) Where a claimant receives an allowance under—

Income Support, Jobseekers' Allowance, etc.

(a) section 68 of the 1992 Act (severe disablement allowance), or
(b) section 70 of that Act (carer's allowance),

the amount of that allowance is to be deducted from the amount of retirement pension income which he is treated as possessing for the purposes of paragraph (1) (or, where applicable, paragraph (1) read with paragraph (1B)).

(1D) A claimant who has attained the qualifying age shall be treated as possessing income from an occupational pension scheme which he elected to defer, but only from the date on which it could be expected to be acquired if a claim for it were made."

In addition, also with effect from October 2, 2006, reg.14(4)(b) of the Social Security (Miscellaneous Amendments) (No. 4) Regulations 2006 (SI 2006/2378) amended reg.18 by inserting new paras (9) and (10) as follows:

"(9) For the purposes of paragraph (6), a person is not to be regarded as depriving himself of income where—
(a) his rights to benefits under a registered pension scheme are extinguished and in consequence of this he receives a payment from the scheme, and
(b) that payment is a trivial commutation lump sum within the meaning given by paragraph 7 of Schedule 29 to the Finance Act 2004.

(10) In paragraph (9), 'registered pension scheme' has the meaning given in section 150(2) of the Finance Act 2004."

p.1171, *amendment to the State Pension Credit Regulations 2002, Sch.II, para.13 (Other housing costs)*

With effect from October 2, 2006, reg.14(5)(a) of the Social Security (Miscellaneous Amendments) (No. 4) Regulations 2006 (SI 2006/2378) amended para.13(1)(a) by omitting the words "and, in Scotland, payments by way of feu duty". 3.122

p.1172, *amendment to the State Pension Credit Regulations 2002, Sch.II, para.14 (Persons residing with the claimant)*

With effect from October 2, 2006, reg.14(5)(b) of the Social Security (Miscellaneous Amendments) (No. 4) Regulations 2006 (SI 2006/2378) amended para.14 by substituting "(1)(b)" for "(1)(c)" in sub-para.(2)(a) and inserting after sub-para.(7)(d) a new sub-para.(7)(dd) as follows: 3.123

"(dd) in respect of whom a deduction in the calculation of a rent rebate or allowance falls to be made under regulation 55 (non-dependant deductions) of the Housing Benefit (Persons who have attained the qualifying age for state pension credit) Regulations 2006; or"

p.1174, *annotation to the State Pension Credit Regulations 2002, Sch.II*

The treatment of service charges for the purposes of entitlement to state pension credit (SPC) was considered by Mr Commissioner Lloyd- 3.124

Income Support, Jobseekers' Allowance, etc.

Davies in joined appeals *CPC/1820/2005* and *CIS/2574/2005* (to be reported as *R(PC) 1/07*). The tribunals in both cases had in effect concluded that as 29 per cent of the service charges in dispute were met by the Supporting People programme, the balance of 71 per cent of the charges were eligible housing costs for SPC purposes under para.13. Setting aside the decisions and remitting the appeals for rehearing, the Commissioner ruled that both tribunals had erred in law in making this assumption. Overall, the evidence before the tribunals lacked "any detail of what the scheme manager did other than in relation to general counselling and support, and nowhere was there any indication of what proportion of his time a scheme manager spent on activities said to relate to the provision of adequate accommodation" (para.18). The Commissioner, whilst noting that "the process described by the Commissioner in paragraph 28 of *CIS/2901/04* may be described as the gold standard for assessing what proportion of charges are eligible or ineligible in cases such as these" (para.23), also observed that he would concur:

> "with the remark of the Commissioner in paragraph 9 of *CPC/968/2005* that a 'broad approach' is called for: for example, a decision-maker or tribunal supplied with the terms of the lease relating to services and service charges, a breakdown of the service charges, details of what service charges (if any) are met by the Supporting People programme, and a statement from the scheme manager as to how his working time is usually divided up should normally be able to make a reasoned estimate of how much of the service charges in dispute are eligible or ineligible. Each case will, however, inevitably turn on its own facts and evidential requirements will vary" (para. 23).

p.1183, *amendment to the State Pension Credit Regulations 2002, Sch.V, para.16(2) (Income from capital)*

3.125 With effect from October 2, 2006, reg.14(6) of the Social Security (Miscellaneous Amendments) (No. 4) Regulations 2006 (SI 2006/2378) amended para.16(2) by substituting a new sub-para.(a) as follows:

"(a) by the High Court or the County Court under Rule 21.11(1) of the Civil Procedure Rules 1998, or the Court of Protection, or on behalf of a person where the payment can only be disposed of by order or direction of any such court;".

In addition, and with effect from the same date, reg.14(6) also amended para.16(2)(b) by omitting the words "Rule 131 of the Act of Sederunt (Rules of the Court, consolidation and amendment) 1965, or under".

p.1204, *Social Fund Cold Weather Payments (General) Regulations 1988, Sch.1 (Identification of stations and postcode districts)*

3.126 With effect from November 1, 2006, reg.3 of the Social Fund Cold Weather Payments (General) Amendment Regulations 2006 (SI 2655/2006) substituted the following Schedule for Sch.1:

Income Support, Jobseekers' Allowance, etc.

"SCHEDULE 1

Regulation 2(1)(a) and (2)

IDENTIFICATION OF STATIONS AND POSTCODE DISTRICTS

Column (1)	*Column (2)*
Meteorological Office Station	*Postcode districts*
1. Aberporth	SA35–48, SA64–65. SY20, SY23–25.
2. Albemarle	DH1–6. DL5, DL16–17. NE1–13, NE15–18, NE20–21, NE23, NE25–43, NE45–46. SR1–7. TS21, TS28–29.
3. Andrewsfield	AL1–10. CB10–11. CM1–9, CM11–24, CM77. CO9. RM14–20. SG1–2, SG9–14.
4. Aultbea	IV21–22, IV26, IV40, IV52–54.
5. Aviemore	AB31, AB33–34, AB36–37. PH18–26.
6. Bedford	LU1–7. MK1–19, MK40–46. NN1–16, NN29. PE19. SG3–7, SG15–19.
7. Bingley	BB3–5, BB8–12, BB18. BD1–24. DE4, DE45. HD1–9. HX1–7. LS21, LS27, LS29. OL1–5, OL11–16. S32–33, S35–36. SK13, SK17, SK22–23. ST13. WF15–17.
8. Bishopton	G1–5, G11–15, G20–23, G31–34, G40–46, G51–53, G60–62, G64–69, G71–78, G81–84. KA1–26, KA28–30. ML1–5. PA1–27, PA30, PA32.
9. Boltshope Park	DH7–9. DL4, DL8, DL11–15. NE19, NE44, NE47–48.
10. Boscombe Down	BA12. RG28. SP1–5, SP7, SP9–11.
11. Boulmer	NE22, NE24, NE61–71. TD12, TD15.
12. Braemar	AB35.
13. Brize Norton	CV36. GL54–56. OX1–8, OX10–18, OX20, OX25–29, OX33, OX39, OX44, OX49. SN7.
14. Capel Curig	LL24–25, LL41.
15. Cardinham (Bodmin)	PL13–17, PL22–35. TR2, TR9.
16. Carlisle	CA1–11, CA16–17. DG12, DG16. LA6–10, LA22–23. NE49.

Income Support, Jobseekers' Allowance, etc.

Column (1)	Column (2)
Meteorological Office Station	*Postcode districts*
17. Cassley	IV27–28. KW11, KW13.
18. Charlwood	BN5–6, BN44. GU5–8, GU26–33, GU35. ME14–20. RH1–20. TN1–20, TN22, TN27.
19. Chivenor	EX22–23, EX31–34, EX39.
20. Coleshill	B1–21, B23–38, B40, B42–50, B60–80, B90–98. CV1–12, CV21–23, CV31–35, CV37, CV47. DY1–14. LE10. WS1–15. WV1–16.
21. Crosby	BB1–2, BB6–7. CH1–8, CH41–49, CH60–66. FY1–8. L1–40. LL11–14. PR1–9, PR25–26. SY14. WA1–2, WA4–12. WN1–6, WN8.
22. Culdrose	TR1, TR3–6, TR10–20, TR26–27.
23. Dundrennan	DG1–2, DG5–7.
24. Dunkeswell Aerodrome	DT6–8. EX1–15, EX24. TA21. TQ1–6, TQ9–14.
25. Dyce	AB10–16, AB21–25, AB30, AB32, AB39, AB41–43, AB51–54. DD8–11.
26. Edinburgh Gogarbank	EH1–42, EH47–49, EH51–55. FK1–21. G63. KY3, KY11–13. PH3–6. TD5, TD11, TD13–14.
27. Eskdalemuir	DG3–4, DG10–11, DG13–14. ML12. TD1–4, TD6–10.
28. Fylingdales	YO11–18, YO21–22, YO25.
29. Great Malvern	GL1–6, GL10–20, GL50–53. HR1–9. NP15, NP25. SY8. WR1–15.
30. Heathrow	BR1–8. CR0, CR2–8. DA1–2, DA4–8, DA14–18. E1–18. E1W. EC1–4. EN1–11. HA0–9. IG1–11. KT1–24. N1–22. NW1–11. RM1–13. SE1–28. SL0, SL3. SM1–7. SW1–20. TW1–20. UB1–10. W1–14. WC1–2. WD1–7, WD17–19, WD23–25.
31. Herstmonceux, West End	BN7–8, BN20–24, BN26–27. TN21, TN31–40.
32. High Wycombe	HP1–23, HP27. OX9. RG9. SL7–9.
33. Hurn (Bournemouth Airport)	BH1–25, BH31. DT1–2, DT11. SP6.
34. Isle of Portland	DT3–5.
35. Kinloss	AB38, AB44–45, AB55–56. IV1–3, IV5, IV7–20, IV30–32, IV36.

Income Support, Jobseekers' Allowance, etc.

Column (1)	Column (2)
Meteorological Office Station	Postcode districts
36. Kirkwall	KW15–17.
37. Lake Vyrnwy	LL20–21, LL23. SY10, SY15–17, SY19, SY21–22.
38. Lerwick	ZE1–3.
39. Leuchars	DD1–7. KY1–2, KY4–10, KY14–16. PH1–2, PH7, PH12–14.
40. Linton on Ouse	DL1–3, DL6–7, DL9–10. HG1–5. LS1–20, LS22–26, LS28. S62–64, S70–75. TS9, TS15–16. WF1–14. YO1, YO7–8, YO10, YO19, YO23–24, YO26, YO30–32, YO41–43, YO51, YO60–62.
41. Liscombe	EX16–21, EX35–38. PL19–20. TA22, TA24.
42. Loch Glascarnoch	IV4, IV6, IV23–24, IV63.
43. Loftus	SR8. TS1–8, TS10–14, TS17–20, TS22–27.
44. Lusa	IV41–49, IV51, IV55–56.
45. Lyneham	BA1–3, BA11, BA13–15. GL7–9. RG17. SN1–6, SN8–16, SN25–26.
46. Machrihanish	KA27. PA28–29, PA31, PA34, PA37, PA41–49, PA60–76. PH36, PH38–41.
47. Manston	CM0. CT1–21. DA3, DA9–13. ME1–13. SS0–17. TN23–26, TN28–30.
48. Marham	IP24–28. PE12–14, PE30–38.
49. Nottingham	CV13. DE1–3, DE5–7, DE11–15, DE21–24, DE55–56, DE65, DE72–75. LE1–9, LE11–14, LE16–19, LE65, LE67. NG1–22, NG25, NG31–34. S1–14, S17–18, S20–21, S25–26, S40–45, S60–61, S65–66, S80–81. ST10, ST14.
50. Pembrey Sands	SA1–8, SA10–18, SA31–34, SA61–63, SA66–73.
51. Plymouth	PL1–12, PL18, PL21. TQ7–8.
52. Rhyl	LL15–19, LL22, LL26–32.
53. St. Athan	BS1–11, BS13–16, BS20–24, BS29–32, BS34–37, BS39–41, BS48–49. CF3, CF5, CF10–11, CF14–15, CF23–24, CF31–36, CF61–64, CF71–72. NP10, NP16, NP18–20, NP26.

Income Support, Jobseekers' Allowance, etc.

Column (1)	Column (2)
Meteorological Office Station	*Postcode districts*
54. St. Catherine's Point	PO30, PO38–41.
55. St. Mawgan	TR7–8.
56. Salsburgh	EH43–46. ML6–11.
57. Scilly, St. Mary's	TR21–25.
58. Sennybridge	CF37–48, CF81–83. LD1–8. NP4, NP7–8, NP11–13, NP22–24, NP44. SA9, SA19–20. SY7, SY9, SY18.
59. Shawbury	ST1–9, ST11–12, ST15–21. SY1–6, SY11–13. TF1–13.
60. South Farnborough	GU1–4, GU9–25, GU46–47, GU51–52. RG1–2, RG4–8, RG10, RG12, RG14, RG18–27, RG29–31, RG40–42, RG45. SL1–2, SL4–6.
61. Stornoway Airport	HS1–9.
62. Thorney Island	BN1–3, BN9–18, BN25, BN41–43, BN45. GU34. PO1–22, PO31–37. SO14–24, SO30–32, SO40–43, SO45, SO50–53.
63. Tiree	PA77–78. PH42–44.
64. Tulloch Bridge	PA33, PA35–36, PA38, PA40. PH8–11, PH15–17, PH30–35, PH37, PH49–50.
65. Valley	LL33–40, LL42–49, LL51–78.
66. Waddington	DN1–22, DN31–41. HU1–20. LN1–13. NG23–24. PE10–11, PE20–25.
67. Walney Island	CA12–15, CA18–28. LA1–5, LA11–21.
68. Wattisham	CB9. CO1–8, CO10–16. IP1–23, IP29–33.
69. West Freugh	DG8–9.
70. Weybourne	NR1–35.
71. Wick Airport	IV25. KW1–3, KW5–10, KW12, KW14.

Income Support, Jobseekers' Allowance, etc.

Column (1)	Column (2)
Meteorological Office Station	Postcode districts
72. Wittering	CB1–8. LE15. NN17–18. PE1–9, PE15–17, PE26–29. SG8.
73. Woodford	BL0–9. CW1–12. M1–9, M11–35, M38, M40–41, M43–46, M50, M90. OL6–11. SK1–12, SK14–16. WA3, WA13–16. WN7.
74. Yeovilton	BA4–10, BA16, BA20–22. BS25–28. DT9–10. SP8. TA1–20, TA23."

p.1207, *Social Fund Cold Weather Payments (General) Regulations 1988, Sch.2 (Specified alternative stations)*

With effect from November 1, 2006, reg.4 of the Social Fund Cold Weather Payments (General) Amendment Regulations 2006 (SI 2655/2006) substituted the following Schedule for Sch.2:

3.127

"SCHEDULE 2

Regulation 2(1A)(a) and 2(1B)(a)

SPECIFIED ALTERNATIVE STATIONS

Column (1)	Column (2)
Meteorological Office Station	Specified Alternative Station
Charlwood	Kenley Airfield
Coleshill	Coventry
Fylingdales	Linton on Ouse
Hurn (Bournemouth Airport)	St. Catherine's Point
Kinloss	Lossiemouth
Linton on Ouse	Church Fenton
St. Athan	Mumbles."

p.1231, *amendment to the Social Fund Maternity and Funeral Expenses (General) Regulations 2005, reg.7(9) (Funeral payments: entitlement)*

With effect from April 30, 2006, reg.8(2) of the Social Security (Persons from Abroad) Amendment Regulations 2006 (SI 2006/1026) amended para.(9) to read as follows:

3.128

"(9) The sixth condition is that the funeral takes place—

Income Support, Jobseekers' Allowance, etc.

(a) in a case where paragraph (10) applies, in a member State of the European Union, Iceland, Liechtenstein[, Norway or Switzerland];
(b) in any other case in the United Kingdom."

pp.1231–1232, *Social Fund Maternity and Funeral Expenses (General) Regulations 2005, reg.7(10) (Funeral payments: entitlement)*

3.129 With effect from April 30, 2006, reg.8(3) of the Social Security (Persons from Abroad) Amendment Regulations 2006 (SI 2006/1026) substituted a new para.(10) reading as follows:

"(10) This paragraph applies where the responsible person or his partner is—
(a) a worker for the purposes of Council Directive No. 2004/38/EC;
(b) a self-employed person for the purposes of that Directive;
(c) a person who retains a status referred to in sub-paragraph (a) or (b) pursuant to Article 7(3) of that Directive;
(d) a person who is a family member of a person referred to in sub-paragraph (a), (b) or (c) within the meaning of Article 2 of that Directive; or
(e) a person who has a right to reside permanently in the United Kingdom by virtue of Article 17 of that Directive".

p.1235, *annotation to the Social Fund Maternity and Funeral Expenses (General) Regulations 2005, reg.7(10) (Funeral payments: entitlement)—Place of funeral*

3.130 In CIS/1335/2004, the claimant's husband died while they were on holiday in Spain. Because she could not afford to have his body flown back to the UK, he was cremated in Spain. His ashes were then interred in England. The Commissioner confirmed the Secretary of State's decision to refuse a funeral payment. The "funeral" was the Spanish cremation and not the subsequent burial of ashes in the UK. Therefore, the actual cost of the burial did not qualify under reg.9(3)(a) and the other UK costs could only qualify as other funeral expenses under reg.9(3)(g) as incidental to, or consequential upon, the cremation in Spain if the claimant was in principle entitled to a funeral payment in respect of that cremation. That was not the case because the claimant was neither a migrant worker nor a family member of such a worker within the provisions set out in para.(10). The result was that the rule treated UK citizens less favourably than citizens of other Member States exercising rights in the UK under EU law. However, that discrimination was not unlawful under EU law or under ECHR Art.14, taken together with Art.1 of the First Protocol.

From April 30, 2006 para.(10) applies to nationals of Norway, Iceland, Liechtenstein and Switzerland—and to members of their families as defined by Article 2 of the Rights of Residence Directive—as if those nationals were EU nationals (see reg.10(g) of SI 1026/2006). The effect

Income Support, Jobseekers' Allowance, etc.

of the change is substantially to reverse the decision of the Tribunal of Commissioners in *CPC/2920/2005*.

p.1238, *annotation to the Social Fund Maternity and Funeral Expenses (General) Regulations 2005, reg.8 (Funeral payments: supplementary): Meaning of "Estrangement"*

In *CIS/4096/2005*, Mrs Commissioner Jupp reviewed the authorities on estrangement (in the context of reg.13(1)(d) of the Income Support Regulations) and concluded that there was no requirement of mutuality in feeling for estrangement to exist, as had been suggested by the Commissioner in *CIS/4498/2001*. Disharmony can arise from one person's attitude to another even though the other party may not wish the situation to be as it is. The position has to be judged from the point of view of (in the context of funeral payments) the surviving immediate family member who is being considered and not from the point of view of the deceased.

3.131

p.1243, *annotation to the Social Fund Maternity and Funeral Expenses (General) Regulations 2005, reg.9 (Amount of funeral payment): Burial and cremation—paras 3(a) and (b).*

See also in this context *CIS/1335/2004* discussed in the commentary to reg.7(10) (above).

3.132

PART IV

**UPDATING MATERIAL
VOLUME III**

**ADMINISTRATION, ADJUDICATION AND
THE EUROPEAN DIMENSION**

p.50, *annotations to the Social Security Administration Act 1992, s.71*

CIS/3605/2005 was concerned with the application of s.71(5A) (para.1.84 of Vol.III) in a case in which the amount of income support to which the claimant was entitled had reduced following the cessation of child benefit. Complications arose when that entitlement had been resurrected for a number of periods. The claimant argued that the revision decision had been made in ignorance of the true position on the dates for which child benefit had been awarded and so was invalid. The Commissioner concluded:

4.001

> "10. It seems to me that the claimant's argument confuses the concepts of correctness and validity. The Secretary of State had statutory power to make the decision of 14th August 2002, even if it was based on an inaccurate understanding of the facts. It was subject to supersession, revision, and appeal, but until one of those events took place it was, in law, a valid decision, and satisfied the requirements of section 71(5A) for the purposes of a recoverability decision.
>
> 11. This approach is consistent with the jurisprudence of the House of Lords in administrative law. Thus, a decision which might traditionally have been regarded as void is nevertheless to be treated as having legal effect until a court has decided that it is void (*Re Racal Communications Ltd* [1980] 2 All ER 634) and an order may be void for one purpose and valid for another (*Calvin v Carr* [1980] AC 574; *R v Wicks* [1998] AC 92)."

CIS/764/2002 and *CIS/3228/2003*, on the need for revision or supersession of all decision authorising payment of benefit during a period of alleged overpayment, have been followed in *CIS/203/2002* (a post-*Hinchy* decision of August 24, 2006).

Following the rejection of her application for leave to appeal, the claimant in *B v Secretary of State* has made an application to the European Court of Human Rights alleging a violation of Convention rights.

In *CIS/4422/2002* the Commissioner has followed the approach adopted in *CIS/1887/2002* in ruling that, in situations where a claimant's benefit is being dealt with inside the same local office, this "does not mean that the claimant has gratuitously to notify it of the actions of its own staff". (para.1). In this case " . . . there was no evidence of any requirement on [the claimant] to send any separate notification to any separately identified section of staff working within what was otherwise presented to him as a single local office of the Department for Work and Pensions . . . " (para.10). The overpayment was accordingly not recoverable. *CIS/3846/2001* has been reported as *R(IS) 4/06*. The decision is authority for four propositions. First, even if the doctrine of *non est factum* applied to social security, which was doubtful, there was no evidence that the form was fundamentally different from the form the claimant thought he was signing and he could reasonably have taken precautions to ascertain its contents and significance (*Lloyds Bank plc v Waterhouse* [1993] 2 FLR 97 followed) (paras 9 to 23). Secondly, there is a difference between acting deliberately and acting dishonestly or fraudulently and it is possible for a claimant to make an innocent misrepresentation by omission (paras 30 and 31). Thirdly, the language of the declaration signed by the claimant could not be read other than as a guarantee that the form had been completed in a way that accurately set out all details that might affect entitlement to the benefit claimed and hence as a misrepresentation and not a failure to disclose (*Chief Adjudication Officer v Sherriff* (reported as *R(IS) 14/96*) followed) (para.39). Finally, in the present case there was no ambiguity or contradiction in the information in the claim form as there was in *CIS/222/1991*, but simply an incompleteness which did not require further investigation by the adjudication officer before deciding the claim and (following *Duggan v Chief Adjudication Officer* (reported as the Appendix to *R(SB) 13/89*)) any failure to investigate by the decision-maker did not relieve the claimant of responsibility for the overpayment (paras 42 to 47).

In *CIS/1867/2006* the claimant sought to rely on telephone advice that the capital limit for income support purposes was £8,000. The claimant, in fact, had capital in excess of £3,000 but below £8,000. As a result of its non-disclosure there was an overpayment of income support. The Commissioner concludes in deciding the case himself that the telephone advice was not given in response to disclosure of possession of capital, and did not relieve the claimant of the obligation to read the disclosure requirements in the back of her payment book. In the course of his decision, the Commissioner indicates that the Secretary of State must, in such cases, provide a copy of the instructions as to disclosure given to a claimant, and must indicate that the diminishing capital rule has been applied (paras 7 and 8 of the decision).

In *C1/06–07(IS)*, a Commissioner in Northern Ireland stresses the importance of the Department's presenting documentary evidence in support of key matters on which the decision to recover overpaid benefit is based. In this case, it was two forms through which the Department claimed to have notified the claimant that he had been found capable of work. Had the claimant disclosed the content of these decisions the overpayment of income support in issue could not have occurred. The Commissioner said:

> "26. . . . In general terms I consider that the Department should supply copies or pro formas of relevant notifications in recoverability cases. In cases where notification is an issue the tribunal should ask to see at least pro formas of these documents if they have not been furnished."

p.52, *annotations to the Social Security Administration Act 1992, s.71*

4.002 *B v Secretary of State* (decision of Court of Appeal and of Tribunal of Commissioners) is reported as *R(IS) 9/06*.

It is understood that CPAG has lodged an application with the European Court of Human Rights in relation to the circumstances of the B case (see para.1.92).

CA/2298/2005 is reported as *R(A) 2/06* (see para.1.92).

p.201, *annotation to the Social Security Act 1998, s.8(3)*

It having been pointed out that there was no power to revise or supersede a decision relating to mobility allowance so as to be able to recover an overpayment (*CDLA/2999/2004*), the Social Security Act 1998 (Prescribed Benefits) Regulations 2006 (SI 2006/2529—see Part I of this Supplement) prescribe a number of benefits payable under the Social Security Act 1975, together with supplementary benefit payable under the Supplementary Benefits Act 1976. The benefits payable under the 1975 Act that are prescribed were all abolished before the 1998 Act came into force and are unemployment benefit, sickness benefit, invalidity benefit, attendance allowance (as paid to those aged under 65), mobility allowance and supplementary benefit.

4.003

p.206, *annotation to the Social Security Act 1998, s.10*

The effect of *CDLA/2999/2004* has now been reversed by the Social Security Act 1998 (Prescribed Benefits) Regulations 2006 (SI 2006/2529), which prescribes mobility allowance (and certain other benefits) for the purposes of s.8(3)(h) of this Act (see Pt I of this Supplement) and by the Social Security Act 1998 (Commencement Nos 9 and 11) (Amendment) Order 2006 (SI 2006/2540), which amends transitional provisions relating to the replacement of sickness and invalidity benefit by incapacity benefit and to the replacement of attendance allowance for people under 65 and mobility allowance by disability living allowance.

4.004

p.206, *annotation to the Social Security Act 1998, s.10(1)*

There are no provisions specifying what constitutes an application for supersession, save that reg.6(5) of the Social Security and Child Support (Decisions and Appeals) Regulations 1999 (SI 1999/991—see p.554 of the main work) provides that the Secretary of State may treat an application for a revision or a notification of a change of circumstances as an application for a supersession. In *CI/954/2006*, the Commissioner doubted that giving information to a medical adviser during an examination was to be treated as an application for supersession, although the Secretary of State could have superseded on his own motion in the light of the information.

Often departmental procedures require a claimant to complete a claim form for what is really a supersession rather than a claim. This can lead to confusion. One example is the practice of requiring claimants of income support who move to a new address to complete a new claim. If this is not done promptly, a claimant may find that there is a gap in benefit payments that is not subsequently made up. The grounds upon which benefit is withheld in those circumstances may be somewhat dubious. In *CI/954/2006*, it was pointed out that where a claimant is in receipt of disablement benefit and suffers another industrial accident, a claim in respect of the subsequent accident may have to be treated in the alternative as an application for supersession of the original award,

4.005

because, following *R(I) 4/03*, aggregation of assessments of disablement is an alternative to the making of two separate awards. One practical difference is that claims may be backdated but supersessions in those circumstances cannot, which the Commissioner suggested is anomalous. The Commissioner also pointed out that an application for supersession of an assessment of disablement needed to be treated also as an application for supersession of the underlying award if proper effect was to be given to any supersession of the assessment of disablement (see the supplemental annotations to regs 6 and 26 of the 1999 Regulations, below).

pp.211–213, *annotation to the Social Security Act 1998, s.12(1)*

4.005a In *CIS/624/2006*, a Tribunal of Commissioners has held that, although an appeal to a tribunal normally lies only against an "outcome decision" (*R(IB) 2/04*), a tribunal hearing an appeal against an "outcome decision" is not always obliged to substitute another such decision.

"When an appeal against an outcome decision raises one issue on which the appeal is allowed but it is necessary to deal with a further issue before another outcome decision is substituted, a tribunal may set aside the original outcome decision without substituting another outcome decision, provided it deals with the original issue raised by the appeal and substitutes a decision on that issue. The Secretary of State must then consider the new issue and decide what outcome decision to give. In that outcome decision, he must give effect to the tribunal's decision on the original issue unless, at the time he makes the outcome decision, he is satisfied that there are grounds on which to supersede the tribunal's decision so as, for instance, to take account of any changes of circumstances that have occurred since he made the decision that was the subject of the appeal to the tribunal. Because his decision is an outcome decision, the claimant will have a right of appeal against it."

The Tribunal of Commissioners gave the following additional guidance—

"Where a tribunal, having dealt with the issues originally raised in an appeal, is not able immediately to give an outcome decision, it must decide whether to adjourn or whether to remit the question of entitlement to the Secretary of State. The technical difficulty of the outstanding issues and the likelihood of a further appeal if the entitlement question is remitted will be relevant considerations. The tribunal should consider whether the Secretary of State would be in a better position to decide the issue and to seek further information from the claimant. It may have to balance the desirability of a decision being made as quickly as possible against the desirability of it being made as accurately as possible, given that an appeal on a point of fact will not lie against a decision of the tribunal on any fresh issue. The wishes of the parties should be taken into account."

Administration, Adjudication and the European Dimension

pp.213–220, *annotation to the Social Security Act 1998, s.12(2)*

An appeal to a tribunal is a rehearing; it is not just a review of the decision under appeal. Therefore, where the Secretary of State has a broad discretion as to the period of disqualification for jobseeker's allowance to be imposed when a person leaves his employment voluntarily without just cause, the tribunal has to substitute its own judgment for that of the Secretary of State, rather than merely considering whether the Secretary of State has acted reasonably (*CJSA/1703/2006*). Moreover, one implication of a tribunal being entitled to correct defects in decisions of the Secretary of State (see p.219 of the main work) is that it may be unnecessary for a tribunal to consider the exact nature of the decision of the Secretary of State that is under appeal; it will usually be enough to consider what he *should* have decided (*CIS/624/2006*).

4.006

There is nothing in s.12 to indicate what powers a tribunal has when it allows an appeal, and it is therefore open to a tribunal to set aside a decision and, in effect, to remit the case to the original decision-maker where that appears to be more appropriate than substituting its own decision. Examples are where the decision under appeal was made without jurisdiction or where a recoverability decision should have been made against a person who is not a party to the appeal (*R(H) 6/06*) or where issues first arise in the course of an appeal (*CIS/624/2006*, where it was made clear that the tribunal must nonetheless deal with the issues originally raised in the appeal—see the supplemental note to s.12(1) above).

At a paper hearing, or a hearing not attended by a claimant, it will always be an error of law for a tribunal to remove an award that has already been made unless the claimant has been given specific notice (in the sense of being focussed on their own particular case) that this is under consideration (*CDLA/1480/2006*).

Although an appeal to a tribunal must be lodged with the Secretary of State or other body from whom the appeal is to be brought, the Secretary of State is not entitled to refuse to refer the case to a tribunal if he considers that the tribunal has no jurisdiction to hear it. It is for the tribunal to determine whether it has jurisdiction to hear a case (*R(I) 7/94*) and, if the Secretary of State were to refuse to refer an appeal lodged at an office of the Department for Work and Pensions to the tribunal, it would be open to the tribunal to consider whether it had jurisdiction and, if it had, to determine the appeal without the appeal having been passed to it by the Secretary of State (*R(H) 1/07*).

In *CH/2484/2006*, the Deputy Commissioner said "it would be unrealistic—especially in a case like this where both parties were represented—to expect tribunals to read every clause of a tenancy agreement in case a representative fails to rely on a clause which might be helpful to his case". He also said—

> "To the extent that the local authority is dissatisfied with the outcome of this case, that perhaps highlights the need for thorough preparation of a local authority's factual case in advance of tribunal hearings, so that all the points can be raised there. Even the most thoroughly

prepared appeal to a Commissioner is not an adequate substitute for doing so, for the reason that, however strongly a Commissioner might doubt the factual correctness of a tribunal decision . . . , the Commissioner's doubts are irrelevant in the absence of an error of law. And it will seldom be an error of law for a tribunal to fail to deal with a point that a local authority representative has not raised before it."

However, it is suggested that overlooking a point that is determinative of a case will usually render a decision erroneous in point of law (as in *R4/01(IS)*, mentioned on p.223 of the main work).

pp.233–239, *annotation to the Social Security Act 1998, s.14(1)*

4.007   The Secretary of State has applied for leave to appeal against *CIS/1363/2005*. Because the claimant's appeal was dismissed by the Commissioner in that case, the Court of Appeal has directed that the application be considered at a hearing in May 2007 where there will be full argument as to the circumstances in which the Court should give leave to appeal to an applicant who does not seek to disturb the final decision being challenged but only the reasoning leading to it.

CI/1804/2005 has been reported as *R(I) 2/06*.

In *CCS/1876/2006*, the Commissioner made the point that the mere fact that a tribunal chairman is not bound to recuse himself when he has previously decided a case against a party before him does not mean that he is not entitled to arrange for the appeal to be heard by another chairman if he considers it desirable do so in order to strengthen the party's confidence in the fairness of the procedures and undue expense will not be involved.

In *CAF/3326/2005*, the Commissioner followed *Chief Supplementary Benefit Officer v Leary* [1985] 1 W.L.R. 84 (also reported as an appendix to *R(SB) 6/85*) in holding that, where a Commissioner exercises a jurisdiction equivalent to that previously exercised by a single judge of the High Court on a statutory appeal, the Commissioner is not bound by the decisions made by judges on such appeals. Single Commissioners approach such cases in the same way as they approach decisions of other single Commissioners, normally following them "in the interests of comity and to secure certainty and avoid confusion on questions of legal principle" but recognising that "a slavish adherence to this could lead to the perpetuation of error" and departing from them when there is a good reason for doing so (*R(I) 12/75*).

pp.240–241, *annotation to the Social Security Act 1998, s.14(8)*

4.008   *CI/1804/2005* has been reported as *R(I) 2/06*.

In *CSIB/808/2005 and CSIB/818/2005*, at paras 66 to 69, the Tribunal of Commissioners said it was wrong to suggest that a Commissioner necessarily had to refer a case to another tribunal, just because no witness had attended to give evidence before the Commissioner and there was a dispute between the parties as to the decision that should be substituted for one that had been set aside. Neither party had suggested there was any material evidence not recorded in the papers or that anything turned on a dispute about that evidence. If the evidence was not in issue, the dispute between the parties was likely to be one of law that a Commissioner should resolve. The Court of Appeal has made a similar point in *Secretary of State for Work and Pensions v Menary-Smith* [2006] EWCA Civ 175. There, a Commissioner had allowed an appeal and referred a case to a tribunal to make further findings of fact but at the same time had expressed some doubt as to effect of the relevant legislation. The Court thought that the tribunal was likely to find its intended role very unclear but felt itself unable to clarify the legal position and was not even sure that it would make any practical difference to the claimant how the legislation was interpreted. "This case needs sorting out, if at all, at Commissioner level." Accordingly, the Court dismissed the appeal before it, save to the extent of directing that the case be determined by a Commissioner rather than a tribunal.

pp.241–242, *annotation to the Social Security Act 1998, s.14(10)*

Where a Commissioner in England refuses leave to appeal in a case that arose in Scotland, or vice versa, both the Court of Session in Scotland and the High Court in England have jurisdiction to consider an application for judicial review. Nonetheless, it is open to a respondent to ask a court to decline jurisdiction on the ground that it would have been more appropriate to bring the proceedings in the other court. In *Tehrani v Secretary of State for the Home Department* [2006] UKHL 47; [2006] 3 W.L.R. 699, where such an issue arose in an immigration case, it was held that the appropriate court would normally be the court in the part of the United Kingdom where the adjudicator (the equivalent of an appeal tribunal) sat. However, there is probably a broader discretion to consider all the circumstances in a social security case, because the House of Lords relied by analogy on the statutory provision defining the appropriate court on an appeal from the Immigration Appeal Tribunal (which depended on where the adjudicator sat), whereas s.15(4) of the Social Security Act 1998 is less prescriptive. 4.009

p.247, *annotation to the Social Security Act 1998, s.16(1)–(3)*

The Secretary of State has applied for leave to appeal against *CIS/ 1363/2005*. See the supplementary annotation to s.14(1) above. 4.010

pp.248–249, *annotation to the Social Security Act 1998, s.17(2)*

In *CIS/3605/2005*, it was held that an erroneous decision on entitlement was a valid revision or supersession decision for the purposes of s.71(5A) of the Social Security Administration Act 1992, so as to enable the Secretary of State to recover an overpayment, but was not conclusive as to the amount of the overpayment, so that only the amount actually overpaid was recoverable. This approach was applied in *CA/2650/2006*, where a tribunal had found a claimant not to be ordinarily resident in 4.011

Great Britain from October 27, 2003, when she had moved abroad, and had upheld a decision superseding her award of attendance allowance from that date. On an appeal against a second tribunal decision to the effect that an overpayment from October 27, 2003 to January 4, 2004 was recoverable from the claimant, the Commissioner found that she had ceased to be ordinarily resident in Great Britain only from January 4, 2004 (even though she was also resident abroad) and so she had not been overpaid benefit as a result of any failure to disclose a material fact. Accordingly, he allowed her appeal. However, under the law as it then stood, the first tribunal ought to have superseded her award only from the date of supersession in February 2004. The Commissioner pointed out that, even if the claimant had in fact ceased to be ordinarily resident in Great Britain on October 27, 2003, the first tribunal would have wrongly decided that she had not been entitled to attendance allowance from then until January 4, 2004, but that decision was final by virtue of s.17(1) of the Social Security Act 1998. Moreover, if she had ceased to be ordinarily resident, she would have actually been overpaid during that period because, had she reported the fact that she had moved overseas straightaway, her award would have been terminated immediately. He considered that, in those circumstances, he would have been bound to find that there had been an overpayment and that it was recoverable, despite the first tribunal's error. That suggestion is, strictly speaking, obiter dicta and the Commissioner did not consider whether a supersession that is technically defective (as opposed to being based on an erroneous finding of fact) might be found to be invalid for the purposes of s.71(5A) so that, even though there was an overpayment, the overpayment would not be recoverable.

In *CIB/3327/2004*, it was pointed out that, although a decision as to whether or not a person is incapable of work that is made on a claim for incapacity benefit is conclusive for the purposes of credits in respect of incapacity for work (by virtue of reg.10 of the Social Security and Child Support (Decisions and Appeals) Regulations 1999, mentioned in the main work), a decision as to whether or not a person is engaged in remunerative work made on a claim for jobseeker's allowance is not conclusive for the purposes of credits in respect of involuntary unemployment.

p.253, *annotation to the Social Security Act 1998, s.20(3)*

4.012   *CIB/3108/2005* has been reported as *R(IB) 2/06*.

p.326, *Civil Partnership Act 2004, s.246*

4.013   With effect from May 11, 2006 the Civil Partnership Act 2004 (Relationships Arising Through Civil Partnership) Order 2006 (SI 2006/1121) applies s.246 to the entry in column (A) of para.7 of Pt 3 of Sch.1 (employment by father, etc.) to the Social Security Categorisation of Earners) Regulations 1978.

Administration, Adjudication and the European Dimension

p.378, *amendment to the Claims and Payments Regulations 1987, reg.4D*

With effect from July 24, 2006, reg.4D was amended by the Social Security (Miscellaneous Amendments) (No. 2) Regulations 2006 (SI 2006/832) as follows: 4.014

(a) in para.(3) the words "by telephone to, or" are omitted;
(b) in para.(6) the words "or by telephone" are omitted;
(c) after para.(6), the following new paragraphs are added:
> "(6A) A claim for state pension credit may be made by telephone call to the telephone number specified by the Secretary of State.
>
> (6B) Where the Secretary of State, in any particular case, directs that the person making the claim approves a written statement of his circumstances, provided for the purpose by the Secretary of State, a claim made by telephone is not a valid claim unless the person complies with the direction.
>
> (6C) A claim made by telephone in accordance with paragraph (6A) is defective unless the Secretary of State is provided, during that telephone call, with all the information he requires to determine the claim.
>
> (6D) Where a claim made by telephone in accordance with paragraph (6A) is defective, the Secretary of State is to provide the person making it with an opportunity to correct the defect.
>
> (6E) If the person corrects the defect within one month, or such longer period as the Secretary of State considers reasonable, of the date the Secretary of State last drew attention to the defect, the Secretary of State shall treat the claim as if it had been duly made in the first instance.";

(d) in para.(12) substitute "Paragraphs (6E) and (11) do" for the words "Paragraphs (11) does".

With effect from October 2, 2006, The Social Security (Miscellaneous Amendments) (No. 3) Regulations 2006 (SI 2006/2377) amended para.(11) by inserting after the word "month" the words "or such longer period as the Secretary of State considers reasonable,".

p.380, *amendment to Claims and Payments Regulations 1987, reg.4F(2)*

With effect from July 24, 2006, reg.4F(2) was amended by the Social Security (Miscellaneous Amendments) (No. 2) Regulations 2006 (SI 2006/832) as follows: 4.015

(a) in sub-para.(b) insert "or (6A)" after the words "4D(3)";
(b) in sub-para.(c) substitute "4D(6E) or (11)" for the words "4D(11)".

p.381, *amendment to the Claims and Payments Regulations 1987, reg.5*

With effect from July 24, 2006, reg.5 was amended by the Social Security (Miscellaneous Amendments) (No. 2) Regulations 2006 (SI   4.016

2006/832) by inserting the words "or 4D(6A)" after the words "regulation 4(11)".

p.382, *amendment to the Claims and Payments Regulations 1987, reg.6.*

4.017 With effect from October 2, 2006, the Social Security (Miscellaneous Amendments) (No. 3) Regulations 2006 (SI 2006/2377) amended reg.6 as follows:

(c) by inserting in sub-para.(19)(b) before the word "re-awarded" the words "awarded or";
(d) by substituting the following for para.(20):
"(20) The circumstances referred to in paragraph (19) are—
(a) that the award of the qualifying benefit has itself been terminated or reduced by means of a revision, supersession, appeal or termination of an award for a fixed period in such a way as to affect the original award; or
(b) at the date the original award was terminated the claimant's claim for a qualifying benefit had not been decided."
(e) by substituting the following for sub-para.(21)(b):
"(b) the further claim is made within three months of the date on which the qualifying benefit is awarded following a claim, whether initially, on revision or on appeal, or re-awarded following revision, supersession, appeal or further claim when an award for a fixed period expires, whether benefit is re-awarded when the further claim is decided or following a revision of, or an appeal against, such a decision."

CIS/2726/2005 is now reported as *R(IS) 10/06* (see para.2.71).

Something has gone wrong with the annotations on p.386 of the main volume relating to paras (24) to (26) of reg.6. Paragraphs (24) to (26) relate to incapacity benefit, and not to the benefits stated in the annotations.

p.382, *annotations to the Claims and Payments Regulations 1987, reg.6*

4.018 *CIS/2726/2005* (see para.2.71) is reported as *R(IS) 10/06*.

CG/2973/2004 has been appealed to the Court of Appeal and upheld in *Levy v Secretary of State for Work and Pensions*, [2006] EWCA Civ 890, reported as *R(G) 2/06*. The Court of Appeal ruled that reg.6(1) was not ultra vires. The next question was whether s.7 of the Interpretation Act 1978 applied. Dyson L.J. (with whom Hallett and Pill L.JJ. agreed) concluded that the provision has no application in this context. Even if s.7 did apply, its application would appear to be excluded by the words "unless the contrary intention appears" in s.7 of the Interpretation Act. The Court of Appeal concludes that "It is plain that regulation 6(1) requires that the claim be received in fact and not merely that it be sent." (para.32 of the judgment). It follows that *CIS/306/2003* and

CG/2973/2004 correctly analyse the legal position and that *CSIS/48/1992* and *CIS/759/1992* are wrong in so far as they suggest otherwise.

p.398, *correction to the Claims and Payments Regulations 1987, text of reg.7(3)*

The text should read: 4.019

"(3) In the case of a claim for working families' tax credit or disabled person's tax credit, the employer of the claimant or, as the case may be, of the partner shall [within one month of being required to do so or such longer period as the Board may consider reasonable] furnish such certificates, documents, information and evidence in connection with the claim or any question arising out of it as may be required by the Secretary of State [Board]."

The words in square brackets are inserted for the purposes of tax credits only.

p.405, *annotations to the Claims and Payments Regulations 1987*

Bhakta and the Commissioner's decisions are now reported as *R(IS) 7/06*. Note that the Government is planning to legislate to reverse the effect of these decisions. 4.020

p.407, *annotations to the Claims and Payments Regulations 1987, reg.13A*

See also *CSDLA/242/2006*. 4.021

p.417, *amendment to the Claims and Payments Regulations 1987, reg.19*

With effect from October 2, 2006, The Social Security (Miscellaneous Amendments) (No.3) Regulations 2006 (SI 2006/2377) amended reg.19 by adding a new sub-paragraph after sub-para.(i) as follows: 4.022

"(j) the claimant was unable to make telephone contact with the appropriate office where he would be expected to notify his intention of making a claim because the telephone lines to that office were busy or inoperative."

p.452, *annotations to the Claims and Payments Regulations 1987, reg.30*

The text of the last two lines of para.(6C) should read, "shall be extended by such period, not exceeding 6 months, as may be specified in the certificate".

In *CDLA/2807/2003* the Commissioner said: 4.023

"It seems to me quite impossible to say in circumstances where the operative decision is that no benefit is payable that any right to payment, let alone a right to payment of any amount that has been quantified, is in existence. There could be no right to payment until that decision has been altered in some way. Regulation 38 simply cannot have any operation in such circumstances."

Administration, Adjudication and the European Dimension

p.472, *amendment to the Claims and Payments Regulations 1987, Sch.9*

4.024 With effect from October 2, 2006, the Social Security (Miscellaneous Amendments) (No. 3) Regulations 2006 (SI 2006/2377) amended Sch.9 as follows:

(f) in para.5(5), by omitting the words from "a sum equal to" to the end and substituting "a sum calculated in accordance with paragraph 8(4);"
(g) by omitting para.5(5A);
(h) in para.6(6) by omitting the words from "a sum equal to" to the end and substituting "a sum calculated in accordance with paragraph 8(4);"
(i) by omitting para.6(6A);
(j) in para.7(8) by omitting the words from "a sum equal to" to the end and substituting "a sum calculated in accordance with paragraph 8(4);"
(k) by omitting para.7(9);
(l) in para.8(2) by omitting the words from "a sum equal to" to the end and substituting "a sum calculated in accordance with sub-paragraph (4);"
(m) by omitting para.8(2A);
(n) by inserting after para.8(3) the following new paragraph:

"(4) The sum referred to in sub-paragraph (2) is—
(a) where the claimant or partner does not receive child tax credit, 25 per cent of—
  (i) in the case of income support, the applicable amount for the family as is awarded under sub-paragraphs (a) to (d) of regulation 17(1) (applicable amounts) or sub-paragraphs (a) to (e) of regulation 18(1) (polygamous marriages) of the Income Support Regulations;
  (ii) in the case of jobseeker's allowance, the applicable amount for the family as is awarded under paragraphs (a) to (e) of regulation 83 (applicable amounts) or sub-paragraphs (a) to (f) of regulation 84(1) (polygamous marriages) of the Jobseeker's Allowance Regulations; or
  (iii) in the case of state pension credit, the appropriate minimum guarantee less any housing costs under Schedule 2 to the State Pension Credit Regulations 2002 which may be applicable in the particular case; or
(b) where the claimant or his partner receives child tax credit, 25 per cent of the sum of—
  (i) the amount mentioned in sub-paragraphs (a)(i) to (iii), which applies to the claimant;
  (ii) the amount of child benefit awarded to him or his partner by the Board under Part 2 of the Tax Credits Act 2002; and

(iii) the amount of child tax credit awarded to him or his partner by the Board under section 8 of that Act."

p.484, *amendment to the Claims and Payments Regulations 1987, Sch.9A*

With effect from October 1, 2006, the Social Security (Miscellaneous Amendments) (No. 4) Regulations 2006 (SI 2006/2378), amended para.8(c) by substituting for the words "Scottish Homes" the words "Communities Scotland".

4.025–
4.026

p.536, *annotation to the Decisions and Appeals Regulations, reg.1(3)*

Since it was decided in *CDLA/1707/2005* that a tribunal is entitled to substitute a revision for a supersession or refusal to supersede (see p.219 of the main work), there have been a number of decision on the meaning of "official error". In *CDLA/393/2006*, the Commissioner regarded the adjudication officer's reliance on the claim form without obtaining further evidence as "a failure in the proper standards of administration" but found that the claimant's mother had contributed to the error by the way in which she had completed the claim form. There was therefore no "official error". He said that "in judging what was a material contribution a common sense approach should be taken, rather than a highly refined analysis of causation" and that the way the claim form had been completed should not be seen as merely the setting for the adjudication officer's error. In *CH/687/2006*, the claimant was overpaid housing benefit because the amount of her partner's incapacity benefit changed due to the length of time he had been incapable of work. The Deputy Commissioner reviewed the cases and held that there was no official error. Although the local authority had known that the incapacity benefit in payment when the award was made was only short-term incapacity benefit, which would inevitably be replaced by a higher rate if the claimant's partner continued to be incapable of work, the local authority had been entitled to presume that any change in the rate of incapacity benefit would be reported to it. This can therefore be seen as another case where the claimant contributed to the error. In *CPC/206/2005*, the Commissioner stated that the term "official error" is not confined to errors of law but said that it "involves more than merely taking a decision that another decision-maker with the same information would not take". He considered that it would not be helpful further to explain what the term meant. However, he found an official error in the case because "no Secretary of State or decision-maker acting reasonably could have [made the decision under appeal]". That would have been an error of law and it is perhaps difficult to envisage an official error that would not be an error of law in its public law sense (see p.233 *et seq.* in the main work).

4.027

p.538, *annotation to the Decisions and Appeals Regulations, reg.2*

Levy v Secretary of State for Work and Pensions [2006] EWCA Civ 890 has been reported as *R(G) 2/06*.

4.028

Administration, Adjudication and the European Dimension

pp.556–562, annotation to the Decisions and Appeals Regulations, reg.6

4.029 In *CI/954/2006*, the Commissioner held that an application to supersede an assessment of disablement should generally be treated as also an application to supersede the underlying award, because, if an award on the ground that a new assessment has been made, the effective date will not be the effective date of the new assessment. He also held that, where a person who had been awarded disablement benefit suffered another industrial accident, a claim for disablement benefit in respect of the second accident might have to be treated in the alternative as an application for supersession of the first award and he pointed out that there is an anomolous difference in the extent to which a claim and an application for supersession can be backdated. He doubted that giving information to a medical advisor during a medical examination amounted to an application for supersession (although a notification of a change of circumstances may be treated as an application for supersession—see para.(5)), but he suggested that the Secretary of State could have made a supsersession decision of his own motion when the information was passed to him.

Although reg.6(2)(a)(i) enables the Secretary of State to supersede a decision on the ground that there has been a change of circumstances "since the decision had effect", a Tribunal of Commissioners has suggested that it would be improper for the Secretary of State to do so where the decision being superseded was that of a tribunal and, because the change of circumstances occurred before the decision under appeal and the tribunal was well aware of it, the tribunal could have taken it into account notwithstanding section 12(8)(b) of the Social Security Act 1998, (*CIS/624/2006*). "The Secretary of State should abide by a tribunal's decision in such circumstances."

p.563, *Decisions and Appeals Regulations, reg.7(2)*

4.030 A new sub-para.(2)(bc) is added to reg.7 by the Social Security (Miscellaneous Amendments) (No. 3) Regulations 2006 (SI 2006/2377), reg.3(2), with effect from October 2, 2006:

> "(bc) where the decision is advantageous to the claimant and is made in connection with the cessation of payment of a carer's allowance, the day after the last day for which that allowance was paid;".

pp.576–577, annotation to the Decisions and Appeals Regulations, reg.7A

4.031 In *CA/2650/2006*, the Commissioner held that the reference to s.64 of the Contributions and Benefits Act (which has a different structure from that in ss.72 and 73) in head (a) of the definition of "disability determination" refers only to "determinations whether the conditions set out in section 64(2) and (3) were satisfied (and possibly extending to age and non-entitlement to DLA)" and so does not extend to determinations as to residence or presence.

Administration, Adjudication and the European Dimension

p.595, *annotation to the Decisions and Appeals Regulations, reg.26*

In *CI/954/2006*, the Commissioner pointed to the difficulties caused as a result of reg.26(c) separating the adjudication of assessments of disablement from the adjudication of awards of benefit and held that an application to supersede an assessment of disablement should generally be treated as also an application to supersede the underlying award so that full effect could be given to any new assessment decision.

4.032

p.599, *annotation to the Decisions and Appeals Regulations, reg.30*

In *CIS/624/2006*, a decision was made in 2003 to the effect that the claimant was not entitled to income support from May 17, 2002. When the claimant appealed, the decision was revised and income support was paid in respect of the period from May 17, 2002 to July 31, 2002. It was held that reg.30(2)(a) did not require the appeal to be treated as having lapsed in respect of the period from August 1, 2002. The Tribunal of Commissioners said—

4.032a

" . . . where a period before the date of the original decision is in issue and a revision affects only part of that period, it seems to us that there are many circumstances in which it can be appropriate to regard the decision as being more advantageous to the appellant only in respect of that part of the period and not the remainder of the period. This is particularly so where the Secretary of State knows very well that the revision does not deal with the main issue raise by the appeal and that it would be a waste of time to treat the appeal as having lapsed and to require the appellant to start all over again."

p.601, *annotation to the Decisions and Appeals Regulations, reg.31(4)*

The Secretary of State has applied for leave to appeal against *CIS/1363/2005*. Because the claimant's appeal was dismissed by the Commissioner in that case, the Court of Appeal has directed that the application be considered at a hearing in May 2007 where there will be full argument as to the circumstances in which the Court should give leave to appeal to an applicant who does not seek to disturb the final decision being challenged but only the reasoning leading to it.

4.033

p.603, *annotation to the Decisions and Appeals Regulations, reg.32(4)*

The Secretary of State has applied for leave to appeal against *CIS/1363/2005*. See the supplemental note to reg.31(4) above.

4.034

pp.614–615, *annotation to the Decisions and Appeals Regulations, reg.39*

At a paper hearing, or a hearing not attended by a claimant, it will always be an error of law for a tribunal to remove an award that has already been made unless the claimant has been given specific notice (in the sense of being focussed on their own particular case) that this is under consideration (*CDLA/1480/2006*).

4.035

Administration, Adjudication and the European Dimension

p.621, *annotation to the Decisions and Appeals Regulations, reg.46*

4.036　　The Secretary of State has applied for leave to appeal against *CIS/ 1363/2005*. See the supplemental note to reg.31(4) above.

p.624, *annotation to the Decisions and Appeals Regulations, reg.49(1)*

4.037　　*CDLA/145/2006* has been reported as *R(DLA) 2/06*.

pp.628–631, *annotation to the Decisions and Appeals Regulations, reg.51*

4.038　　There is no general rule that an appeal to a tribunal should be postponed while related criminal proceedings are pending (*R(IS) 1/07*). The wishes of the parties will be relevant but will not be determinative. Often a claimant will not wish an appeal to be heard while criminal proceedings are pending lest anything he says at the tribunal hearing is used against him in the criminal trial. However, another claimant may prefer an appeal to be heard first because a finding that he or she was entitled to benefit is likely to undermine a prosecution for obtaining the same benefit by deception.

Adjournments are sometimes necessary because a member of the tribunal is obliged to stand down to avoid an appearance of bias (see pp.237–8 of the main work). In *CCS/1876/2006*, the Commissioner suggested that there might be occasions when it was prudent for a member of a tribunal to stand down in order to strengthen a party's confidence in the fairness of the procedures, even if there was no strict legal duty to do so, but he did acknowledge that the expense of an adjournment had to be kept in mind.

p.632, *annotation to the Decisions and Appeals Regulations, reg.53(1)*

4.038a　　Where an appeal is against an "outcome decision" expressed in terms of a claimant's entitlement to benefit, a decision notice "should make it absolutely clear whether the tribunal has made an outcome decision (subject, in some cases, to the precise amount being calculated by the Secretary of State) or has remitted the final decision on entitlement to the Secretary of State" (*CIS/624/2006*, in which it was suggested that the President of appeal tribunals might wish to consider whether the form of decision notice usually issued in income support and similar cases should be altered to assist chairmen with that task).

p.636, *annotation to the Decisions and Appeals Regulations, reg.53(4)*

4.039　　Erratum: *CIS/1814/2004* was an erroneous reference. The correct reference is now *R(I) 2/06*.

p.642, *annotation to the Decisions and Appeals Regulations, reg.55(1)*

4.039a　　Because a statement of reasons ought to deal with the principal points raised by the parties but a tribunal is not always required to consider points that have not been explicitly raised, the record of proceedings may be an important document on an appeal to a Commissioner, as it should record the parties' arguments. It may, however, be supplemented. In *CH/2484/2006*, the Deputy Commissioner said—

> "I appreciate that a record of proceedings is not a complete *verbatim* note and that it is possible for points to be omitted, but if an appellant to the Commissioner wishes to base a submission on the overlooking of evidence or submissions and the evidence or submission are not recorded in the record, it seems to me to be necessary as a general rule for it to equip itself with evidence (such as a statement by someone who was present) that that piece of evidence or submission was in fact made. It should also raise the matter with the other side in advance, so as to avoid surprise and facilitate agreement on the position if possible."

In that case, the local authority was the appellant. Where a claimant is an appellant and the Secretary of State was not present at the hearing before the tribunal, the Secretary of State will not be in a position to dispute a statement by the claimant as to what occurred at that hearing. It will be open to a Commissioner to seek the views of the tribunal but he or she will not be obliged to do so.

pp.645–647, *annotation to the Decisions and Appeals Regulations, reg.57(1)*

An appeal against *CG/2973/2004* was dismissed by the Court of Appeal (*Levy v Secretary of State for Work and Pensions* [2006] EWCA Civ 890 (reported as *R(G) 2/06)*). 4.040

p.660, *amendment to the Decisions and Appeals Regulations, Sch.3A, para.3*

A new para.3(h) is added to Sch.3A by the Social Security (Miscellaneous Amendments) (No. 3) Regulations 2006 (SI 2006/2377), reg.3(3), with effect from October 2, 2006. 4.041

"(h) regulation 9 of the Social Security (Disability Living Allowance) Regulations 1991 (persons in certain accommodation other than hospitals) applies, or ceases to apply, to the claimant for a period of less than one week."

p.676, *amendment to the General Benefit Regulations 1982, reg.16*

With effect from October 1, 2006, the Social Security (Miscellaneous Amendments) (No. 4) Regulations 2006, (SI 2006/2378) substituted the sum of "£4,472" for the sum "£4,212". 4.041a

p.704, *amendment to the Jobcentre Plus Interviews Regulations, reg.2*

With effect from April 24, 2006, the Social Security (Working Neighbourhoods) Miscellaneous Amendment Regulations 2006 (SI 4.042

2006/909), amended reg.2(3) by omitting the words from "or where a person" to the words "regulation 2(3) of those Regulations,".

p.715, *amendment to the Jobcentre Plus Interviews Regulations, reg.16*

4.043 With effect from April 24, 2006, the Social Security (Working Neighbourhoods) Miscellaneous Amendment Regulations 2006 (SI 2006/909), amended reg.16 by omitting the words from "and except where a person" to "regulation 2(3) of those regulations."

p.716, *amendment to the Jobcentre Plus Interviews Regulations, reg.2*

4.044 With effect from April 24, 2006, the Social Security (Working Neighbourhoods) Miscellaneous Amendment Regulations 2006 (SI 2006/909) amend reg.2(2) by omitting the words from "Except in a case where" to "regulation 2(3) of those Regulations."

p.812, *amendment to the Work-focussed Interviews Regulations, reg.4*

4.045 With effect from April 24, 2006, The Social Security (Working Neighbourhoods) Miscellaneous Amendment Regulations 2006 (SI 2006/909) amend reg.4 as follows:

(o) in para.(1)(c) the words ", the Social Security (Working Neighbourhoods) Regulations 2004" are omitted;
(p) para.(2) is omitted.

p.816, *revocation of the Working Neighbourhoods Regulations*

4.046 With effect from April 24, 2006, these regulations (save for regs 22, 24, 25(1), (2) and (4) and 26(1) and (3)) were revoked by the Social Security (Working Neighbourhoods) Miscellaneous Amendment Regulations 2006 (SI 2006/909), subject to transitional provisions for employment zones (which came to an end on October 31, 2006) to be found in reg.4 of these amending regulations.

The explanatory note to the amending regulations provides:

"These Regulations revoke most of the Social Security (Working Neighbourhoods) Regulations 2004 ("the Neighbourhoods Regulations") (S.I. 2004/959) from 24th April 2006. Regulation 2 makes consequential revocations to other legislation.Regulation 3(2) keeps small parts of the Neighbourhoods Regulations in force so that other legislation operates correctly in two ways. Firstly, regulations 22 and 24 of the Neighbourhoods Regulations amend the Social Security (Claims and Payments) Regulations 1987 (S.I. 1987/1968) and the Social Security and Child Support (Decisions and Appeals) Regulations 1999 (S.I. 1999/991) so that they refer to all Regulations made under certain powers. Without those amendments, the Regulations amended would only apply to specified Regulations made under those powers. Secondly, regulations 25 to 27 of the Neighbourhoods Regulations amend other Regulations which require claimants to take part in work-focused interviews. Without those amendments, claimants could be required to take part in an interview under those other Regulations immediately after these Regulations come into force. Regulation 4 contains transitional provisions. The parts of the Neighbourhoods Regulations relating to employment zones continue to apply to a claimant who is participating in an employment zone programme under those Regulations on 23rd April 2006. The transitional provisions will end by 31st October 2006."

p.912, *annotations to the European Communities Act 1972, s.2*

Walker-Fox is now reported as *R(IS) 3/06* (see para.3.13).   4.047

p.924, *annotation to Art.18 EC*

In case C–406/04 *De Cuyper*, judgment of July 18, 2006, the Court of Justice ruled that freedom of movement and residence, conferred on citizens of the Union under Art.18 EC, does not preclude a residence clause, which is imposed on an unemployed person over 50 years of age who is exempt from the requirement of providing that he is available for work, as a condition for the retention of his entitlement to unemployment benefit. De Cuyper, a Belgian national, was born in 1942. He was no longer required to "submit to the local control procedures" in connection with his entitlement to unemployment benefit because he was over 50 years of age. Following a routine check, it was established that he spent considerable periods each year living in France. He was subsequently refused unemployment benefit. The Court of Justice concluded that the benefit in question was an unemployment benefit (as distinct from a pre-retirement benefit) and that, although the restriction on his right of movement if he was to remain entitled to unemployment benefit was a restriction on his right to free movement, the requirement for residence was objectively justifiable having regard to the need to monitor the employment and family situation of unemployed persons. There was no less restrictive measure capable of meeting the monitoring requirement.   4.048

Collins in the Court of Justice and in the Court of Appeal is now reported as *R(JSA) 3/06* (see para.3.31).

A series of cases decided by a Tribunal of Commissioners (*CIS/3573/2005; CPC/2920/2005; CIS/2559/2005; CIS/2680/2005* and *CH/2484/2005*) has determined that non economically active nationals of the Member States (and of the EEA countries) do not acquire a right to reside under Community law and any discrimination which arises as a consequence of such nationals being required to establish a right to reside is objectively justified and proportionate. A memorandum (Memo DMG Vol.2 01/06) from the Department for Work and Pensions indicates that the changes consequent upon the entry into force of Directive 2004/38/EC (the "Citizenship Directive") do not alter the position. Three of these cases (*CIS/3573/2005; CPC/2920/2005* and *CH/2484/2005)* are under appeal to the Court of Appeal as *Abdirahman, Abdirahman and Uluslow v Secretary of State for Work and Pensions.* See also the Northern Ireland decision in *C 6/05–06 (IS)* to similar effect in the case of a Polish worker who had ceased to work; this case is under appeal to the Northern Ireland Court of Appeal as *Zalewska v Department for Social Development*.

In *CIS/3875/2005* the Commissioner found that a French national could not claim a right to reside in Community law based on his being a recipient of services. It may be significant that the Commissioner did not consider the *Carpenter* case (C–60/00 *Carpenter v Secretary of State for the Home Department,* [2002] ECR I-6279). See also *CIS/3182/2005* which concerned a Dutch national who had worked for about six weeks before giving up work because she was pregnant. The Commissioner concluded that she had no right to reside under the United Kingdom regulations. See also *CH/3314/2005 and CIS/3315/2005* which concerned a person who claimed to be seeking work, but who had worked from mid-July to mid-October 2004; the Commissioner ruled that she nevertheless had no "right to reside" in the United Kingdom.

CH/1400/2006 concerned a woman who was a Slovenian national. She had entered the United Kingdom with her three children in September 2003. She began a postgraduate course in contemporary cinema cultures in September 2004. In July 2005 she applied for housing benefit, and had appealed against its refusal. The tribunal had held that she had a right to reside under Community law as a person receiving services, namely the education on the course on which she was enrolled at the time of her claim. The Commissioner allowed the local authority's appeal on the grounds that the claimant was a person from abroad. In coming to that conclusion, he relied on Case C–263/86 *Humbel,* [1988] ECR 5365, and Case C–109/92, *Wirth,* [1993] ECR I-6447 in concluding that the provision of education was not the provision of services. It is certainly possible to read paras 18 and 19 of the Luxembourg Court's ruling in *Wirth* as *not applying* to the provision of a course in a University where a student is paying (as in this case) full cost fees because she has the status of an overseas student. The Commissioner went on to consider whether the claimant had a right to reside as a student under the terms of the Students Directive (Directive 93/96/EEC) but concluded that this Directive required a student to have "sufficient resources to avoid becoming a burden on the social assistance system of the host Member State". However, in coming to that conclusion the Commissioner does not refer to Case C-184/99 *Grzelczyk* (see para.3.31 of Vol.III) where the Court accepted that, in the case of students, what was required was an assurance of sufficient resources, which may be frustrated by the passage of time, and which does not preclude access to national assistance. The Commissioner also rejected a final argument based on Regulation 1408/71. It seems that no argument was presented based upon Case C-456/02 *Trojani* (see para.3.31 of Vol.III) on the grounds that the claimant was lawfully resident in the United Kingdom, and on these grounds alone was entitled to equal treatment.

In *W (China) and X (China) v Secretary of State for the Home Department,* [2006] EWCA Civ 1494, rather surprisingly, distinguished the decision of the Court of Justice in the *Chen* case (Case C-200/02, *Zhu and Chen*, [2004] ECR I-9925) in which it had held that third country nationals who were the parents of a Union citizen—in this case a baby born in Northern Ireland who thereby became entitled to Irish citizenship—had a right to reside in a Member State since otherwise the entitlement of the child to reside would be rendered nugatory. The Court of Appeal indicated disagreement with the decision in the *Chen* case on the grounds that certain matters were not argued. In approaching the case the way it did, the Court of Appeal focused exclusively on the technical requirements of Directive 90/364, giving it a priority which the Court of Justice had not, and arguably failed to give sufficient weight to the growing case law on rights flowing from Union citizenship provided in the Treaty.

In Case C-1/05 *Yunying Jia v Migrationsverket*, judgment of January 9, 2007, the Court of Justice ruled:

"Article 1(1)(d) of Council Directive 73/148/EEC of 21 May 1973 on the abolition of restrictions of movement and residence within the Community for nationals of Member States with regard to establishment and the provision of services is to be interpreted to the effect the 'dependent on them' means that members of the family of a Community national established in another Member State within the meaning of Article 43 EC need the material support of that Community national or his or her spouse in order to meet their essential needs in the State of origin of those family members or the State from which they have come at the time when they apply to join that Community national. Article 6(b) of that directive must be interpreted as meaning that proof of the need for material support may be adduced by any appropriate means, while a mere undertaking from the Community national or his or her spouse to support the family members concerned need not be regarded as establishing the existence of the family members' situation of real dependence."

p.927, *annotation to Art.39*

A person does not cease to be a worker for the purposes of Art.39 simply by ceasing to be employed. So a German worker whose employment ended not long after it had started when she suffered a back injury did not, by that reason alone, cease to be a worker: *CIS/3890/2005*. Note that Art.7(3)(a) of the Citizenship Directive expressly provides that a person temporarily unable to work by reason of illness or accident retains the status of a worker. Furthermore, Art.17(1)(b) affords a right of permanent residence to those who become permanently incapacitated for work after a continuous period of residence in the host Member State for two years.

4.049

p.942, *annotation to Art.7, Reg.1612/68*

Collins in the Court of Justice and in the Court of Appeal is now reported as *R(JSA) 3/06* (see para.3.57).

4.050

p.950, *annotation to Dir. 2004/38/EC*

4.051 Note that The Immigration (European Economics Are) Regulations 2006 (SI 2006/1003) implement in United Kingdom law the requirements of the Directive.

p.953, *annotation to Art.1, Citizenship Directive*

4.052 See notes under p.924 above on Commissioners' decisions on the "right to reside".

p.982, *annotation to Art.4, Reg.1408/71*

4.053 *Walker-Fox*, in which *CIS/488/2004* was over-turned, is now reported as *R(IS) 3/06* (see para.3.113).
CIS/1491/2004 is now reported as *R(IS) 8/06*.

p.991, *annotation to Art.13, Reg.1408/71*

4.054 *CF/1727/2006* contains guidance on the procedure for obtaining a formal decision of the National Insurance Contributions Office as to a person's liability to pay national insurance contributions. That is important for Regulation 1408/71, since it will also determine which law is applicable to a claim for child benefit.

p.1192, *annotations to Art.1, Reg.859/2003*

4.055 The House of Lords overruled the Court of Appeal in *Szoma*, and held that persons admitted to the United Kingdom who are subject to immigration control are lawfully present in the United Kingdom: [2005] UKHL 64, reported as *R(IS) 2/06*.

p.1200, *annotations to Art.7, Dir.79/7/EEC*

4.056 *Richards* is now reported as *R(P) 1/07*.

p.1211, *annotation to Human Rights Act 1998, s.2*

4.057 *Kay v London Borough of Lambeth, Leeds City Council v Price* [2006] UKHL 10, [2006] 2 WLR 570 provides guidance for courts and tribunals when faced with a judgment of the Court of Human Rights which conflicts with an earlier binding authority of a national court. Both Justice and Liberty were permitted to intervene in the case. The court rejected the argument that a lower court could depart from what would otherwise be a binding precedent of a higher court where there was a later judgment of the Court of Human Rights which was clearly inconsistent with the judgment of the higher court. The effect of the House of Lords ruling is that the development of case law will be influenced by the judgments of the Court of Human Rights, but that legal certainty can only be maintained if conflicts between decisions of the Court of Human

Rights and those of national courts are determined within the hierarchy of courts in the national legal order.

There are aftershocks of this decision in the social security context in the context of whether non-contributory benefits are "possessions" within Art.1 of Protocol 1. So, for example, both *Couronne* and *CIS/ 1757/2006* (para.40) decide that they were bound to follow *Reynolds* and *Campbell R(H) 1/06* in the Court of Appeal to the effect that non-contributory benefits are not possessions, notwithstanding the decision of the Grand Chamber to the contrary in *Stec*. It is understood that CPAG are concerned about this approach and have raised the matter with the Department for Work and Pensions. There is certain to be further case law on this point in the social security context. In such litigation it would be argued that the special circumstances of the post-Court of Appeal litigation in *Reynolds* would provide grounds for *not* following the general rule laid down in *Price*.

p.1220, *annotations to Human Rights Act 1998, s.3*

Esfandiari is now reported as *R(IS) 11/06*.   4.058

p.1239, *annotations to Art.6 ECHR*

Gillies in the House of Lords is reported as *R(DLA) 5/06* (see para.4.62).   4.059

In *C5/05–06 (IB)* a Commissioner in Northern Ireland set aside the decision of a tribunal where the claimant had asked for an oral hearing but did not attend. The claimant subsequently indicated that he had not received notification of the hearing, nor had his solicitors. The Commissioner, following *CDLA/5413/1999*, appears to consider that in such circumstances there had been a breach of Art.6.

In *Elo v Finland* (App. 30742/02) the Court of Human Rights was considering a complaint that the lack of an oral hearing before an Accident Board whose task was to determine the level of disability following an accident at work. The Court found no breach of Art.6. It stated the general proposition, " . . . unless there are exceptional circumstances that justify dispensing with a hearing, the right to a public hearing under Article 6(1) implies a right to an oral hearing at least before one instance." (para.34). The Court went on:

> "1. The Court reiterates that the character of the circumstances that may justify dispensing with an oral hearing essentially comes down to the nature of the issues to be decided by the competent national court not to the frequency with which such issues come before the courts. This does not mean that refusing to hold an oral hearing may be justified only in rare cases (see *Miller v. Sweden*, no. 55853/00, § 29, 8 February 2005). Thus, the Court has recognised that disputes concerning benefits under social-security schemes are generally rather technical and their outcome usually depends on the written opinions

given by medical doctors. Many such disputes may accordingly be better dealt with in writing than in oral argument. Moreover, it is understandable that in this sphere the national authorities should have regard to the demands of efficiency and economy. Systematically holding hearings could be an obstacle to the particular diligence required in social-security cases (see *Schuler-Zgraggen v. Switzerland*, cited above, pp.19–20, § 58).

2. Turning to the particular circumstances of the present case, the Court observes that the jurisdiction of the Accident Board and the Insurance Court was not limited to matters of law but also extended to factual issues. The issue before them was whether the applicant's injuries attained the category 7 disability on the scale of injuries and whether his injuries could have been assessed under the general title "the lower extremities as a whole" as alleged by the applicant. The question is whether hearing oral evidence from the applicant and the doctors treating him could have produced anything relevant and decisive which was not already encompassed in the written evidence and submissions. The Accident Board found an oral hearing manifestly unnecessary. Nor did the Insurance Court find an oral hearing necessary as the decisive factor for reaching a decision in the applicant's case was the medical opinions on the applicant's injuries.

3. The Court observes that under the Ministry's decision the personal circumstances of a claimant are not taken into account when assessing the disability category to be attributed. Thus the Accident's Board's and Insurance Court's assessments were entirely based on the medical evidence in the case, presented in the form of written medical certificates issued by the applicant's doctors. The medical certificates on which the applicant relied supported his claim. It does not appear that the doctors' opinions differed (see, *mutatis mutandis*, *Döry v. Sweden*, cited above, § 42). The Court sees no reason to differ from the finding of the Insurance Court that the applicant's entitlement to compensation had to be based on the evaluation of the injuries sustained to his heels and ankles, which assessment could be made on the basis of the written medical evidence. Further, there is no indication that a hearing was needed in order to hear oral testimony (see *Ringel v. Sweden* (Dec.), no. 13599/03, 23 March 2004).

4. In these circumstances, it must be concluded that the dispute in the case concerned the correct interpretation of written medical evidence. The Court considers that the Accident Board and the Insurance Court could adequately resolve this issue on the basis of the medical certificates before them and the applicant's written submissions.

5. Having regard to the foregoing, the Court finds that there were circumstances which justified dispensing with a hearing in the applicant's case."

Tsfayo v United Kingdom (App.60860) judgment of November 14, 2006, is now largely of historical interest, but a violation of Art.6 was found on the grounds that the Housing Benefit Review Board was not an independent and impartial tribunal.

p.1258, *annotations to Art.8 ECHR*

In *Grant v United Kingdom* (App.32570/03), judgment of May 23, 2006, the Court of Human Rights ruled that there was a violation of Art.8 from the day of its judgment in the *Goodwin* and *I* cases, where the United Kingdom refused to make State pension payments to a post-operative male to female transsexual at the age of 60. The violation of Convention rights arose from the breach of her right to respect for her private life as a woman.

4.060

In *C1/05–06 (WB), C2/05–06 (WB), and C3/05–06 (WB)*, a Commissioner in Northern Ireland concluded that an absolute three months time limit for claiming widow's benefit does not violate Art.8. She said:

"17. . . . I am doubtful that the three month time limit for claiming a benefit can in any way be linked to or have a "meaningful connection" with an Article 8 right in the absence of any Article 14 discrimination. However, even if a link exists, it is too tenuous to be within the ambit of the right. The right is not to the benefit but to the respect set out in Article 8. The time limit in no way violates that respect."

p.1263, *annotation to Art.14, ECHR*

On August 22, 2006, the Court of Human Rights handed down its judgments in *Pearson v United Kingdom* and *Walker v United Kingdom* (opera. 4.76 of Vol.III). In both cases, the Court followed its decision in *Stec*, in ruling that differential State pensionable ages, and a requirement for men to continue to make national insurance contributions must be regarded as pursing a legitimate aim and as being reasonably and objectively justified.

4.061

In *H E Manning v Revenue and Customs Commissioners*, SpC552, decision of July 3, 2006, the Special Commissioner held, in the face of claims by a self-employed person that there was a breach of Art.14 read together with Art.1 of Protocol 1, that it was not discriminatory that national insurance contributions for the employed ceased at the age of 65 whereas Class 4 contributions for the self-employed ceased if the person had attained that age at the beginning of the tax year. The Special Commissioner noted that admissibility decisions of the European Commission of Human Rights had held that difference in treatment between the employed and self-employed was justified, and that any difference in treatment was wholly in favour of self-employed people.

Esfandiari is now reported as *R(IS) 11/06* (see paras 4.77 and 4.80).
Francis is now reported as *R(IS) 6/06* (see paras 4.76 and 4.80).
CIS/1916/2005 is now reported as *R(IS) 12/06* (see para.4.80).

R(G) 1/06 (the reported decision of *CG/2054/2004*) concerned entitlement of an elderly widower to a bereavement payment. Section 36(1)(a) of the Contributions and Benefits Act provides that, even where the contribution conditions are met, there is no entitlement to a bereavement payment when the bereaved party is over pensionable age at the time of the relevant death, and the spouse who has died was getting their own Category A retirement pension. The Commissioner explains the historical origins of this limiting condition. It was argued on behalf of the claimant that the restrictive condition operated to discriminate between deceased spouses who had or had not opted for a Category B rather than a Category A retirement pension, and that this was contrary to Art.14 when read with either Art.8 or Art.1 of Protocol 1. The Commissioner found that he could not interpret the relevant statutory provisions in a manner compatible with this interpretation. However, he was not persuaded that three was discrimination in breach of the Convention. He ruled:

"28.... In a system as complicated and interlocking as the insured benefits scheme under the United Kingdom social security system it is inevitable that differences of treatment, even anomalies and incongruities, may arise at the boundaries between one set of facts and another. Such things are inherent in the system but it is clear on the authority of the House of Lords in *R (Carson) v. Secretary of State* [2005] UKHL 37, [2006] 1 AC 173 that the mere existence of such dividing lines, not raising questions of differential treatment between categories of human beings on the "suspect" grounds, such as sex, race, and so forth or otherwise offensive to accepted notions of the respect due to the individual, does not constitute unlawful discrimination in the human rights context.

29. The dividing lines drawn in a contributory insurance system between the benefits for those who are themselves just under or over pensionable age, those whose deceased partners happen to have just under or over the 25% level of contributions to qualify them for a Category A retirement pension (or for that matter those whose deceased partners had a 100% contribution record, or 99% or something less, on the alternative construction put forward), or those whose partners had or had not happened to elect under section 43 to forgo their own contributory pension benefit on their own contributions and receive a Category B pension on their spouse's contributions instead, are all in my judgment squarely within the area that is left to be determined by the national legislation; and the same applies to deciding whether or in what way what may now be viewed largely as an historical anomaly in section 36(1)(a) should be eliminated. If the effect of the condition is now "incongruous" as suggested in the tribunal chairman's statement of reasons at pages 42 to 43 of file CG 1614/05, that is a matter those concerned for claimants in this position must take up in some other forum than this."

In *R (on the application of RJM) v Secretary of State for Work and Pensions*, [2006] EWHC 1761 (Admin), the claimant had mental health problems and was in receipt of income support including a disability premium. The disability premium was removed when the claimant was sleeping rough, since he was then without accommodation. The claimant argued that the removal of the disability premium constituted unlawful discrimination contrary to Art.14 when read with Art.1 of Protocol 1. He appeared to base his complaint on unwarranted distinctions between those with and without accommodation. The Court ruled that having accommodation was not a personal characteristic. Being disabled was a personal characteristic, but this was not the basis of the distinction drawn in the benefit regulations. The distinction was based on whether a person had or did not have accommodation. Consequently, Art.14 was not engaged. Even if it were, there would be objective and reasonable justification for the differences in payment of the disability premium.

In *Couronne v Secretary of State for Work and Pensions, Bontemps v Secretary of State for Work and Pensions* [2006] EWHC 1514 (Admin), it was argued that the refusal to award jobseekers allowance to British Citizens arriving from Mauritius (whose parents had been displaced from the Chagos Islands) constituted discrimination in breach of Art.14 when read with Art.8 and/or Art.1 of Protocol 1. It was argued, inter alia, that the comparator group (British Citizens of Irish ethnic origin) are exempt from the habitual residence test, whereas the claimants were not. Bennett J. concluded:

"96. In my judgment the aim of the habitual residence test is a legitimate one. Both the ECJ and the Court of Appeal have said so, at least in the context of community law. If the aim, as explained in the evidence, is to protect the British taxpayer from claims by persons who have no genuine or real intention of settling in the UK, if it has been the subject of wide debate and consultation, and if Parliament itself has debated the matter in 1999, it is a nonsense to suggest that the habitual residence test does not have a legitimate aim. The real complaint of the Claimants is, in my judgment, that the implementation of the habitual residence test in relation to the Chagossians, given their special history, is not a proportionate means of achieving the legitimate aim.

97. The word "proportionate" to my mind imports the notion of a balanced response to a given situation. I do not see how it can be said that the inclusion of British citizens of Irish national or ethnic origin within the habitual residence test is not proportionate to the legitimate aim. The complaint of the Chagossians must be that they were not exempted from the scope of the habitual residence test, particularly in the light of their exile and being granted British citizenship. But that, with all due respect, is, as Mr Howell submitted, not the question. The question is whether the habitual residence test is a proportionate means of achieving a legitimate aim given the particular disadvantage to which it is said to put other British citizens not of Irish national or ethnic origin only if an exception is made for the Chagossians. I am afraid that the brutal reality is that the Chagossians are seeking to be treated better than their comparator group and thus seeking a complete exemption from the habitual residence test. The argument as to exile (particularly as British citizens) has no relevance, because it is an exemption that they would have to seek even if the habitual residence test was framed solely in terms of habitual residence in the United Kingdom; and, as is apparent, the Claimants could not (and do not) object to a habitual residence test framed solely in those terms. The distinction made by the UK Government between the plight of the people of Montserrat and of the Chagossians is one about which argument will rage. But hard and difficult decisions have to be made.

Administration, Adjudication and the European Dimension

There may be no 'right' answer, only a least wrong one. The question is whether the refusal of the UK Government to exempt them from the habitual residence is a proportionate response. In my judgment it is . . ."

In *Barrow v United Kingdom* (App.42735/02), judgment of August 22, 2006, the Court of Human Rights has followed the judgment of the Grand Chamber in *Stec* in finding that the change from incapacity benefit to State retirement pension for a woman at the age of 60, which results in her receiving less money than a man in a similar position, does not breach either Art.1 of Protocol 1, nor Art.14 when read together with Art.1 of Protocol 1.

p.1275, *annotation to Art.1, Protocol 1*

4.062   In *R(P) 1/06*, the Commissioner ruled that the three months time limit on the backdating of a claim for retirement pension did not constitute a deprivation of property contrary to Art.1 of Protocol 1. Nor was there any question of a claim based on discrimination by reading Art.14 together with Art.1 of Protocol 1.

In *C8/06–07(IB)* a Commissioner in Northern Ireland said:

"15. I consider there is no merit in the submission based on Article 1 of Protocol 1. There is no inbuilt Convention right to any State benefit. A State is not obliged to provide benefit. The right to benefit only arises when the conditions therefore (which are provided under domestic legislation) are satisfied. In this case they were not so satisfied. The claimant was not entitled to the benefit because he worked and his work did not fall within the categories of exempt work. The basic rule in relation to IB is that those who work are not entitled to it. The benefit is, after all, an incapacity for work benefit. There are exceptions to this basic rule but they relate only to certain categories of work. The relevant category here includes that the work be work of which the required notice is given. Working on the assumption that the domestic law requirement of written notice within 42 days is valid, there is no entitlement to IB if work is done which does not come within an exempt category. Article 1 of Protocol 1 is not therefore invoked, there being no property to enjoy. The claimant is not being asked to repay benefit incorrectly paid. His benefit entitlement is merely being determined according to the applicable statutory conditions of entitlement."

PART V

UPDATING MATERIAL
VOLUME IV

TAX CREDITS, CHILD TRUST FUNDS AND EMPLOYER-PAID SOCIAL SECURITY BENEFITS

Tax Credits, Child Trust Funds and Employer-Paid Social Security Benefits

p.8, *amendment to the Taxes Management Act 1970, s.9A (Notice of enquiry)*

With effect from April 1, 2004, Finance Act 2004, s.30(9) and Sch.5, para.1 amended s.9A to read as follows:

5.001

"(4) An enquiry extends to—
(a) anything contained in the return, or required to be contained in the return, including any claim or election included in the return,
(b) [omitted]
(c) [omitted]
(5) If the notice of enquiry is given as a result of an amendment of the return under section 9ZA of this Act—
(a) at a time when it is no longer possible notice of enquiry under subsection (2)(a) or (b) above, or
(b) after the enquiry into the return has been completed,
the enquiry into the return is limited to matters to which the amendment relates or which are affected by the amendment.
(6) In this section "the filing date" means the day mentioned in section 8(1A) or, as the case may be section 8A(1A) of this Act."

p.28, *amendment to the Income and Corporation Taxes Act 1988, s.336 (Temporary residents in the United Kingdom)*

As a result of amendments by the Finance Act 2004, s.281 and Sch.35, para.13 (with effect from April 6, 2006) and Taxation of Pension Schemes (Consequential Amendments) (No. 2) Order 2006 (SI 2006/1963), art.4 (with effect from August 11, 2006), s.336(1A)(b) is amended to read as follows:

5.002

"(b) the charge under Part 9 of ITEPA 2003 (pension income) in respect of—
  (i) income to which section 573, 609, 610, 611, or 629 of the Act applies,
  (ia) an annuity under a registered pension scheme fell within paragraph 1(1)(f) of Schedule 36 to the Finance Act 2004, or
  (ii) an annual payment to which section 633 of the Act applies that is made by or on behalf of a person who is outside the United Kingdom; . . . and".

p.50, *amendments to the Social Security Contributions and Benefits Act 1992, s.165 (The maternity pay period)*

With effect from October 1, 2006, s.1 of the Work and Families Act 2006 amended subs. (1) by substituting "52 weeks" for "26 weeks" as the maximum length of the maternity pay period. Also with effect from October 1, 2006, s.11 and Sch.1, para.7(2) of the Work and Families Act 2006 substituted new subss.(2) and (3) as follows:

5.003

Tax Credits, Child Trust Funds and Employer-Paid Social Security Benefits

"(2) Subject to subsections (3) and (7), the maternity pay period shall begin with the 11th week before the expected week of confinement.

(3) Cases may be prescribed in which the first day of the period is to be a prescribed day after the beginning of the 11th week before the expected week of confinement, but not later than the day immediately following the day on which she is confined."

In addition, and again with effect from the same date, s.11 and Sch.1, para.7(3) of the Work and Families Act 2006 inserted at the beginning of subs.(4) the words "Except in such cases as may be prescribed," while para.7(4) inserted after subs.(7) a new subs.(8) as follows:

"(8) In subsections (1), (4) and (6) 'week' means a period of seven days beginning with the day of the week on which the maternity pay period begins."

p.51, *amendments to the Social Security Contributions and Benefits Act 1992, s.166 (Rate of statutory maternity pay)*

5.004   With effect from October 1, 2006, s.11 and Sch.1, para.8(2) of the Work and Families Act 2006 inserted after subs.(1) a new subs.(1A) as follows:

"(1A) In subsection (1) "week" means any period of seven days."

In addition, and with effect from the same date, s.11 and Sch.1, para.8(3) inserted after subs.(3) a new subs.(4) as follows:

"(4) Where for any purpose of this Part of this Act or of regulations it is necessary to calculate the daily rate of statutory maternity pay, the amount payable by way of statutory maternity pay for any day shall be taken as one seventh of the weekly rate."

p.56, *amendments to the Social Security Contributions and Benefits Act 1992, s.171 (Interpretation of Pt XII and supplementary provisions)*

5.005   With effect from October 1, 2006, s.11 and Sch.1, para.9 of the Work and Families Act 2006 amended subs.(1) by omitting the definition of "week" and inserting after subs.(1) a new subs.(1A) as follows:

"(1A) In this Part, except section 165(1), (4) and (6), section 166(1) and paragraph 3(2) of Schedule 13, 'week' means a period of 7 days beginning with Sunday or such other period as may be prescribed in relation to any particular case or class of case."

p.62, *amendment to the Social Security Contributions and Benefits Act 1992, s.171ZE (Rate and period of pay)*

5.006   With effect from October 1, 2006, s.11 and Sch.1, para.16(1) and (3) of the Work and Families Act 2006 amended s.171ZE by inserting after subs.(10) a new subs.(10A) as follows:

"(10A) Where for any purpose of this Part of this Act or of regulations it is necessary to calculate the daily rate of ordinary statutory paternity pay, the amount payable by way of ordinary statutory paternity pay for any day shall be taken as one seventh of the weekly rate."

p.66, *amendment to the Social Security Contributions and Benefits Act 1992, s.171ZJ (Part XIIA: supplementary)*

With effect from October 1, 2006, reg.49(1) and Sch.8, Pt 1, para.11(2) of the Employment Equality (Age) Regulations 2006 (SI 2006/1031) substituted a new definition of "employer" in subs.(1) as follows: 5.007

" 'employer', in relation to a person who is an employee, means a person who—
(a) under section 6 above is, liable to pay secondary Class 1 contributions in relation to any of the earnings of the person who is an employee; or
(b) would be liable to pay such contributions but for—
    (i) the condition in section 6(1)(b), or
    (ii) the employee being under the age of 16;".

With effect from October 1, 2006, reg.49(1) and Sch.8, Pt 1, para. 11(3) of the Employment Equality (Age) Regulations 2006 (SI 2006/1031) also omitted subs.(2)(b) and the word "and" preceding it. However, by virtue of para.11(4) of the Employment Equality (Age) Regulations 2006 (SI 2006/1031), the amendments made by para.11(2) and (3) above apply only in relation to an entitlement to—

"(a) statutory paternity pay (birth) in respect of children whose expected week of birth begins on or after 14th January 2007;
(b) statutory paternity pay (adoption) in respect of children—
    (i) matched with a person who is notified of having been matched on or after the commencement date; or
    (ii) placed for adoption on or after the commencement date."

p.69, *amendment to the Social Security Contributions and Benefits Act 1992, s.171ZL (Entitlement)*

With effect from October 1, 2006, art.3(a) of the Adoption and Children Act 2002 (Consequential Amendment to Statutory Adoption Pay) Order 2006 (SI 2006/2012) amended subs.(4)(b) to read as follows: 5.008

"(b) he falls within subsection (4A);"

In addition, art.3(b) inserted after subs.(4) the following new subss.(4A) and (4B):

"(4A) A person falls within this subsection if—
(a) the child is, or is expected to be, placed for adoption with him as a member of a couple;
(b) the other member of the couple is a person to whom the conditions in subsection (2) above apply; and
(c) the other member of the couple has elected to receive statutory adoption pay.

(4B) For the purposes of subsection (4A), a person is a member of a couple if—
: (a) in the case of an adoption or expected adoption under the law of England and Wales, he is a member of a couple within the meaning of section 144(4) of the Adoption and Children Act 2002;
: (b) in the case of an adoption or an expected adoption under the law of Scotland or of Northern Ireland, he is a member of a married couple."

These amendments have effect only in relation to a person with whom a child is expected to be placed for adoption, where the placement is expected to occur on or after October 1, 2006; and for this purpose the date on which the child is actually placed for adoption is immaterial.

p.71, *amendment to the Social Security Contributions and Benefits Act 1992, s.171ZN (Rate and period of pay)*

5.009   With effect from October 1, 2006, s.2 of the Work and Families Act 2006 amended subs.(2) by substituting "52 weeks" for "26 weeks" as the maximum length of the adoption pay period. In addition, and as from the same date, Sch.1, para.21 of the 2006 Act amended subs.(3) by inserting at the beginning "Except in such cases as may be prescribed," and by inserting after subs.(6) a new subs.(6A) as follows:

"(6A) Where for any purpose of this Part of this Act or of regulations it is necessary to calculate the daily rate of statutory adoption pay, the amount payable by way of statutory adoption pay for any day shall be taken as one seventh of the weekly rate."

p.74, *amendment to the Social Security Contributions and Benefits Act 1992, s.171ZS (Pt XIIB: supplementary)*

5.010   With effect from October 1, 2006, reg.49(1) and Sch.8, Pt 1, para.12(2) of the Employment Equality (Age) Regulations 2006 (SI 2006/1031) substituted a new definition of "employer" in subs.(1) as follows:

" 'employer', in relation to a person who is an employee, means a person who—
: (a) under section 6 above is liable to pay secondary Class 1 contributions in relation to any of the earnings of the person who is an employee; or
: (b) would be liable to pay such contributions but for—
  : (i) the condition in section 6(1)(b), or
  : (ii) the employee being under the age of 16;".

With effect from October 1, 2006, reg.49(1) and Sch.8, Pt 1, para. 12(3) of the Employment Equality (Age) Regulations 2006 (SI 2006/1031) also omitted subs.(2)(b) and the word "and" preceding it. However, by virtue of para.12(4) of the Employment Equality (Age) Regulations 2006 (SI 2006/1031), the amendments made by para.12(2)

and (3) above apply only in relation to an entitlement to statutory adoption pay in respect of children—
- "(a) matched with a person who is notified of having been matched on or after the commencement date; or
- (b) placed for adoption on or after that commencement."

p.77, *amendment to the Social Security Contributions and Benefits Act 1992, Sch.11 (Circumstances in which periods of entitlement to statutory sick pay do not arise)*

With effect from October 1, 2006, reg.49(1) and Sch.8, Pt 1, para.13(1) of the Employment Equality (Age) Regulations 2006 (SI 2006/1031) omitted para.(2)(a) (period of entitlement not to arise if at the relevant date the employee is over 65), subject to the following:

5.011

"(2) Sub-paragraph (1) applies in relation to a period of incapacity for work which—
- (a) begins on or after the commencement date, or
- (b) begins before and continues on or after the commencement date.

(3) But in a case falling within sub-paragraph (2)(b), sub-paragraph (1) does not affect the application of paragraph 1 of Schedule 11 to the 1992 Act in relation to the part of the period of incapacity for work that falls before the commencement date."

There is a consequential amendment to Statutory Sick Pay Act 1994, s.1(2) with effect from October 1, 2006, by reg.49(1) and Sch.8, Pt 1, para.17 of the Employment Equality (Age) Regulations 2006 (SI 2006/1031). Statutory Sick Pay Act 1994, s.1(2) had amended Social Security Contributions and Benefits Act 1992, Sch.11, para.2(a).

p.80, *amendment to the Social Security Contributions and Benefits Act 1992, Sch.13 (Relationship of statutory maternity pay with benefits and other payments, etc.)*

With effect from October 1, 2006, s.11 and Sch.1, para.23 of the Work and Families Act 2006, amended para.3 (contractual remuneration) by inserting after sub-para.(2) a new sub-para.(2A) as follows:

5.012

"(2A) In sub-paragraph (2) 'week' means a period of seven days beginning with the day of the week on which the maternity pay period begins."

p.134, *annotations to the Tax Credits Act 2002, s.6: Changes that must be reported*

HMRC has issued new advice following amendments to reg.21 of the Tax Credits (Claims and Notifications) Regulations 2002 (SI 2002/2014) by reg.3 of the Tax Credits (Claims and Notifications) (Amendment) Regulations 2006 (SI 2006/2689), which took effect from November 1, 2006 (see note to p.488 of the main volume below). In a

5.013

campaign being run either side of the introduction of the changes, HMRC advised all recipients to tell HMRC "straight away" (by telephoning 0845 300 3900) of the following changes, which they must report:

"(1) Your work and income:
— if you were working 30 hours or more a week and now you're working less
— if you were working between 16 and 30 hours and now you're working less
(2) Your children:
— if a child leaves home
— if a child over 16 leaves full-time school or college or goes to university
— if for any other reason you can no longer claim child tax credit
— if childcare costs go down for more than 4 weeks
(3) Your household:
— if a partner moves in or out
— if you leave the country for 8 weeks or more."

HMRC have adopted a high profile approach to this simplified statement of the need to report changes. This may counteract some of the failures by claimants currently to report changes. The very general description of "a partner moving in or out" is not further explained in the main literature but is designed to cover both marriages and civil partnerships and their informal equivalents. This is likely to remain the most problematic of the changes that must be reported within three months, as discussed in the commentary to s.3 at para.1.290 in the main volume (p.128).

p.164, *annotations to the Tax Credits Act 2002, s.29 (Recovery of overpayments): General Note*

5.014   HMRC issued a further new edition of COP 26, *What happens if we have paid you too much tax credit?* in mid 2006. See the note below to p.877 of the main volume. The relevant telephone numbers for following up on overpayments are also set out there.

A report of the House of Commons Treasury Select Committee issued in June 2006, *The Administration of Tax Credits* (HC 811, Sixth Report, Session 2005–06), examined again the many criticisms of the way that HMRC has been handling tax credits and in particular its treatment of overpayments. It reported that HMRC had been under the impression that the absence of any appeal rights for tax credits was in line with the approach taken for other social security benefits. The Select Committee put that somewhat surprising misapprehension right and repeated the recommendation previously made by the Parliamentary Ombudsman that there should be a right of appeal to an independent tribunal about overpayments. The most recent version of COP26 makes the ability to appeal the underlying decision rather clearer than was previously the case. The report also detailed the efforts of HMRC to streamline the

Tax Credits, Child Trust Funds and Employer-Paid Social Security Benefits

handling of overpayment cases since September 2005, a process that has led to significant further overpayments of tax credits being written off. This was confirmed by figures showing that for 2004–05, as well as 2003–04, the total overpayment of tax credits was in the order of £2 billion. The Government's response to the Select Committee's report was published in November 2006 (*The administration of tax credits: Government Response to the Committee's Sixth Report of Session 2005–06*, HC 49, First Special Report of Session 2006–07).

p.174, *annotation to the Tax Credits Act 2002, s.38 (Appeals)*

In *CTC/31/2006* a Commissioner rejected an argument for the appellant that there should be read into s.38 a right of appeal against a decision of HMRC under reg.5(2)(b) of the Claims and Notifications Regulations about the form in which a claim for tax credits could be made. The argument was based in part on the Human Rights Act 1998, but the Commissioner considered that judicial review was an adequate remedy for any unreasonable decision about the form of a claim and refused to extend the rights of appeal.

5.014a

p.214, *amendment to the Income Tax (Earnings and Pensions) Act 2003, s.3 (Structure of employment income Parts)*

With effect from April 6, 2003, Finance Act 2003, s.140, Sch.22, para.16(1) amended the description of Pt 7 in subs.(1) to read as follows:

5.015

"Part 7 deals with income and exemptions relating to securities and securities options acquired in connection with an employment".

p.215, *amendment to the Income Tax (Earnings and Pensions) Act 2003, s.6 (Nature of charge to tax on employment income)*

With effect from April 6, 2005, Income Tax (Trading and Other Income) Act 2005 s.882(1) and Sch.1, para.585 amended subs.(5) (exception to charge to tax on employment income for income of divers and diving supervisors) by omitting the words from "Case I" to "ICTA" and substituting "Part 2 of ITTOIA 2005 (trading income) by virtue of section 15 of that Act".

5.016

p.238, *amendment to the Income Tax (Earnings and Pensions) Act 2003, s.327 (Deductions from earnings general)*

With effect from April 6, 2006, ss.281(1) and 326 and Sch.35, para.60 and Sch.42, Pt 3 of the Finance Act 2004 amended subss.(4) and (5) to read as follows:

5.017

"(4) Further provision about deductions from earnings is made in—
    section 232 (giving effect to mileage relief;
    . . .

Tax Credits, Child Trust Funds and Employer-Paid Social Security Benefits

section 262 of CAA 2001 (capital allowances to be given effect by treating them as deductions from earnings).

(5) Further provisions about deductions from income including earnings is made in—

Part 12 (payroll giving); and

Sections 188 to 194 of FA 2004 (contributions to registered pension schemes)."

p.248, *amendment to the Income Tax (Earnings and Pensions) Act 2003, s.655 (Structure of Pt 10)*

5.018   With effect from April 6, 2005, s.882(1) and Sch.1, paras 584 and 612 of the Income Tax (Trading and Other Income) Act 2005, substituted in subs.(2), for the entries relating to ss.84 and 85 of the Finance Act 2000, the following:

"section 781 of ITTOIA 2005 (exemption from income tax for payments under New Deal 50plus);

section 782 of ITTOIA 2005 (exemption from income tax for payments under employment zone programmes)."

p.260, *amendment to the Income Tax (Earnings and Pensions) Act 2003, s.679 (Taxable social security income)*

5.019   With effect from April 6, 2005, s.882(1) and Sch.1, paras 584 and 613 of the Income Tax (Trading and Other Income) Act 2005 has amended s.679 to read as follows:

"(1) If section 678 applies, the taxable social security income for a taxable benefit for a tax year is the full amount of the social security income arising in the tax year, but subject to subsection (2).

(2) That income is treated as relevant foreign earnings for the purposes of Chapters 2 and 3 of part 8 of ITTOIA 2005 (relevant foreign income: remittance basis and deductions and reliefs).

(3) See also Chapter 4 of that Part (unremittable income)."

p.323, *amendment to the Income Tax (Trading and Other Income) Act 2005, s.619 (Charge to tax under Chapter 5)*

5.020   With effect from December 5, 2005, reg.186 of the Tax and Civil Partnership Regulations 2005 (SI 2005/3229) substituted "relevant" for "unmarried minor" in subs.(1)(b).

p.324, *amendment to the Income Tax (Trading and Other Income) Act 2005, s.619 (Charge to tax under Chapter 5)*

5.021   With effect from April 6, 2006, Finance Act 2006, s.89 and Sch.13, para.5 substituted a new subs.(2) for subss.(2) to (4) as follows:

"(2) For the purposes of sections 1 to 1B of ICTA, where income of another person is treated as income of the settlor and is charged to tax under subsection (1)(a) or (b) above, it shall be charged in accordance

Tax Credits, Child Trust Funds and Employer-Paid Social Security Benefits

with whichever provisions of the Tax Acts would have been applied in charging it if it had arisen directly to the settlor."

p.331, *amendment to the Income Tax (Trading and Other Income) Act 2005, s.783 (General disregards of exempt income for income tax purposes)*

With effect from July 19, 2006, Finance Act 2006, s.64(3) amended subss.(2) and (3) to read as follows:

5.022

"(2) There are exceptions to this in the following cases.

(2A) Interest on deposits in ordinary accounts with the National Savings Bank which is exempt under this Part from every charge to income tax is not to be ignored for the purpose of providing information.

(2B) Interest paid to or in respect of victims of National-Socialist persecution which is so exempt is not to be ignored for the purposes of sections 17 and 18 of TMA 1970 (information provisions relating to interest).

(3) These express exceptions to subsection (1) are without prejudice to the existence of other implied or express exception to that subsection (whether in connection with the provision of information or otherwise)."

p.380, *annotation to the Working Tax Credit (Entitlement and maximum Rate) Regulations 2002, reg.14 (Entitlement to childcare element of working tax credit)*

In *C1/05–06 (TC)(T)* a Tribunal of Commissioners in Northern Ireland rejected the argument that reg.14(2)(c) is incompatible with the European Convention on Human Rights. The appeal concerned the claimant's request for the childcare costs incurred in relation to her son to be taken into account in assessing her entitlement to working tax credit (WTC). The son, aged three, had been diagnosed with a severe learning disability, epilepsy and autistic spectrum disorder. Attempts to place the boy with mainstream registered childcare providers broke down because of the difficulties posed by his behaviour. Therefore the claimant and her partner arranged childcare privately, employing a team of four helpers on an ad hoc basis, all of whom were non-registered childminders, and who looked after the boy in the parents' home. The Northern Ireland legislation then in force expressly provided that someone who looked after a child in the home of her employer could not be treated as, and therefore registered as, a child minder (Children (Northern Ireland) Order 1995 (1995 No. 755 (N.I.2), Art.119(4) and (6)). As a result, the claimant's request for her childcare costs to be accepted for the purposes of her WTC claim was rejected by HMRC, given the terms also of reg.14(2)(c). An appeal tribunal upheld the HMRC's decision. The claimant's further appeal was dismissed by the Tribunal of Commissioners. The Tribunal of Commissioners acknowledged that children with very severe disabilities may not be able to take advantage of registered childcare, but took the view that this did not amount to discrimination as such (paras 26–28). Moreover, there were objective and

5.023

justifiable reasons for any differences in treatment, given for example the need to protect against arrangements designed to abuse the tax credits scheme for assisting with childcare costs (paras 29–30), and such anti-abuse measures were within the margin of appreciation for the national authorities (para.31). These conclusions were not undermined by the fact that the relevant legislation has now been modified, so that since April 6, 2006 childcare provided in the child's own home in Northern Ireland may be regarded as registered childcare (see Tax Credits (Approval of Home Care Providers) Scheme (Northern Ireland) 2006, SR 2006/64), a position which was reached earlier in England: see Tax Credits (Approval of Home Care Providers) Scheme 2005 (SI 2005/93).

p.401, *amendment to the Tax Credits (Definition and Calculation of Income) Regulations 2002, reg.2 (Interpretation)*

5.024 With effect from April 6, 2006, art.26(2)(a) of the Taxation of Pension Schemes (Consequential Amendments) Order 2006 (SI 2006/745) substituted "registered pension scheme" for "personal pension scheme or a retirement annuity contract" in the definition of "pension fund holder" and omitted "or contract" at the end. In addition, art.26(2)(b) omitted the definition of "personal pension scheme" and art.26(2)(d) omitted the definitions of "retirement annuity contract" and "retirement benefits scheme". Finally, art.26(2)(c) inserted after the definition of "qualifying young person" the following new definition:

> " 'registered pension scheme' has the meaning given by section 150(2) of the Finance Act 2004; and".

p.403, *amendment to the Tax Credits (Definition and Calculation of Income) Regulations 2002, reg.3 (Calculation of income of claimant)*

5.025 With effect from April 6, 2006, art.26(3) of the Taxation of Pension Schemes (Consequential Amendments) Order 2006 (SI 2006/745) amended para.(7)(b)–(d) to read as follows:

> "(b) the grossed up amount of any banking qualifying donation (within the meaning of section 25 of the Finance Act 1990 (donations to charities by individuals) made by the claimant or, in the case of a joint claim, by either or both of the claimants; and
> (c) the amount of any contribution made by the claimant or, in the case of a joint claim, by either or both of the claimants to a registered pension scheme together with the amount of any tax relief due on those contributions.
> (d) ... ".

p.413, *amendment to the Tax Credits (Definition and Calculation of Income) Regulations 2002, reg.5 (Pension income)*

5.026 With effect from April 6, 2006, art.26(4)(a) of the Taxation of Pension Schemes (Consequential Amendments) Order 2006 (SI 2006/745)

Tax Credits, Child Trust Funds and Employer-Paid Social Security Benefits

amended para.(1) by substituting for sub-paras (d) and (e) the following:

"(d) any pension, annuity or income withdrawal to which section 579A of ITEPA applies;
(e) any unauthorised member payments to which section 208(2)(a) or (b) of the Finance Act 2004 applies;".

In addition, art.26(4)(b) amended para.(1) by omitting sub-paras (g), (h), (i) and (j) and art.26(4)(c) substituted for sub-para.(k) the following:

"(k) any annuity paid under a retirement annuity contract to which Chapter 9 of Part 9 of ITEPA applies;".

p.414, *amendment to the Tax Credits (Definition and Calculation of Income) Regulations 2002, reg.5 (Pension income), Table 2*

With effect from April 6, 2006, Art.26(4)(d) of the Taxation of Pension Schemes (Consequential Amendments) Order 2006 (SI 2006/745) substituted "section 636A of ITEPA" for "section 637 of ITEPA" in item 10 of Table 2.

5.027

p.440, *amendment to the Tax Credits (Definition and Calculation of Income) Regulations 2002, reg.19 (General disregards in the calculation of income), Table 6*

With effect from November 1, 2004, reg.12 and Sch.2, para.3 of the Community Care, Services for Carers and Children's Services (Direct Payments) (Wales) Regulations 2004 (SI 2004/1748) inserted after "Health and Personal Social Services (Direct Payments) (Northern Ireland) Order" in item 14 of Table 6 the following:

5.028

"or regulations made under section 57 of the Health and Social Care Act 2001 (direct payments)".

p.450, *amendment to the Child Tax Credit Regulations 2002, reg.3 (Circumstances in which a person is or is not responsible for a child or qualifying young person)*

With effect from May 24, 2006, reg.2(2) of the Child Tax Credit (Amendment No. 2) Regulations 2006 (SI 2006/1163) inserted a new Case F in reg.3 after Case E as follows:

5.029

"**Case F**
The child (having attained the age of sixteen) or the qualifying young person claims and receives working tax credit in his or her own right (whether alone or on a joint claim).
This Case does not apply in the case of a child or qualifying young person, for whom another ("the recipient"), had made a claim for child tax credit before, and was entitled to receive child tax credit immediately before, the making of these Regulations, until—

Tax Credits, Child Trust Funds and Employer-Paid Social Security Benefits

      (a) the child or qualifying young person ceases to receive relevant education or approved training (in each case within the meaning of regulation 1(3) of the Child Benefit (General) Regulations 2006),
      (b) the recipient ceases to receive child tax credit for any other reason, or
      (c) 24th August 2006,
whichever occurs first."

p.452, *annotation to the Child Tax Credit Regulations 2002, reg.3 (Circumstances in which a person is or is not responsible for as child or qualifying young person)*

5.030   This rule has proved to be even more controversial than the equivalent rules for child benefit. In *CTC/2065/2004* a Commissioner considered a challenge alleging that the unfairness of the provisions was discriminatory under Art.14 of the European Convention of Human Rights. After hearing full argument and fully reviewing the relevant case law, the Commissioner decided that the status of being a minority carer was not a personal characteristic for the purposes of Art.14. In that case one of the parents had responsibility for the children for seven months of the year and the other for five months. In *CTC/4390/2004* the Commissioner dealt with conflicting claims to the same child tax credit in a case where, in terms of shared timing, the parents agreed to a court order giving them equal responsibility. The tribunal in that case found that "it was virtually impossible to say who had the main responsibility". The Commissioner took the view that the legislation required that the tribunal establish that one of the two had the main responsibility. In a case where the usual criteria failed to identify the person with main responsibility and HMRC had to decide under rule 3, the Commissioner agreed with the argument of HMRC that it was appropriate to consider that responsibility should rest with the person who would receive the greater amount of child tax credit. This solution may present problems to tribunals because they may only have one of the conflicting claimants before them. In *CTC/4390/2004* this was solved by the tribunal chairman joining separate appeals by the two claimants. The Commissioner confirmed that approach, with the agreement of HMRC, and referred the case back to a tribunal with both claimants as parties.

It is understood that another solution acceptable to HMRC where the claim is for two or more children is for the claims to be shared, in the sense that one person claims for one or more of the children while the other claims for the other or others, using rule 3.

p.478, *annotation to the Tax Credits (Claims and Notifications) Regulations 2002, reg.5(2) (Manner in which claims to be made)*

5.030a   In *CTC/31/2006* the Commissioner refused to extend the rights of appeal under s.38 of the Act to include a right of appeal against a decision about reg.5(2)(b). HMRC had refused to accept a claim made on an income tax return. The Commissioner considered that the merits of that decision were not justiciable and susceptible only to judicial review. The Commissioner decided that a tribunal therefore had no jurisdiction to hear an appeal from a decision by HMRC not to accept a claim on the grounds that it was not properly made. He distinguished decision *R(IS) 6/04* to the opposite effect for the similar rule for income support. He rejected the attempt to widen s.38 to cover this decision by reference to Art.6 of the European Convention on Human Rights. The HMRC decision, if not that of the Commissioner, raises the question whether there is any operative link between income tax and child tax credits other than the calculation of a claimant's income.

p.479, *annotation to the Tax Credits (Claims and Notifications) Regulations 2002, reg.7 (Time limit for claims)*

In *CTC/869/2006* the Commissioner rejected an attempt to challenge the time limit under the European Convention of Human Rights and the Human Rights Act 1998 on the grounds that a self-employed person did not receive proper notification of the changes. The Commissioner decided that even if there were an argument based on unfairness it did not call the terms of the legislation into question, and the Human Rights Act 1998 provided no remedy.

5.031

p.488, *amendment to the Tax Credits (Claims and Notifications) Regulations 2002, reg.21 (Requirement to notify changes of circumstances which may decrease the rate at which a person or persons is or are entitled to tax credit or mean that entitlement ceases)*

With effect from November 1, 2006, reg.3 of the Tax Credits (Claims and Notifications) (Amendment) Regulations 2006 (SI 2006/2689) amended reg.21(1A) by substituting "27(2), (2A) or (3) for "27(1)". In addition, reg.4 substituted a new provision for reg.21(2) as follows:

5.032

"(2) The changes of circumstances described by this paragraph are those where—
(a) entitlement to the tax credit ceases by virtue of section 3(4), or regulations made under section 3(7), of the Act;
(b) there is a change in the relevant child care charges which falls within regulation 16(1)(b) (omitting paragraph (i)) of the Working Tax Credit Regulations;
(c) a person ceases to undertake work for at least 16 hours per week for the purposes of—
  (i) the Second Condition in regulation 4(1) (read with regulations 4(3) to (5) and 5 to 8), or
  (ii) regulation 13(1),
  of the Working Tax Credit Regulations;
(d) a person ceases to undertake work for at least 30 hours per week for the purposes of the Second Condition in regulation 4(1) of the Working Tax Credit Regulations (read with regulations 4(3) to (5) and 5 to 8), except in a case where he still falls within the terms of paragraph (a) or (b) of that Condition;

Tax Credits, Child Trust Funds and Employer-Paid Social Security Benefits

    (e) a person ceases to undertake, or engage in, qualifying remunerative work for at least 16 hours per week for the purposes of—
        (i) regulation 9(1)(a) (disability element),
        (ii) regulation 10(2)(d) (30 hour element), or
        (iii) regulation 18(3)(c) (50 plus element),
    of the Working Tax Credit Regulations;
    (f) a person ceases to engage in qualifying remunerative work for at least 30 hours per week, for the purposes of—
        (i) regulation 10(1) (30 hour element), or
        (ii) regulation 11(2)(c) (second adult element), in a case where the other claimant mentioned in that provision is not so engaged for at least 30 hours per week,
    of the Working Tax Credit Regulations;
    (g) a couple cease to engage in qualifying remunerative work for at least 30 hours per week, for the purposes of regulation 10(2)(c) (30 hour element) of the Working Tax Credit Regulations;
    (h) a person ceases to be treated as responsible for a child or qualifying young person, for the purposes of child tax credit or of the Working Tax Credit Regulations;
    (i) in a case where a person has given advance notification under regulation 27(2B) that a child is expected to become a qualifying young person, the child does not become a qualifying young person for the purposes of Part 1 of the Act;
    (j) a person ceases to be a qualifying young person for the purposes of Part 1 of the Act, other than by attaining the age of twenty; or
    (k) a child or qualifying young person dies."

In addition, and with effect from the same date, reg.5 of the Tax Credits (Claims and Notifications) (Amendment) Regulations 2006 (SI 2006/2689) amended reg.21(3) to read as follows:

"(3) The time prescribed by this paragraph is the period of 3 months beginning on the date on which the change of circumstances occurs or (except in the case of paragraph (2)(j)), if later, the period of 3 months beginning on the date on which the person first becomes aware of the change in circumstances."

Finally, note that with effect from April 6, 2007, the period of "3 months" will be amended to read "1 month" by virtue of reg.6 of the Tax Credits (Claims and Notifications) (Amendment) Regulations 2006 (SI 2006/2689).

p.488, *annotation to the Tax Credits (Claims and Notifications) Regulations 2002, reg.21 (requirement to notify changes of circumstances etc)*

5.033   See also the note to s.6 of the 2002 Act for the changes that are required to be reported under this and other regulations.

Tax Credits, Child Trust Funds and Employer-Paid Social Security Benefits

p.489, *annotation to the Tax Credits (Claims and Notifications) Regulations 2002, reg.22 (Manner in which notifications to be given)*

GENERAL NOTE

HMRC strongly recommend in their general publicity for this to be done by telephone to their helpline on 0845 300 3900. One advantage of reporting such matters by telephone is that the calls are all recorded. If the claimant keeps details of the call, some advisers demand a copy of the record in the event of any dispute about whether the call was made and what was said at the time.

5.034

p.494, *amendment to the Tax Credits (Claims and Notifications) Regulations 2002, reg.27 (Advance notification)*

With effect from November 1, 2006, reg.7 of the Tax Credits (Claims and Notifications) (Amendment) Regulations 2006 (SI 2006/2689) amended reg.27 by substituting "to" for ", (2A) and" and by inserting, after para.(2A), a new para.(2B) as follows:

5.035

"(2B) The circumstances prescribed by this paragraph are those where a child is expected to become a qualifying young person for the purposes of Part 1 of the Act."

p.575, *annotation to the Tax Credits (Approval of Home Child Care Providers) Scheme 2003*

This scheme has now been entirely replaced by provisions in the Tax Credits (Approval of Child Care Providers) Scheme 2005 (SI 2005/93), set out at p.611 of the main volume.

5.036

p.638, *amendment to the Statutory Sick Pay (General) Regulations 1982, reg.16 (Meaning of "employee")*

With effect from October 1, 2006, reg.49(1) and Sch.8, Pt 2, para.50(2) of the Employment Equality (Age) Regulations 2006 (SI 2006/1031) amended reg.16(1), inserting at the beginning the words "Subject to paragraph (1ZA)," and omitting the words "over the age of 16". With effect from the same date Sch.8, Pt 2, para.50(3) of the Employment Equality (Age) Regulations 2006 (SI 2006/1031) inserted after para.(1) a new reg.16(1ZA) as follows:

5.037

"(1ZA) Any person under the age of 16 who would have been treated as an employed earner or, as the case may be, would have been treated otherwise than as an employed earner by virtue of the Social Security (Categorisation of Earners) Regulations 1978 had he been aged 16 or over, shall be treated as if he is aged 16 or over for the purposes of paragraph (1)."

p.639, *amendment to the Statutory Sick Pay (General) Regulations 1982, reg.17 (Meaning of "earnings")*

With effect from October 1, 2006, reg.49(1) and Sch.8, Pt 2, para.51 of the Employment Equality (Age) Regulations 2006 (SI 2006/1031)

5.038

Tax Credits, Child Trust Funds and Employer-Paid Social Security Benefits

amended reg.17(1) by inserting at the end of sub-para.(a) the words "(or would have been so excluded had he not been under the age of 16)" and at the end of sub-para.(b) the words "(or where such a payment or amount would have been so excluded and in consequence he would not have been entitled to statutory sick pay had he not been under the age of 16)".

p.670, *amendment to the Statutory Maternity Pay (General) Regulations 1986, reg.2 (The Maternity Pay Period)*

5.039   With effect from October 1, 2006, and in relation to women whose expected week of confinement falls on or after April 1, 2007, reg.3(2) of the Statutory Maternity Pay, Social Security (Maternity Allowance) and Social Security (Overlapping Benefits) (Amendment) Regulations 2006 (SI 2006/2379) amended reg.2 by substituting a new reg.2 as follows:

"2. —(1) Subject to paragraphs (3) to (5), where—
(a) a woman gives notice to her employer of the date from which she expects his liability to pay her statutory maternity pay to begin; and
(b) in conformity with that notice ceases to work for him in a week which is later than the 12th week before the expected week of confinement,
the first day of the maternity pay period shall be the day on which she expects his liability to pay her statutory maternity pay to begin in conformity with that notice provided that day is not later than the day immediately following the day on which she is confined.

(2) The maternity pay period shall be a period of 39 consecutive weeks.

(3) In a case where a woman is confined—
(a) before the 11th week before the expected week of confinement; or
(b) after the 12th week before the expected week of confinement and the confinement occurs on a day which precedes that mentioned in a notice given to her employer as being the day on which she expects his liability to pay her statutory maternity pay to begin,
section 165 of the Contributions and Benefits Act shall have effect so that the first day of the maternity pay period shall be the day following the day on which she is so confined.

(4) In a case where a woman is absent from work wholly or partly because of pregnancy or confinement on any day—
(a) which falls on or after the beginning of the 4th week before the expected week of confinement; but
(b) not later than the day immediately following the day on which she is confined,
the first day of the maternity pay period shall be the day following the day on which she is so absent.

(5) In a case where a woman leaves her employment—

(a) at any time falling after the beginning of the 11th week before the expected week of confinement and before the start of the maternity pay period, but

(b) not later than the day on which she is confined,

the first day of the maternity pay period shall be the day following the day on which she leaves her employment."

p.674, *insertion of Statutory Maternity Pay (General) Regulations 1986, reg.9A (Working for not more than 10 days in the Maternity Pay Period)*

With effect from October 1, 2006, and in relation to women whose expected week of confinement falls on or after April 1, 2007, reg.3(3) of the Statutory Maternity Pay, Social Security (Maternity Allowance) and Social Security (Overlapping Benefits) (Amendment) Regulations 2006 (SI 2006/2379) inserted after reg.9 (no liability to pay statutory maternity pay) a new reg.9A as follows:

5.040

"Working for not more than 10 days in the Maternity Pay Period

9A. In a case where a woman does any work under a contract of service with her employer on any day, but for not more than 10 days (whether consecutive or not), during her maternity pay period, statutory maternity pay shall continue to be payable to the employee by the employer."

p.679, *amendment to the Statutory Maternity Pay (General) Regulations 1986, reg.17 (Meaning of "employee")*

With effect from October 1, 2006, reg.49(1) and Sch.8, Pt 2, para.53(2) of the Employment Equality (Age) Regulations 2006 (SI 2006/1031) amended reg.17(1), inserting at the beginning the words "Subject to paragraph (1A)," and omitting the words "over the age of 16". With effect from the same date Sch.8, Pt 2, para.53(3) of the Employment Equality (Age) Regulations 2006 (SI 2006/1031) inserted after para.(1) a new reg.17(1A) as follows:

5.041

"(1A) Any woman under the age of 16 who would have been treated as an employed earner or, as the case may be, would have been treated otherwise than as an employed earner by virtue of the Social Security (Categorisation of Earners) Regulations 1978 had she been aged 16 or over, shall be treated as if she is aged 16 or over for the purposes of paragraph (1)."

p.680, *amendment to the Statutory Maternity Pay (General) Regulations 1986, reg.20 (Meaning of "earnings")*

With effect from October 1, 2006, and in relation to any case where the expected week of confinement begins on or after January 14, 2007, reg.49(1) and Sch.8, Pt 2, para.53 of the Employment Equality (Age) Regulations 2006 (SI 2006/1031), amended reg.20(2) by inserting at the

5.042

end of sub-para.(a) the words "(or would have been so excluded had she not been under the age of 16)" and at the end of sub-para.(b) the words "(or where such a payment or amount would have been so excluded and in consequence she would not have been entitled to statutory maternity pay had she not been under the age of 16)".

p.687, *amendment to the Statutory Maternity Pay (General) Regulations 1986, reg.28 (Rounding to avoid fractional amounts)*

5.043 With effect from October 1, 2006, and in relation to women whose expected week of confinement falls on or after April 1, 2007, reg.3(4) of the Statutory Maternity Pay, Social Security (Maternity Allowance) and Social Security (Overlapping Benefits) (Amendment) Regulations 2006 (SI 2006/2379) substituted a new reg.28 as follows:

> "28. Where any payment of statutory maternity pay is paid for any week or part of a week and the amount due includes a fraction of a penny, the payment shall be rounded up to the next whole number of pence."

p.712, *amendment to the Statutory Paternity Pay and Statutory Adoption Pay (Weekly Rates) Regulations 2002, reg.4 (Rounding of fractional amounts)*

5.044 With effect from October 1, 2006, reg.4 of the Statutory Paternity Pay and Statutory Adoption Pay (General) and the Statutory Paternity Pay and Statutory Adoption Pay (Weekly Rates) (Amendment) Regulations 2006 (SI 2006/2236) amended reg.4 by substituting a new reg.4 as follows:

> "4. Where any payment of—
> (a) statutory paternity pay is made on the basis of a calculation at—
>   (i) the weekly rate specified in regulation 2(b); or
>   (ii) the daily rate of one-seventh of the weekly rate specified in regulation 2(a) or (b); or
> (b) statutory adoption pay is made on the basis of a calculation at—
>   (i) the weekly rate specified in regulation 3(b); or
>   (ii) the daily rate of one-seventh of the weekly rate specified in regulation 3(a) or (b),
> and that amount includes a fraction of a penny, the payment shall be rounded up to the next whole number of pence."

By virtue of reg.2 of the Statutory Paternity Pay and Statutory Adoption Pay (General) and the Statutory Paternity Pay and Statutory Adoption Pay (Weekly Rates) (Amendment) Regulations 2006 (SI 2006/2236), the above amendment applies in relation to an entitlement to—

> "(a) statutory paternity pay (birth) in respect of children whose expected week of birth begins on or after 1st April 2007;

(b) statutory paternity pay (adoption) and statutory adoption pay in respect of children expected to be placed for adoption, where the placement is expected to occur on or after 1st April 2007."

p.741, *amendment to the Statutory Paternity Pay and Statutory Adoption Pay (General) Regulations 2006, reg.21 (adoption pay period)*

With effect from October 1, 2006, reg.4 of the Statutory Paternity Pay and Statutory Adoption Pay (General) and the Statutory Paternity Pay and Statutory Adoption Pay (Weekly Rates) (Amendment) Regulations 2006 (SI 2006/2236) amended reg.21 by substituting "39" for "26" in para.(5). For the application of this amendment, see also the qualification made by reg.2 of the Statutory Paternity Pay and Statutory Adoption Pay (General) and the Statutory Paternity Pay and Statutory Adoption Pay (Weekly Rates) (Amendment) Regulations 2006 (SI 2006/2236), noted at p.712 above.

5.045

p.743, *insertion of Statutory Paternity Pay and Statutory Adoption Pay (General) Regulations 2006, reg.27A (Working for not more than 10 days during an adoption pay period)*

With effect from October 1, 2006, reg.5 of the Statutory Paternity Pay and Statutory Adoption Pay (General) and the Statutory Paternity Pay and Statutory Adoption Pay (Weekly Rates) (Amendment) Regulations 2006 (SI 2006/2236) inserted after reg.27 (cases where there is no liability to pay statutory adoption pay) a new reg.27A as follows:

5.046

"**Working for not more than 10 days during an adoption pay period**

27A. In the case where an employee does any work under a contract of service with his employer on any day for not more than 10 such days during his adoption pay period, whether consecutive or not, statutory adoption pay shall continue to be payable to the employee by the employer."

For the application of this amendment, see also the qualification made by reg.2 of the Statutory Paternity Pay and Statutory Adoption Pay (General) and the Statutory Paternity Pay and Statutory Adoption Pay (Weekly Rates) (Amendment) Regulations 2006 (SI 2006/2236), noted at p.712 above.

p.744, *amendment to the Statutory Paternity Pay and Statutory Adoption Pay (General) Regulations 2002, reg.32 (Treatment of persons as employees)*

With effect from October 1, 2006, reg.49(1) and Sch.8, Pt 2, para.60 of the Employment Equality (Age) Regulations 2006 (SI 2006/1031) amended reg.32(1), inserting at the beginning the words "Subject to paragraph (1A)," and omitting the words "over the age of 16". With effect from the same date Sch.8, Pt 2, para.50(3) of the Employment

5.047

Equality (Age) Regulations 2006 (SI 2006/1031) inserted after para.(1) a new reg.32(1A) as follows:

"(1A) Any person under the age of 16 who would have been treated as an employed earner or, as the case may be, would have been treated otherwise than as an employed earner by virtue of the Social Security (Categorisation of Earners) Regulations 1978 had he been aged 16 or over, shall be treated as if he is aged 16 or over for the purposes of paragraph (1)."

p.748, *amendment to the Statutory Paternity Pay and Statutory Adoption Pay (General) Regulations 2002, reg.39 (Meaning of "earnings")*

5.048   With effect from October 1, 2006, reg.49(1) and Sch.8, Pt 2, para.61 of the Employment Equality (Age) Regulations 2006 (SI 2006/1031) amended reg.39 by inserting at the end of sub-para.(a) the words "(or would have been so excluded had he not been under the age of 16)" and at the end of sub-para.(b) the words "(or where such a payment or amount would have been so excluded and in consequence he would not have been entitled to statutory paternity pay and statutory adoption pay had he not been under the age of 16)".

p.817, *amendment to the Child Trust Funds Regulations 2004, reg.33 (Information about "looked after children" from Local Authorities)*

5.049   With effect from October 31, 2006, reg.3 of the Child Trust Funds (Amendment No. 2) Regulations 2006 (SI 2006/2684) inserted after para.(3)(e) a new sub-para.(ea) as follows:

"(ea) the full name and address of the child's mother, if known (or failing that, the same information for the child's father, if known), unless the local authority considers the child's situation to be particularly sensitive;"

With effect from October 31, 2006, reg.4 of the Child Trust Funds (Amendment No. 2) Regulations 2006 (SI 2006/2684) substituted "ten" for "five" in reg.33(4).

p.819, *amendment to the Child Trust Funds Regulations 2004, reg.33A (The Official Solicitor or Accountant of Court to be the person who has the authority to manage an account)*

5.050   With effect from October 31, 2006, reg.5 of the Child Trust Funds (Amendment No. 2) Regulations 2006 (SI 2006/2684) inserted in reg.33A(2) at the end a new Condition 6 as follows:

"*Condition 6* In England and Wales, an adoption agency or local authority has been authorised to place the child for adoption under section 19, or by a placement order under section 21, of the Adoption and Children Act 2002, or in Northern Ireland, an Order has been made under Article 17 or 18 of the Adoption (Northern Ireland) Order 1987 to free the child for adoption."

Tax Credits, Child Trust Funds and Employer-Paid Social Security Benefits

p.826, *amendment to the Child Trust Funds Regulations 2004, Sch.(Stakeholder accounts)*

With effect from October 31, 2006, reg.6 of the Child Trust Funds (Amendment No. 2) Regulations 2006 (SI 2006/2684) inserted at the end of para.2(2)(ba) the following: ", except where cash is held temporarily on deposit in the course of dealing in investments under the account".

5.051

p.877, *Code of Practice 26, What happens if we have paid you too much tax credit?*

HMRC have reissued this Code of Practice. It has been rewritten to generalise from the provisions for the first year currently set out in the main volume. This can be obtained, along with the form TC846 used for asking HMRC to reconsider overpayments, at *www.hmrc.gov.uk/menus/tax_credits.htm*. The leaflet also sets out the telephone numbers for enquiries. These are: 0845 300 3900 for the general enquiry lines, 0845 302 1429 for setting up repayment arrangements, 08459 0004004 to obtain the leaflets about appeals and appeal rights and about complaints, 0845 300 3909 for Minicom/Textphone, 0845 302 1489 yng Nghymraeg, and 00 44 28 9080 8316 from overseas.

5.052

PART VI

FORTHCOMING CHANGES AND UP-RATING OF BENEFITS

FORTHCOMING CHANGES

This section aims to give users of Social Security Legislation 2006 some information on significant changes coming into force between December 6, 2006—the date to which this Supplement is up to date—and mid-April 2007, the date to which the 2007 edition will be up to date. The information here reflects our understanding of sources available to us as at January 22, 2007, and users should be aware that there will no doubt be further legislative amendment between then and mid-April 2007. This section of the Supplement will at least enable users to access the relevant legislation on the TSO website (*www.hmso.gov.uk/ legis.htm*).

6.001

ACT

The Work and Families Act 2006

The Work and Families Act 2006 (c.18) received the Royal Assent on June 21, 2006. It extends the maternity pay period and adoption pay period, makes provision for additional paternity leave and pay, and also extends various employment rights in relation to flexible working and annual leave. Those provisions which have already been brought into force at the time of writing are noted above at the relevant pages for Volume IV. The two Commencement Orders issued to date are the Work and Families Act 2006 (Commencement No. 1) Order 2006 (SI 2006/1682) and the Work and Families Act 2006 (Commencement No. 2) Order 2006 (SI 2006/2232). Those provisions which are as yet not in force include ss.6 to 10 inclusive of the 2006 Act, which insert new ss.171ZEA to 171ZEE in the SSCBA 1992. These sections provide for the introduction of "additional statutory paternity pay", which will enable a mother to transfer a proportion of her maternity pay to her partner. Similar provision is made for "additional statutory adoption pay". In both cases full details as to entitlement will be contained in secondary legislation.

6.002

REGULATIONS

Tax Credits (Claims and Notifications) (Amendment) Regulations 2006 (SI 2006/2689)

The Tax Credits (Claims and Notifications) (Amendment) Regulations 2006 (SI 2006/2689) are mostly in force as from November 1,

6.003

2006 and are noted above at the relevant pages to Vol.IV. These include amendments to reg.21 of the Tax Credits (Claims and Notifications) Regulations 2002 (SI 2002/2014), which governs the circumstances in which a change must be reported that may have the effect of reducing or ending entitlement to tax credits. There is a further amendment to reg.21(3) of the 2002 Regulations by reg.6 of the 2006 Regulations, which will have the effect as from April 6, 2007 of reducing the time within which such changes must be reported from three months to one month.

The Social Security (Incapacity Benefit Work-focused Interviews) Amendment (No. 2) Regulations 2006 (SI 2006/3088)

6.004 These amended the Social Security (Incapacity Benefit Work-focused Interviews) Regulations 2003 with effect from December 29, 2006. The explanatory memorandum to the amending regulations states:

"4.1 The 2003 Regulations introduced a mandatory Work-Focused Interview ("WFI") regime for claimants of incapacity benefits ("IBs") i.e. Incapacity Benefit, Income Support on the grounds of incapacity and Severe Disablement Allowance. They require these claimants to meet a Departmental official to discuss the prospects of a return to work and to access help to make such a return more realistic (the WFI) as part of the Department's Pathways to Work pilot scheme. The 2003 Regulations introduced the WFI regime for new claimants in 7 pilot areas only from either October 2003 or April 2004.

4.2 The Social Security (Incapacity Benefit Work-focused Interviews) Amendment Regulations 2005 amended the 2003 Regulations to cover claimants who made a claim in the two years before October 2003 or April 2004, as applicable. These claimants have a number of different WFI requirements, such as having to take part in 3 WFIs rather than 6. Also a claimant may claim one of the IBs before October 2003 and another of the IBs after October 2003. Such claimants can be entitled to two IBs at the same time. The 2003 Regulations specify whether such claimants have to take part in 3 or 6 WFIs by reference to whether they made a claim for an IB on or after 7th February 2005.

4.3 The Social Security (Incapacity Benefit Work-focused Interviews) Amendment (No. 2) Regulations 2005 extended the 2003 regulations to cover new and repeat claimants in approximately one third of the country. Those claimants are required to take part in a WFI if they make a claim from October 2005, April 2006 or October 2006, depending on where they live.

4.4 The Social Security (Incapacity Benefit Work-focused Interviews) Amendment Regulations 2006 extended the 2003 Regulations to cover: (a) claimants who made a claim between two and six years before October 2003 (or April 2004) in six of the areas; and (b) all claimants in one of the areas. They also extended the 2003 Regulations so that they apply to additional areas for some claimants making a new claim after April 2006.

4.5 This latest amendment to the 2003 Regulations allows for the introduction of the IBs WFI regime for new and repeat claimants to the remaining areas of the country. It also provides for the mandatory WFI regime to continue when participating claimants move from one designated Pathways to Work area to another such area."

The Social Security (Claims and Payments) Amendment (No. 2) Regulations 2006 (SI 2006/3188)

These amend the Claims and Payments Regulations with effect from December 27, 2006. The explanatory memorandum to the Regulations states: 6.005

"4.1 These regulations amend Schedule 9 of the Social Security (Claims and Payments) Regulations 1987 to include the Eligible Loan Deduction Scheme as a third party deduction. Previous announcements relating to the scheme were made in the Budget 2005 and in the document *Promoting Financial Inclusion* published as part of the Pre-Budget Report 2004. In the 2006 Budget, Ministers announced that the scheme would be in operation by the end of 2006."

Social Security (Miscellaneous Amendments) (No. 5) Regulations 2006 (SI 2006/3274)

With effect from January 8, 2007, these Regulations make amendments to the Income Support (General) Regulations 1987, the Jobseeker's Allowance Regulations 1996, and the State Pension Credit Regulations 2002. 6.006

The Regulations clarify the start date for the four benefit week period ("the period") during which housing costs in relation to income support, jobseeker's allowance and state pension credit, and rent in relation to housing benefit, may be paid in respect of two dwellings in cases where the claimant is treated as occupying both dwellings as his home if he could not have avoided liability in respect of those two dwellings.

The Social Security (Bulgaria and Romania) Amendment Regulations 2006 (SI 2006/3341)

These Regulations amend from January 1, 2007 the Income Support (General) Regulations 1987, the Jobseeker's Allowance Regulations 1996 and the State Pension Credit Regulations 2002 because of the accession to the European Union on that date of Bulgaria and Romania. 6.007

Forthcoming Changes

The income-related benefit regulations provide that a claimant is ineligible for benefit where he or she is a "person from abroad" or, in the case of state pension credit, a "person not in Great Britain". A person is a person from abroad or a person not in Great Britain if he or she is not habitually resident in the United Kingdom, the Channel Islands, the Isle of Man or the Republic of Ireland. No person shall be treated as habitually resident without a relevant right to reside in the place where he or she is habitually resident. However, certain categories of persons are exempt from this habitual residence test.

These Regulations insert a new category of persons who are exempt from the habitual residence test, namely nationals of Bulgaria and Romania who are subject to the worker authorisation scheme established by the Accession (Immigration and Worker Authorisation) Regulations 2006 (SI 2006/3317) and who are treated as workers pursuant to those Regulations.

NEW BENEFIT RATES FROM APRIL 2007

(Benefits covered in Volume I)

	April 2006 £ pw	April 2007 £ pw
Disability benefits		
Attendance allowance		
higher rate	62.25	64.50
lower rate	41.65	43.15
Disability living allowance		
care component		
highest rate	62.25	64.50
middle rate	41.65	43.15
lowest rate	16.50	17.10
Mobility component		
higher rate	43.45	45.00
lower rate	16.50	17.10
Carer's allowance	46.95	48.65
Severe disablement allowance		
basic rate	47.45	49.15
age related addition—higher rate	16.50	17.10
age related addition—middle rate	10.60	11.00
age related addition—lower rate	5.30	5.50
Maternity benefits		
Maternity allowance		
standard rate	108.85	112.75
Bereavement benefits and retirement pensions		
Widowed parent's allowance or widowed mother's allowance	84.25	87.30
Bereavement allowance or widow's pension		
standard rate	84.25	87.30
Retirement pension		
Category A	84.25	87.30
Category B (higher)	84.25	87.30
Category B (lower)	50.50	52.30
Category C (higher)	50.50	52.30

6.008

New Benefit Rates from April 2007

	April 2006 £ pw	April 2007 £ pw
Category C (lower)	30.20	31.30
Category D	50.50	52.30

Incapacity benefit

	April 2006 £ pw	April 2007 £ pw
Long-term incapacity benefit		
basic rate	78.50	81.35
increase for age—higher rate	16.50	17.10
increase for age—lower rate	8.25	8.55
invalidity allowance—higher rate	16.50	17.10
invalidity allowance—middle rate	10.60	11.00
invalidity allowance—lower rate	5.30	5.50
Short-term incapacity benefit		
under pension age—higher rate	70.05	72.55
under pension age—lower rate	59.20	61.35
over pension age—higher rate	78.50	81.35
over pension age—lower rate	75.35	78.05

Dependency increases

	April 2006 £ pw	April 2007 £ pw
Adult		
carer's allowance	28.05	29.05
severe disablement allowance	28.05	29.05
maternity allowance	36.60	37.90
retirement pension	50.50	52.30
long-term incapacity benefit	46.95	48.65
short-term incapacity benefit under pension age	36.60	37.90
short-term incapacity benefit over pension age	45.15	46.80
Child	11.35*	11.35*

Industrial injuries benefits

	April 2006 £ pw	April 2007 £ pw
Disablement benefit		
aged 18 and over or under 18 with dependants—100%	127.10	131.70
90%	114.39	118.53
80%	101.68	105.36
70%	88.97	92.19
60%	76.26	79.02
50%	63.55	65.85
40%	50.84	52.68
30%	38.13	39.51
20%	25.42	26.34
aged under 18 with no dependants—100%	77.90	80.70
90%	70.11	72.63
80%	62.32	64.56
70%	54.53	56.49
60%	46.74	48.42
50%	38.95	40.35

New Benefit Rates from April 2007

	April 2006 £ pw	April 2007 £ pw
40%	31.16	32.28
30%	23.37	24.21
20%	15.58	16.14
Unemployability supplement		
basic rate	78.50	81.35
increase for adult dependant	46.95	48.65
increase for child dependant	11.35*	11.35*
increase for early incapacity—higher rate	16.50	17.10
increase for early incapacity—middle rate	10.60	11.00
increase for early incapacity—lower rate	5.30	5.50
Constant attendance allowance		
exceptional rate	101.80	105.40
intermediate rate	76.35	79.05
normal maximum rate	50.90	52.70
part-time rate	25.45	26.35
Exceptionally severe disablement allowance	50.90	52.70
Reduced earnings allowance		
maximum rate	50.84	52.68
Death benefit		
widow's pension		
higher rate	84.25	87.30
lower rate	25.28	26.19
widower's pension	84.25	87.30

Benefits in respect of children

	April 2006	April 2007
Child benefit		
only, elder or eldest child (couple)	17.45	18.10
only, elder or eldest child (lone parent)	17.55	18.10
each subsequent child	11.70	12.10
Child's special allowance	11.35*	11.35*
Guardian's allowance	12.50	12.95

* These sums payable in respect of children are reduced if payable in respect of the only, elder or eldest child for whom child benefit is being paid (see reg.8 of the Social Security (Overlapping Benefits) Regulations 1979).

NEW BENEFIT RATES FROM APRIL 2007

(Benefits covered in Volume II)

	April 2006 £ pw	April 2007 £ pw
Contribution-based jobseeker's allowance		
Attendance allowance		
personal rates—*aged under 18*	34.60	35.65
aged 18 to 24	45.50	46.85
aged 25 or over	57.45	59.15
Income support and income-based jobseeker's allowance		
personal allowances		
single person—*aged under 18 (usual rate)*	34.60	35.65
aged under 18 (higher rate)	45.50	46.85
aged 18 to 24	45.50	46.85
aged 25 or over	57.45	59.15
lone parent *aged under 18 (usual rate)*	34.60	35.65
aged under 18 (higher rate)	45.50	46.85
aged 18 or over	57.45	59.15
couple *both aged under 18*	34.60	35.65
both aged under 18, one disabled	45.50	46.85
both aged under 18, with a child	68.65	70.70
one aged under 18, one aged 18 to 24	45.50	46.85
one aged under 18, one aged 25 or over	57.45	59.15
both aged 18 or over	90.10	92.80
child—*birth to September following 16th birthday*	45.58	47.45
September following 16th birthday to under 19	45.58	47.45
premiums		
family—*ordinary*	16.25	16.43
lone parent	16.25	16.43
pensioner—*single person (JSA only)*	56.60	59.90
couple	83.95	88.90
enhanced pensioner	83.95	88.90
higher pensioner—*single person (JSA only)*	56.60	59.90
couple	83.95	88.90

New Benefit Rates from April 2007

disability—*single person*	24.50	25.25
couple	34.95	36.00
enhanced disability—*single person*	11.95	12.30
couple	17.25	17.75
child	18.13	18.76
severe disability—*single person*	46.75	48.45
couple (one qualifies)	46.75	48.45
couple (both qualify)	93.50	96.90
disabled child	45.08	46.69
carer	26.80	27.15

Pension credit

Standard minimum guarantee		
single person	114.05	119.05
couple	174.05	181.70
Additional amount for severe disability		
single person	46.75	48.45
couple (one qualifies)	46.75	48.45
couple (both qualify)	93.50	96.90
Additional amount for carers	26.35	27.15
Savings credit threshold		
single person	84.25	87.30
couple	134.75	139.60
Maximum savings credit		
single person	17.88	19.05
couple	23.58	25.26

NEW TAX CREDIT AND EMPLOYER-PAID BENEFIT RATES 2007–08

(Benefits covered in Volume IV)

6.010

	2006–07 £ pa	2007–08 £ pa
Working tax credit		
Basic element	1,665	1,730
Couple and lone parent element	1,640	1,700
30 hour element	680	705
Disabled worker element	2,225	2,310
Severe disability element	945	980
50+ Return to work payment (under 30 hours)	1,140	1,185
50+ Return to work payment (30 or more hours)	1,705	1,770
Child tax credit		
Family element	545	545
Family element, baby addition	545	545
Child element	1,765	1,845
Disabled child element	2,350	2,440
Severely disabled child element	945	980
Tax credit income thresholds		
Income disregard	2,500	2,500
First threshold	5,220	5,220
First threshold for those entitled to child tax credit only	14,155	14,495
First withdrawal rate - 37%		
Second threshold	50,000	50,000
Second withdrawal rate—6.67%		

	2006–07 £pw	2007–08 £pw
Employer paid benefits		
Standard rates		
Statutory sick pay	70.05	72.55
Statutory maternity pay	108.85	112.75
Statutory paternity pay	108.85	112.75
Statutory adoption pay	108.85	112.75
Income threshold	84.00	87.00